BIG BOOK
OF GAMES PUZZLES AND ACTIVITIES FOR MOTIVATING BEGINNING READERS

Jerry J. Mallett, Ed.D.

Professor of Education
Findlay College
Findlay, Ohio

The Center for Applied Research in Education, Inc.
West Nyack, New York 10994

©1981, by

The Center for Applied
Research in Education, Inc.

West Nyack, New York

ALL RIGHTS RESERVED.

For Tippy Pettibone,
a friend who also happens to be
my mother-in-law.

Library of Congress Cataloging in Publication Data

Mallett, Jerry J.
  Big book of games, puzzles, and activities for
motivating beginning readers.

   Includes index.
  1. Reading games—Handbooks, manuals, etc.
  2. Reading (Primary)—Handbooks, manuals, etc.
  3. Creative activities and seat work—Handbooks,
manuals, etc.   I. Title.
  LB1525.55.M34   372.4'1   81-4899
  ISBN 0-87628-184-6   AACR2

Printed in the United States of America

About the Author

Jerry J. Mallett, Ed.D., is a nationally known authority in the field of reading instruction. His experience in education includes over 17 years as an elementary classroom teacher, reading specialist, school principal, and professor. Awarded his doctorate by the University of Toledo in 1972, he is presently Professor of Education at Findlay College in Findlay, Ohio.

Dr. Mallett is the author of many articles on reading instruction and the editor of *The Reading Clinic*, a monthly publishing program which provides practical new ideas, techniques, and materials for elementary reading instruction. He is also the author of many books and other teaching aids for teaching reading, among them *Classroom Reading Games Activities Kit* (1975) and the series *Reading Skills Activity Puzzles* (1980), both published by The Center for Applied Research in Education.

About This Book

The purpose of the *Big Book of Games, Puzzles and Activities for Motivating Beginning Readers* is to help you expand children's interest in reading and reinforce specific reading skills. To achieve this purpose and assist you in selecting specific activities, the book is divided into the following six sections:

I. Games for Individual Instruction

II. Games for Group Instruction

III. Puzzle Pages

IV. Bulletin Boards

V. Learning Boards

VI. Special Motivators

Each activity focuses on a specific skill, is keyed to appropriate grade levels for use, and provides all of the details and directions you need to use or adapt it successfully in your own classroom. Moreover, the games include many full-size patterns of game components you can copy just as they are. Most of the puzzle pages are self-correcting and can be duplicated just as they appear for immediate use with individual pupils or groups of children with similar needs. The bulletin boards and learning boards can be easily reproduced with an opaque projector.

You will find that the *Big Book of Games, Puzzles and Activities for Motivating Beginning Readers* ...

- Helps you motivate children to explore and read a wide variety of books
- Offers a practical and simple way to stimulate children to do the necessary drill of reading skills
- Provides interesting and productive activities for both individual children and groups of children
- Is especially helpful in motivating those "hard-to-interest" reluctant readers
- Includes activities to help children learn over 20 specific reading skills, including recognizing consonant blends, distinguishing fact from fantasy, predicting outcomes, understanding story sequence, compound word usage, medial vowel usage, and sight word knowledge

It is hoped that this *Big Book of Games, Puzzles and Activities for Motivating Beginning Readers* will become an integral part of your reading program.

Jerry J. Mallett

Table of Contents

I. Games for Individual Instruction 1

    The Pumpkin Parade 3
    Marble Match 5
    Button Up 7
    Snowman Shapes 9
    Ladybug Match 12
    Diving for Pearls 15
    Peek in the Windows 18
    Mitten Match 20
    Beautiful Butterflies 22
    Sailing, Sailing 26
    The Lost Caboose 28
    Bigger Than I Am 30
    Something in Common 33
    Word Fit 36
    Stop and Go 37
    Swimmy Flips His Fins 40
    Inside—Outside 42
    Busy As a Bee 46
    Turn On the Light 48
    Let Toby Help 50
    Do a Daisy 53
    Mail the Letters 56
    Meet the Frog Family 59
    Polly Wants a Cracker 62
    Take Daffy Swimming 65
    Time for Baseball 68
    Form a Picture 71
    Marching Toy Soldiers 73
    Ride the Streetcar 75
    Help the Bluebird 77
    Silly Seal 80

II. Games for Group Instruction ... 83

- Eggs in the Basket ... 85
- Sew an Alphabet ... 87
- Bunch of Balloons ... 89
- Birds in the Tree ... 92
- Build a Ship ... 95
- Elmo's Peanut Game ... 97
- The Magic Hat ... 99
- Roll a Blend ... 102
- Road Signs ... 104
- Flying High ... 106
- Magic Pictures ... 107
- A Flock of Birds ... 109
- Egg Carton Picture Game ... 112
- Toby's Problem ... 114
- Watch the Forest Grow ... 116
- The Long Train ... 119
- Crossing the Ocean ... 122
- Picture Plus ... 125
- Old Oak Tree ... 126
- Going Fishing ... 129

III. Puzzle Pages ... 133

- Choo Choo! ... 134
- Colorful Garden ... 136
- The Island ... 138
- Wild Windows ... 140
- Follow Suzy ... 142
- Can You See It? ... 144
- All Aboard! ... 146
- Rocket Puzzle ... 148
- Twirl a Vowel ... 150
- Blend Box ... 152
- What Will We Ride Next? ... 154
- Into the Harbor ... 156
- What Do You Want to Play? ... 158
- Are You Hungry? ... 160
- Can You Find the Animals? ... 162
- My Favorite Day ... 164
- Help Henry ... 166
- Who Is Chickie Looking For? ... 168
- Flying High ... 170
- Who Did It? ... 172
- Going Swimming ... 174
- What Happened at the Zoo? ... 176
- Crazy Mixed-Up Words! ... 178

    Let's Take a Walk 180
    Compound Pictures 182
    Our Picnic Mess 184

IV. Bulletin Boards **187**

    Balloon Fun! 188
    Shivers Up Your Spine 192
    You've Seen Them on TV 196
    Children's Book Week 198
    Gerald Knows ... Do You? 200
    A Hoppin' Good Book 203
    How High Can We Build the Tower? 206
    Reach for the Stars 209
    Vote for Your Favorite Dr. Seuss Book! 212
    It's Grrreat to Write to an Author! 215

V. Learning Boards **217**

    Find Humpty-Dumpty's Cousins! 218
    Marvin Mouse and His Friends 221
    Bells Are Ringing 224
    Fido's Treat 227
    Spin a Vowel 230
    Jack and the Beanstalk 233
    Down the Chute! 236
    Panda's Problem 239
    Help Henrietta Find Her Baby! 241
    Fish Bubbles 244
    Hang Glider 247
    Fill 'er Up 249
    Hello ... Operator 252
    Apples, Apples, and More Apples 254
    The Old Train 257

VI. Special Motivators **261**

    Shhh ... I Can't Hear What the Book's Saying! ... 262
    I Think I Can 262
    Book Displays 264
    A "Bunch" of Mysteries 267
    Magic Well 269
    Bertrum Bug's Book Club 271
    Bookmark Factory 273
    Fabulous Foxy Award 274
    Month of the Super Sillies 278
        Book List 279
        Super Sillies Activity Sheet 280
        Super Sillies Bulletin Board 281

Super Silly Mobile 282
　　Super Silly Button 282
　　Super Silly Reading Center 283
　　Super Silly Reading Game 284
　The Tiger's Tale 286
　And the Books Roll On 288
　Read All About It! 288
　Want Ads 290
　Hidden Books! 290

Reading Skills Index **293**

I
Games for Individual Instruction

Because of the current educational emphasis on individualized instruction, many classroom teachers have begun to reorganize their rooms to include learning centers. Whether the children work directly in the learning center or simply use it as an area from which to obtain instructional material, the fact remains that a wide variety of individualized learning games must be available. While some school systems are able to purchase large quantities of commercially made teaching games, many other systems can often provide only a bare minimum of these normally expensive materials.

The purpose of this section, therefore, is to provide kindergarten and primary teachers with many individualized readiness and reading games which can be easily and inexpensively produced. The only materials necessary for most of the games found in this section are lightweight posterboard, scissors, and a felt-tipped pen. Other items that are required for several of the games are such easily found items as small pictures (from catalogs or readiness workbooks), glue, and shoestrings. In order to help you reproduce these games quickly and easily, detailed instructions for constructing them are provided. You will also notice that most of the game directions include actual-size patterns for simple copying.

The following readiness and reading skills are reinforced by the designated games.

Game	Reading Skill	Grade Level
The Pumpkin Parade	visual discrimination	low primary
Marble Match	visual discrimination	low primary
Button Up	visual discrimination	low primary
Snowman Shapes	visual discrimination	low primary
Ladybug Match	visual discrimination	low primary
Diving for Pearls	auditory discrimination	low primary
Peek in the Windows	auditory discrimination	low primary
Mitten Match	auditory discrimination	low primary

Game	*Reading Skill*	*Grade Level*
Beautiful Butterflies	alphabet knowledge	low primary
Sailing, Sailing	alphabet knowledge	low primary
The Lost Caboose	alphabet knowledge	low primary
Bigger Than I Am	categorization	low primary
Something in Common	categorization	low primary
Word Fit	sight word knowledge	primary
Stop and Go	sight word knowledge	primary
Swimmy Flips His Fins	sight word knowledge	primary
Inside-Outside	sight word knowledge	primary
Busy As a Bee	sight word knowledge	primary
Turn On the Light	sight word knowledge	primary
Let Toby Help	initial consonants	primary
Do a Daisy	initial consonants	primary
Mail the Letters	final consonants	primary
Meet the Frog Family	final consonants	primary
Polly Wants a Cracker	medial vowels	primary
Take Daffy Swimming	consonant blends	primary
Time for Baseball	word meaning	primary
Form a Picture	word sequence	primary
Marching Toy Soldiers	word sequence	primary
Ride the Streetcar	context clue usage	high primary
Help the Bluebird	context clue usage	high primary
Silly Seal	sentence structure	high primary

The Pumpkin Parade

Skill Reinforced: visual discrimination
Grade Level: low primary
Materials Needed:
    16 sheets of 6″ × 6″ orange posterboard
    scissors
    felt-tipped pen

Construction Directions:

1. Cut out the posterboard pieces using the pumpkin pattern.

2. Copy each of the pumpkin faces on the next page onto *two* pieces of the posterboard. Place the same color markers on the backs of the jack-o'-lanterns that have identical faces.

Game Play:

1. Look at one of the pumpkins. See how the eyes, nose, mouth, and stem are made. Now, spread all of the pumpkins out on a flat surface.
2. Look through all of the pumpkins and try to find another one that is made just like the first one. When you think you have found it, turn over the two pumpkins and see if you are right. If the color markers match, you are correct.
3. Continue to do this with all of the jack-o'-lanterns.

Marble Match

Skill Reinforced: visual discrimination
Grade Level: low primary
Materials Needed:

    10 sheets of 6" × 8" blue posterboard
    30 posterboard circles with 1¼" diameters in various colors
    scissors
    felt-tipped pen
    paper hole punch
    10 white shoelaces

Construction Directions:

1. Print each of the following words on three different circles.

sit	that
off	too
cat	bat
new	own
all	two

2. Cut the blue posterboard pieces using the marble bag pattern as shown on the following page. Punch two holes and string the shoelaces through the marble bags as shown in the illustration.
3. Print each of the words in the above list on a different marble bag as shown in the illustration.
4. Place the same color markers on the backs of the bags and marbles that have identical words.

Game Play:

1. Make two piles, one with the marble bags and one with the marbles.
2. Take one of the marble bags and place it in front of you. See that there is a word at the top of the bag. Find three marbles with the same word on each of them.
3. When you have done this with all of the marble bags and marbles, turn them over. If the colors are the same, you are correct.

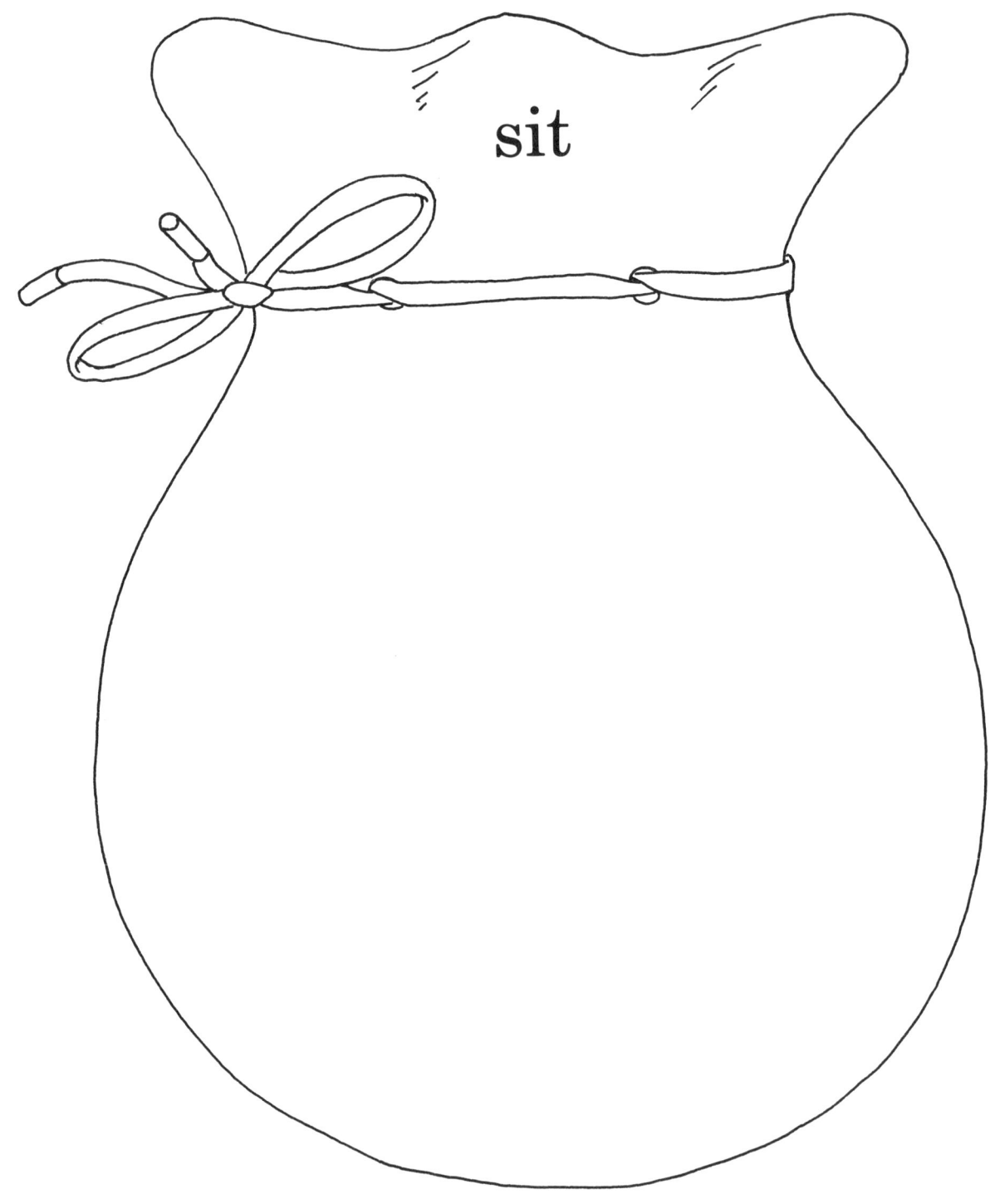

sit

Button Up

Skill Reinforced: visual discrimination
Grade Level: low primary
Materials Needed:

    6 sheets of 9″ × 11″ dark blue posterboard
    18 light blue posterboard circles with 1¼″ diameters
    scissors
    ruler
    felt-tipped pen
    color markers

Construction Directions:

1. Mark each of the following forms on three of the circles.

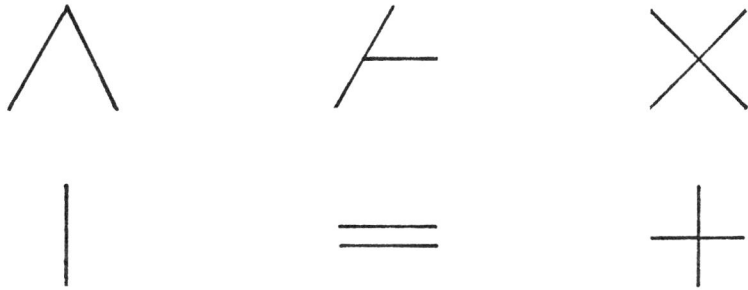

2. Cut and mark the large posterboard pieces using the coat pattern on the following page. Glue one button with a different form to each of the coats as shown in the illustration.
3. Place the same color markers on the backs of the coats and buttons that have the same forms.

Game Play:

1. Make two piles, one with the coats and the other with the buttons.
2. Look at one of the coats. You will see that it already has one button on it. Find two more buttons for the coat. Make sure that they match the button that is already on the coat.
3. When you think you have buttoned up all of the coats, turn the pieces over and see if the colors match. If they do, you are correct. Now, hurry up so that no one catches a cold!

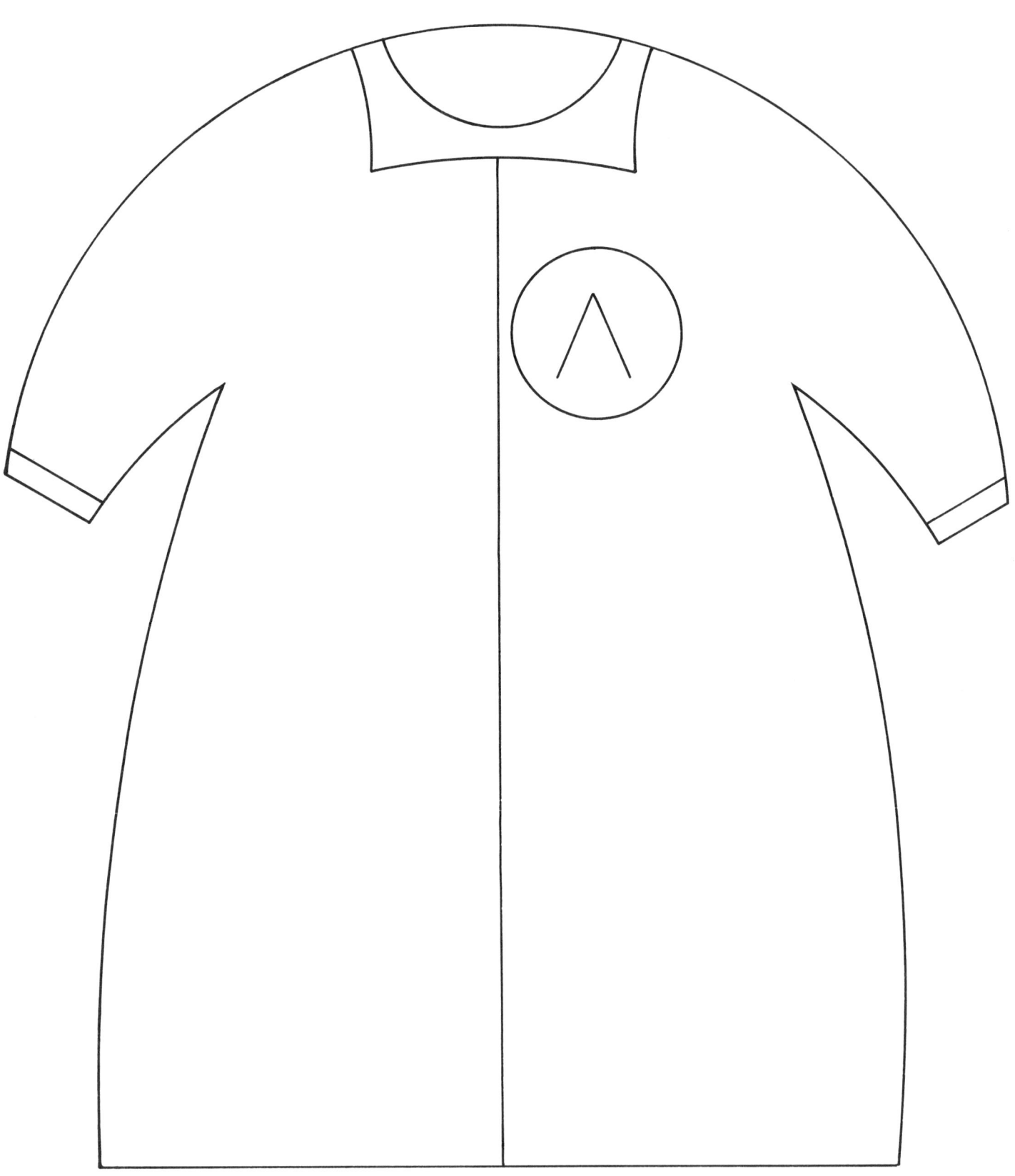

Snowman Shapes

Skill Reinforced: visual discrimination
Grade Level: low primary
Materials Needed:

    9 sheets of 5″ × 5″ white posterboard
    9 sheets of 4″ × 4″ white posterboard
    9 sheets of 3″ × 3″ white posterboard
    9 sheets of 3″ × 4½″ green posterboard
    scissors
    felt-tipped pen
    color markers

Construction Directions:

1. Cut and mark the 5″ × 5″ posterboard pieces as shown here. Use a different mark on each of the pieces. The marks are listed next to the cutout below.

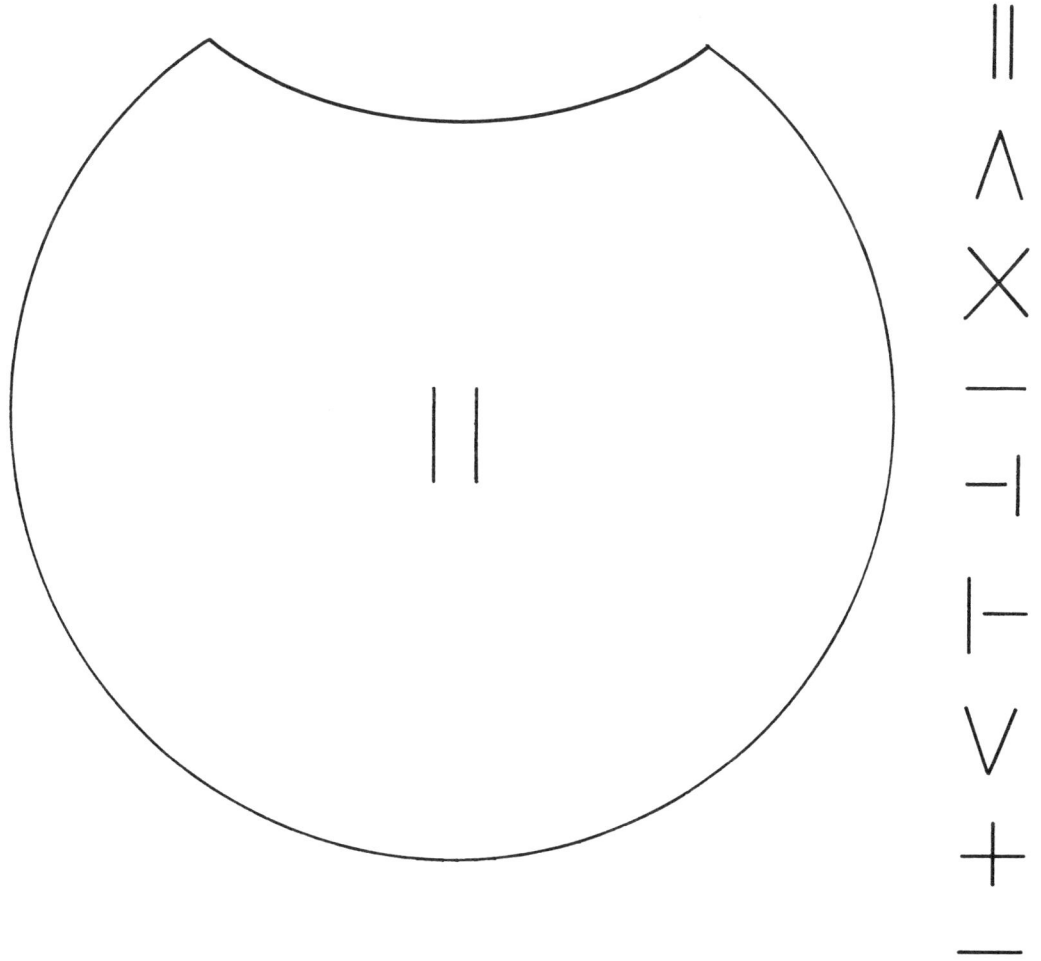

2. Cut the 4" × 4" posterboard pieces as shown here. Mark them the same way as was done before.

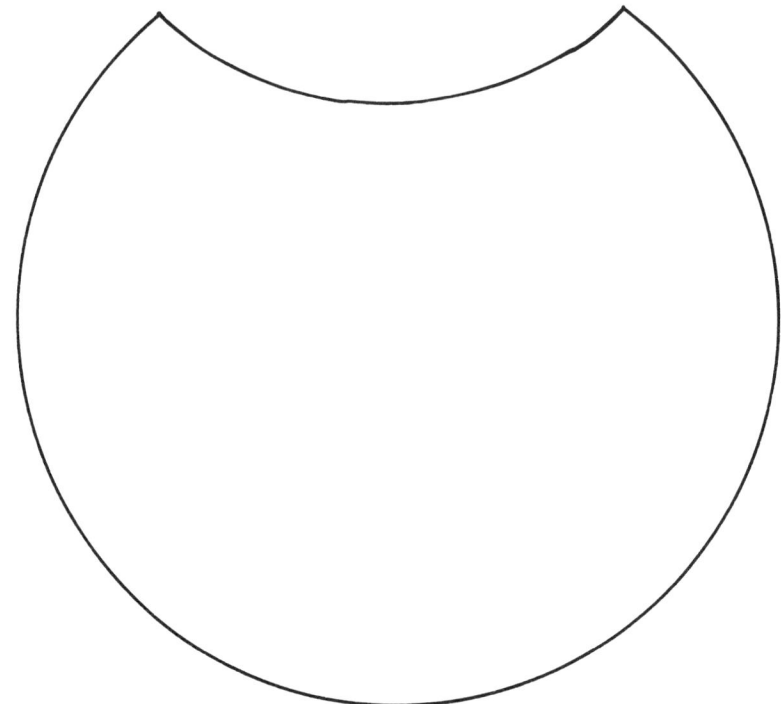

3. Cut the 3" × 3" posterboard pieces as shown here. Mark them the same way as was done before.

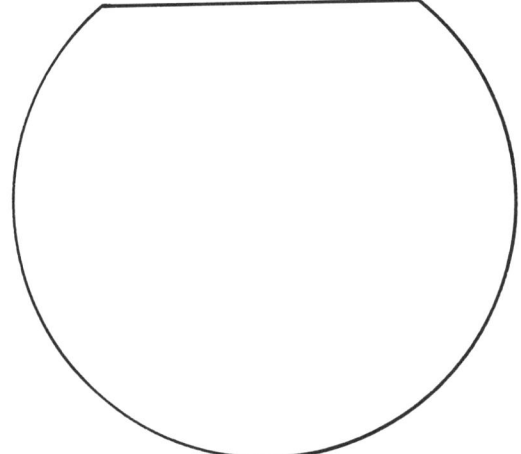

4. Cut the green posterboard pieces as shown here. Mark them the same way as was done before.

5. Place the same color markers on the backs of the pieces with the same marks on their fronts.

Game Play:

1. Make four piles: one with the large, round, white pieces; one with the small, round, white pieces; one with the middle-size, round, white pieces; and one with the green hats.
2. These four pieces will fit together to form a snowman. But in order to do it right you must match the lines that are drawn on the pieces. Take one of the large, round, white pieces. Look at the shape of the lines. Now, look through each of the other piles and find pieces that have this same shape.
3. When you think you have found them, fit them together and form a snowman. Turn them over and see if you are right. If the color markers are all the same color, you are right. Do the rest of the snowmen in the same way.

Ladybug Match

Skill Reinforced: visual discrimination
Grade Level: low primary
Materials Needed:
    26 sheets of 5" × 6½" red posterboard
    scissors
    felt-tipped pen

Construction Directions:
1. Cut and mark the posterboard pieces using the ladybug pattern shown here.

2. Print the upper-case alphabet and cut on the dotted lines as shown here.

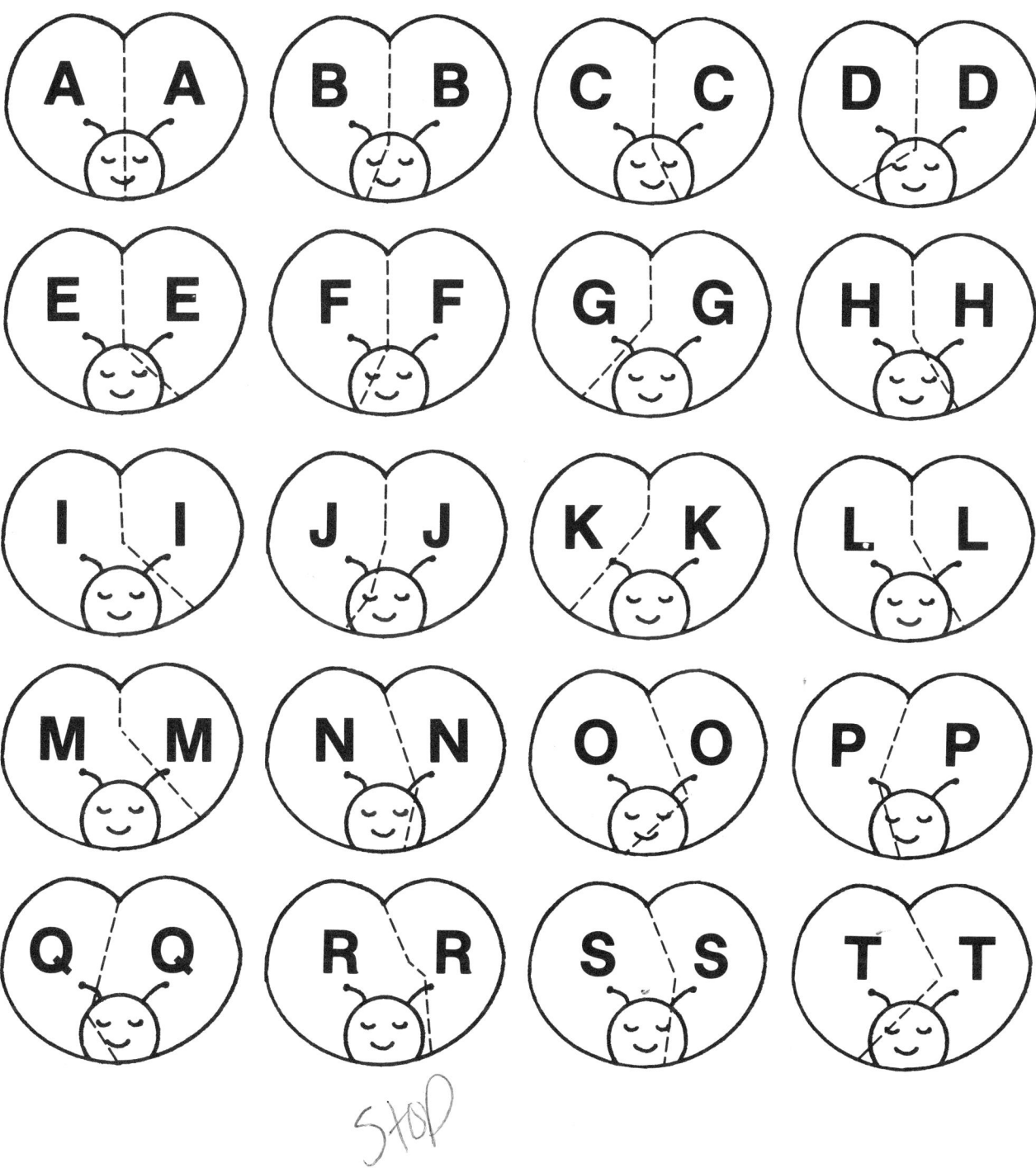

Game Play:

1. Look at one of the ladybug pieces. You will see a letter written on it. Do you know what letter it is?
2. Look through all of the other ladybug pieces and see if you can find another letter just like that one.
3. When you think you have found one, place it next to the first piece. If it fits and makes a complete ladybug, you are right. Continue to do the same with the other ladybug pieces.

Diving for Pearls

Skill Reinforced: auditory discrimination
Grade Level: low primary
Materials Needed:
>13 sheets of 6″ × 6″ pink posterboard
>13 white posterboard circles with 2½″ diameters
>scissors
>felt-tipped pen

Construction Directions:
>1. Cut the pink posterboard pieces using the oyster pattern shown here.

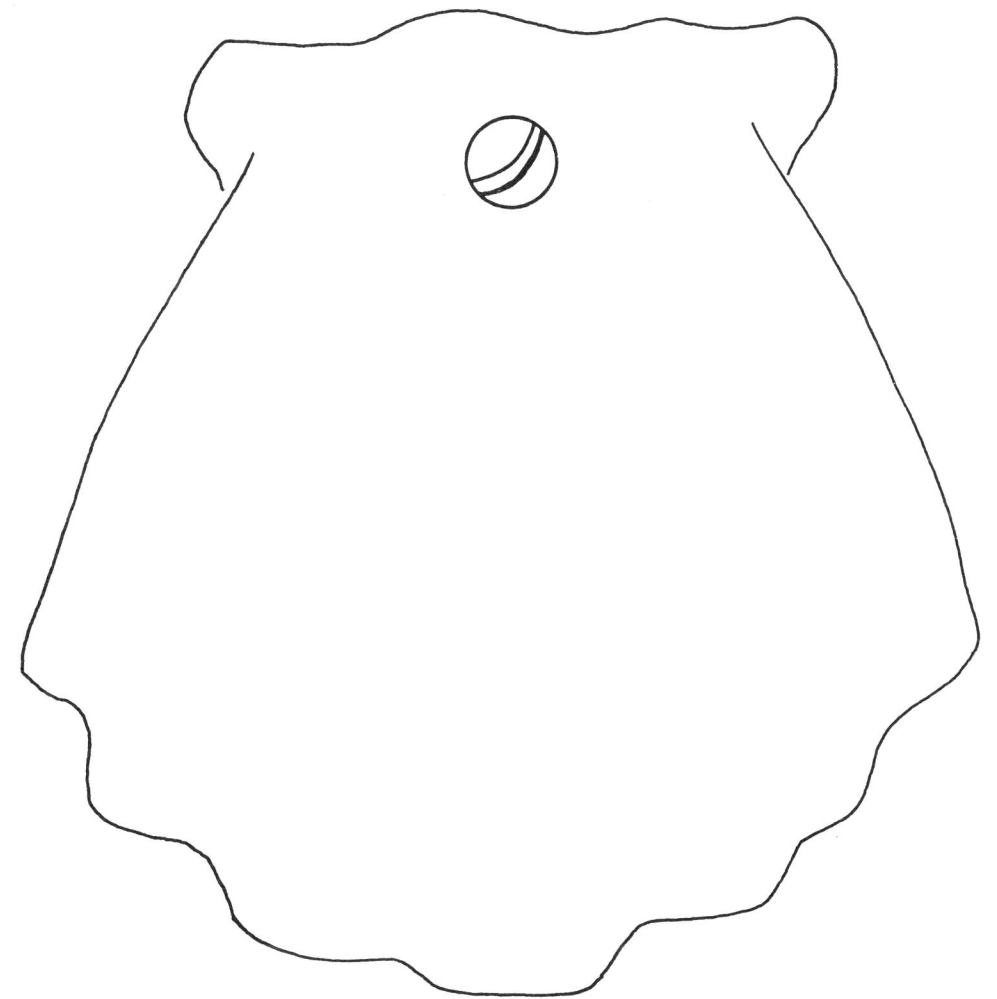

15

2. Draw the following on either the oyster shells or the pearls, as indicated. Mark the corresponding numerals on the backs of both. The figures should be drawn in the center of the pearls and at the top of the oyster shells as shown in the oyster pattern.

	Oyster	*Pearl*
1	rain	ring
2	10	tent
3	sock	soap
4	pen	pig
5	bird	bow
6	ghost	gate
7	nose	needle
8	lamp	lightning
9	fish	feather
10	watch	wind
11	house	hat
12	cat	can
13	ball	bat

Game Play:

1. Make two piles, one with the pink oyster shells and one with the pearls.
2. Look at the drawing on one of the pink oyster shells. Say the word for this picture quietly to yourself. Say it again and listen to the sound at the beginning of the word.
3. Now look through the pearls, saying each of the picture words. Do this until you find one that you think begins with the same sound as the picture word on your first oyster. Place this pearl on top of your oyster and continue to do the same with the rest of the oysters and pearls.
4. When you finish, turn over the oysters and pearls. If the numerals are the same, you are correct.

Peek in the Windows

Skill Reinforced: auditory discrimination

Grade Level: low primary

Materials Needed:

    7 sheets of 7" × 10" yellow posterboard

    scissors

    felt-tipped pen

    small pictures from a catalog or readiness workbook

    glue

Construction Directions:

1. Cut out small pictures from a catalog or readiness workbook. Look for pictures of things that rhyme or belong to the same word family. For example, you should easily be able to find pictures of fish—dish, duck—truck, star—car, sun—gun, hose—rose, fan—pan.
2. You will need seven pairs of rhyming words. You will also need to cut out seven pictures that do *not* rhyme.
3. Cut and mark the seven posterboard pieces using the house pattern shown on the following page. Glue a rhyming pair of pictures plus one nonrhyming picture to each house as shown in the illustration.
4. Mark a star behind the window that is above the rhyming word.

Game Play:

1. Look at the top picture on one of the houses. Say the word for this picture quietly to yourself. Say it again and see how the word ends.
2. Look at the two pictures below the windows. Say each word. Which one of these words rhymes or ends just like the top picture word?
3. When you think you know, open the window above the picture you choose. If you are right, you will find a star.

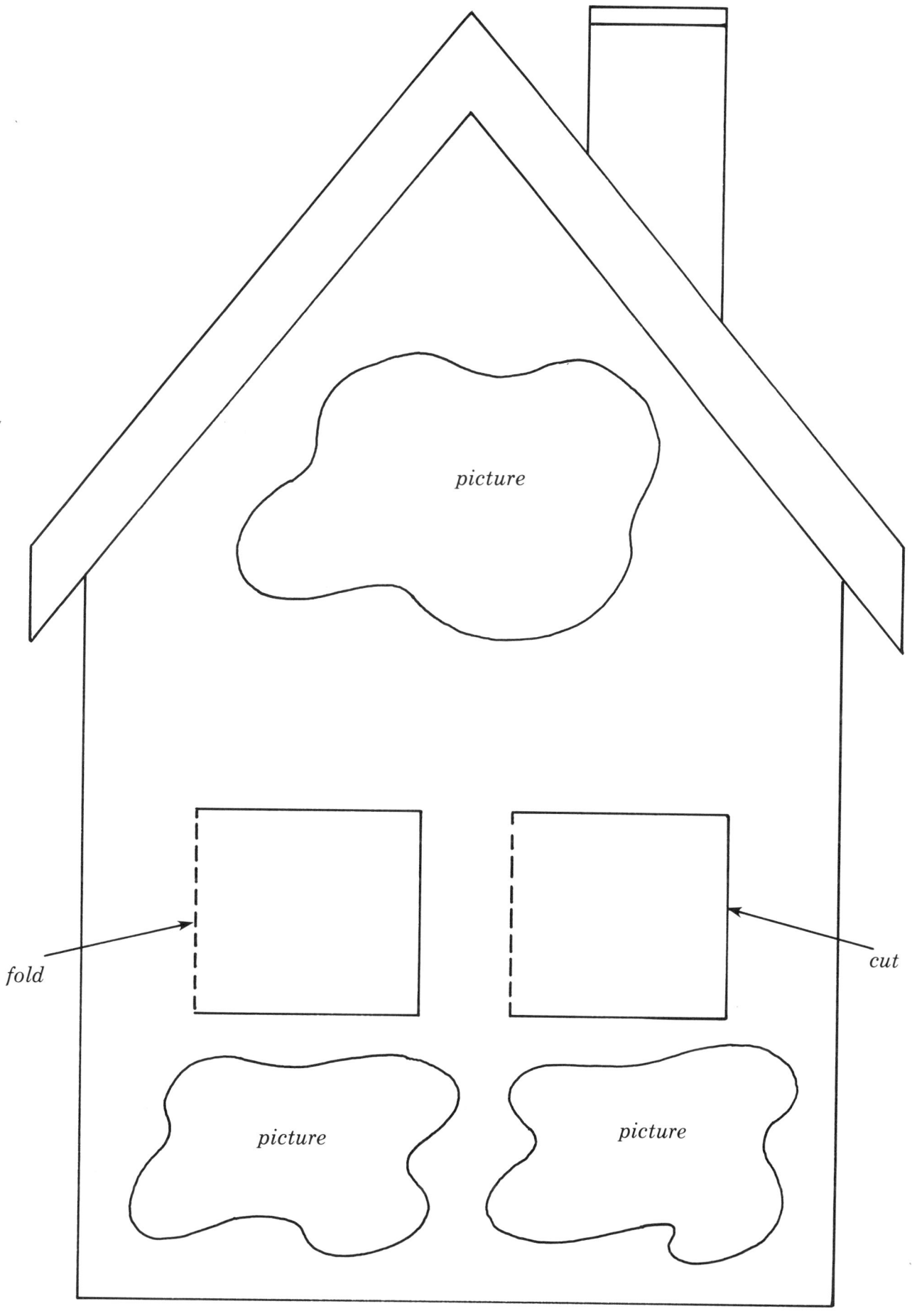

Mitten Match

Skill Reinforced: auditory discrimination
Grade Level: low primary
Materials Needed:
   12 sheets of 6″ × 8″ blue posterboard
   scissors
   felt-tipped pen

Construction Directions:
   1. Cut the posterboard pieces using the mitten pattern on the following page.
   2. Divide the mittens into pairs. On each pair of mittens draw the following pictures. Mark the corresponding numerals on the backs of both.

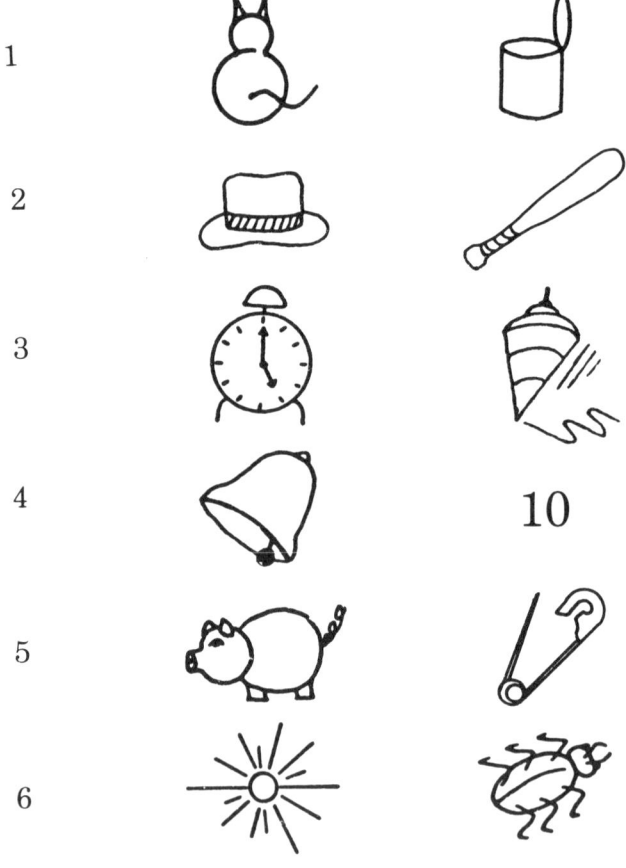

Game Play:
   1. Look at the drawing on one of the mittens. Say the word for this drawing. Say it again and listen for the vowel sound in the middle of the word.

2. Look through the other mittens and try to find a drawing that has a word with the same vowel sound in the middle.
3. When you think you have found one, turn over the mittens. If the numerals are the same, you are correct. Continue to do this with all of the mittens.

Beautiful Butterflies

Skill Reinforced: alphabet knowledge
Grade Level: low primary
Materials Needed:
  18 sheets of 4″ × 8″ orange posterboard
  9 sheets of 2″ × 8″ green posterboard
  scissors
  felt-tipped pen
  color markers

Construction Directions:

1. Cut and mark the green posterboard pieces as shown on the next page. Print each of the following lower-case letters on one of the green pieces as shown in the illustration. Mark the corresponding numerals on the backs of the green pieces.

    b - 1   k - 6
    d - 2   m - 7
    e - 3   n - 8
    g - 4   s - 9
    i - 5

2. Cut nine of the orange posterboard pieces as shown at the left on page 24. Print each of the following lower-case letters on one of these pieces. Mark the corresponding numerals on the backs.

    a - 1   c - 2
    d - 3   f - 4
    h - 5   j - 6
    l - 7   m - 8
    r - 9

3. Cut nine of the orange posterboard pieces as shown at the right on page 24. Print each of the following lower-case letters on one of these pieces. Mark the corresponding numerals on the backs.

    c - 1   e - 2
    f - 3   h - 4
    j - 5   l - 6
    n - 7   o - 8
    t - 9

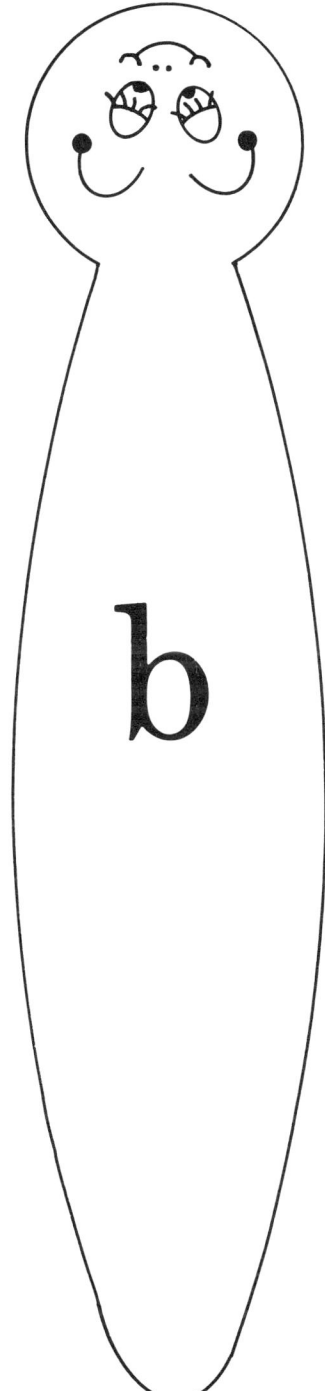

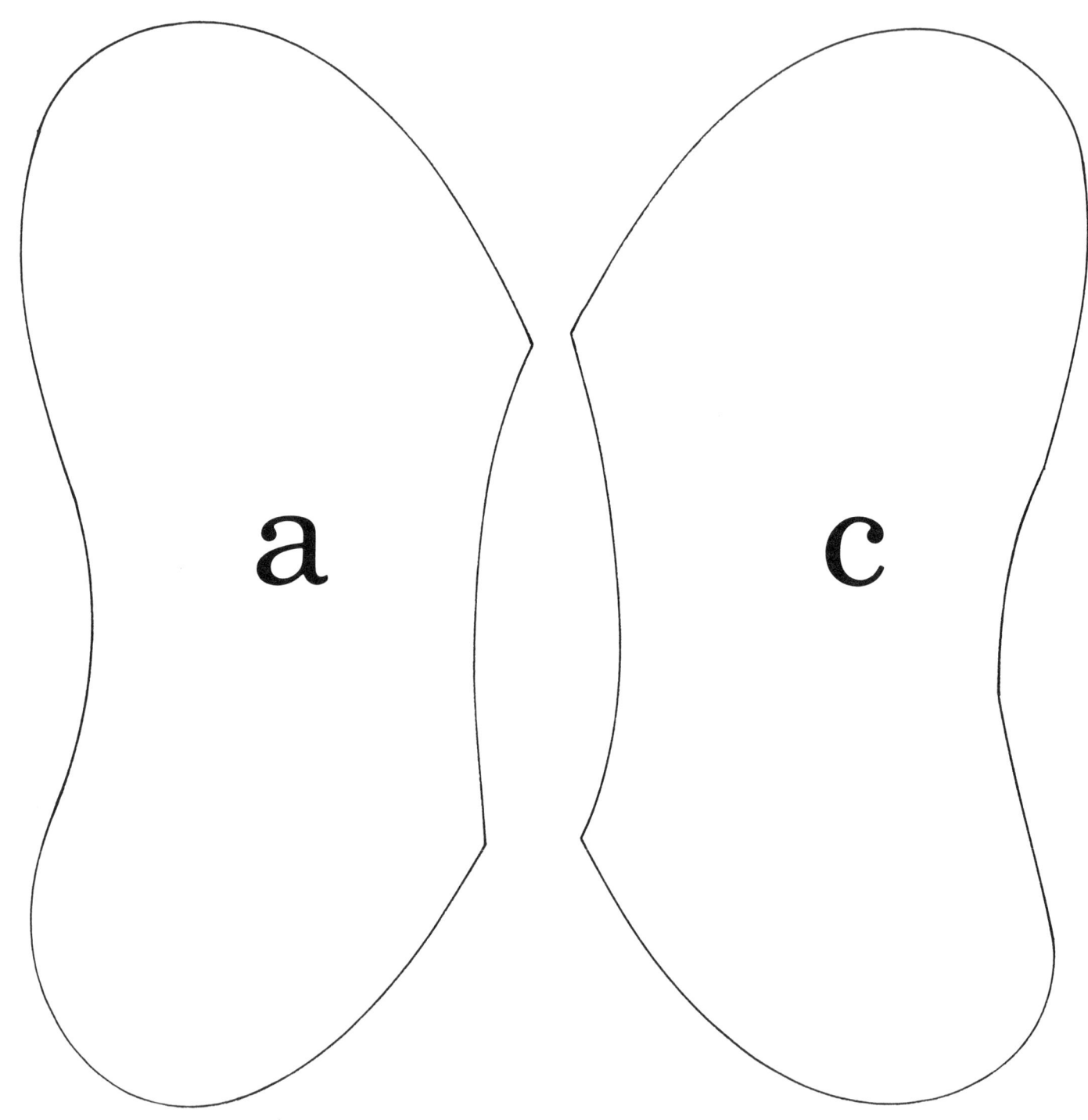

Game Play:

1. Make two piles, one with the green butterfly bodies and one with the wings.
2. Look at one of the green bodies. What letter is on it? Try to find the wings for this butterfly. You can only use the wings with letters of the alphabet that come before and after the letter on the green body.
3. For example, if the body had the letter "b" on it, the wings would have to have the letters "a" and "c."
4. When you are finished, turn over the pieces in order to see if you are correct. The numerals should be the same.

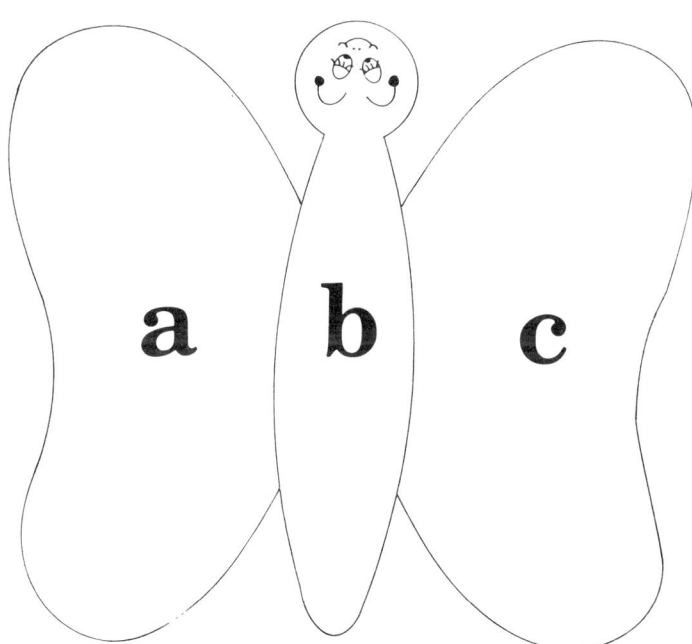

Sailing, Sailing

Skill Reinforced: alphabet knowledge

Grade Level: low primary

Materials Needed:

11 sheets of 2″ × 10″ posterboard in various colors

11 sheets of 4″ × 6″ white posterboard

scissors

felt-tipped pen

color markers

Construction Directions:

1. Cut the 2″ × 10″ posterboard pieces using the boat pattern at the right of the following page.
2. Mark each of the following letter groups on one of the boat pieces as shown in the illustration.

a	b	c	d e
c	d	e	f g
d	e	f	g h
f	g	h	i j
h	i	j	k l
p	q	r	s t
r	s	t	u v
t	u	v	w x
j	k	l	m n
n	o	p	q r
l	m	n	o p

3. Cut the white posterboard pieces using the sail pattern shown at the left of the next page.
4. Mark each of the following letters on one of the sails as shown in the illustration.

f	s	h	i	k m
o	u	w	y	q

5. Place self-checking color markers on the backs of the correct pairs.

Game Play:

1. Make two piles, one with the boats and one with the sails.
2. Choose one of the boats and read the letters of the alphabet. Were you correct? Well, do it again and see if you know what letter comes next after the last letter on the boat. If you do, try to find it on one of the sails.
3. When you think you have found it, turn them over. If the color markers are the same, you are correct. Continue to do this with all of the boats and sails. Don't get seasick!

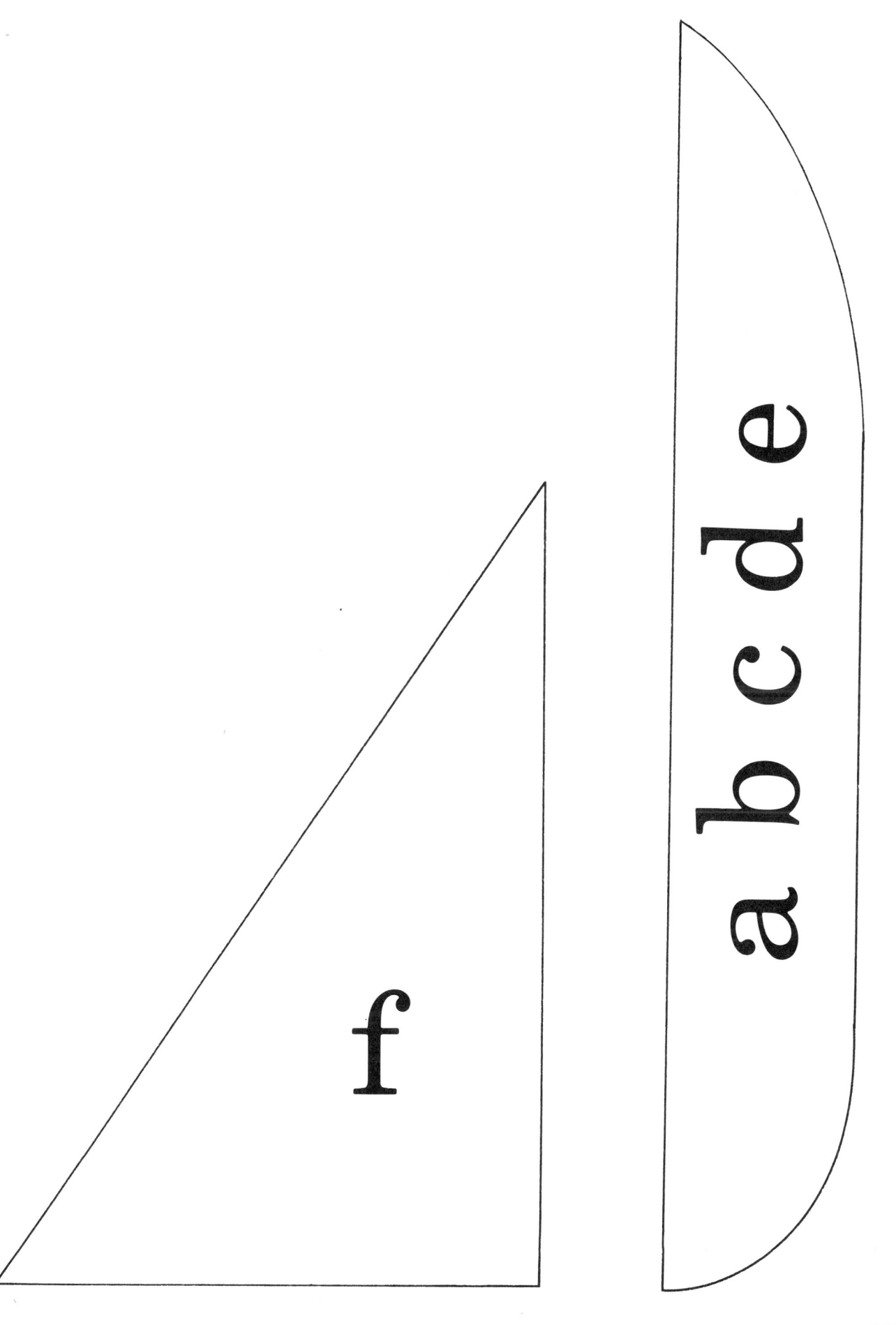

The Lost Caboose

Skill Reinforced: alphabet knowledge
Grade Level: low primary
Materials Needed:
   10 sheets of 5" × 7" gray posterboard
   10 sheets of 5" × 7" red posterboard
   scissors
   felt-tipped pen
   color markers

Construction Directions:
   1. Cut and mark the gray posterboard pieces using the engine pattern shown here.
   2. Print each of the following upper-case letters on one of the engines as shown in the illustration.
      A B C D E F G H I J

3. Cut and mark the red posterboard pieces using the caboose pattern shown here.
4. Print each of the following lower-case letters on one of the cabooses as shown in the illustration.

a b c d e f g h i j

5. Place self-checking color markers on the backs of the correct pairs.

Game Play:

1. Make two piles, one with engines and one with cabooses.
2. Take the first engine and look at the capital letter on it. Help this engine to find his lost caboose. You must look through all of the cabooses until you find the one with the same letter as the one on the engine. You will see that the letters on the cabooses are all small letters.
3. When you think you have found the missing caboose, turn over the two pieces and make sure. If the color markers are the same, you are right.

Bigger Than I Am

Skill Reinforced: categorization
Grade Level: low primary
Materials Needed:
    1 sheet of 7" × 8" red posterboard
    1 blue posterboard circle with 7" diameter
    20 sheets of posterboard (size varies according to pictures)
    scissors
    felt-tipped pen
    pictures from a catalog or readiness workbook
    glue
    color markers

Construction Directions:
1. Cut and mark the red posterboard piece using the house pattern on the following page.
2. Mark the blue posterboard circle using an enlargement of the ball pattern shown here.

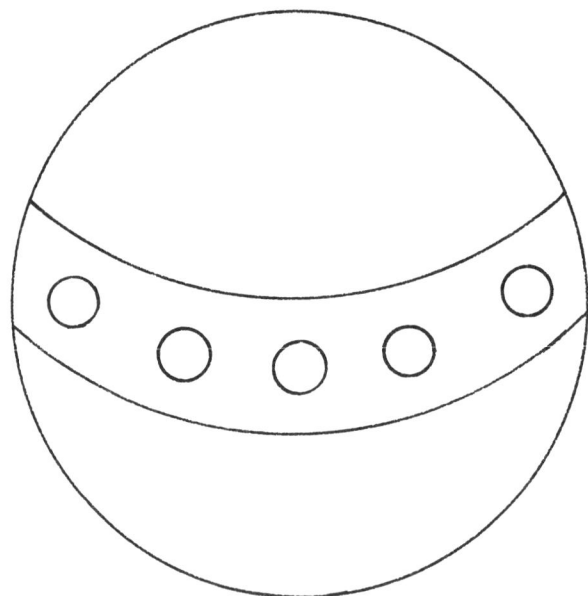

3. Cut out and mount 20 pictures to the smaller posterboard pieces. Ten pictures should be of items that are smaller than a child; for example, a toothbrush, a toy car, a wristwatch. The other ten pictures should be of items that are larger than a child; for example, a bed, a tree, an airplane.
4. Place color markers on the backs of the pieces for self-checking.

Game Play:

1. Place the red house and the blue ball in front of you.
2. Look at one of the picture cards. What is it? If you really had one of these objects, would it be bigger or smaller than you are? If you think it would be bigger, place it on the red house. If you think it would be smaller, place it on the ball. Do this with all of the picture cards.
3. When you are finished, turn over the cards. If the colors are the same in each pile, you are right.

Something in Common

Skill Reinforced: categorization
Grade Level: low primary
Materials Needed:
  11 posterboard circles with 6" diameters
  11 shoelaces
  felt-tipped pen
  paper hole punch
  tape

Construction Directions:

1. Punch holes and attach the shoelaces to the posterboard circles as shown here.

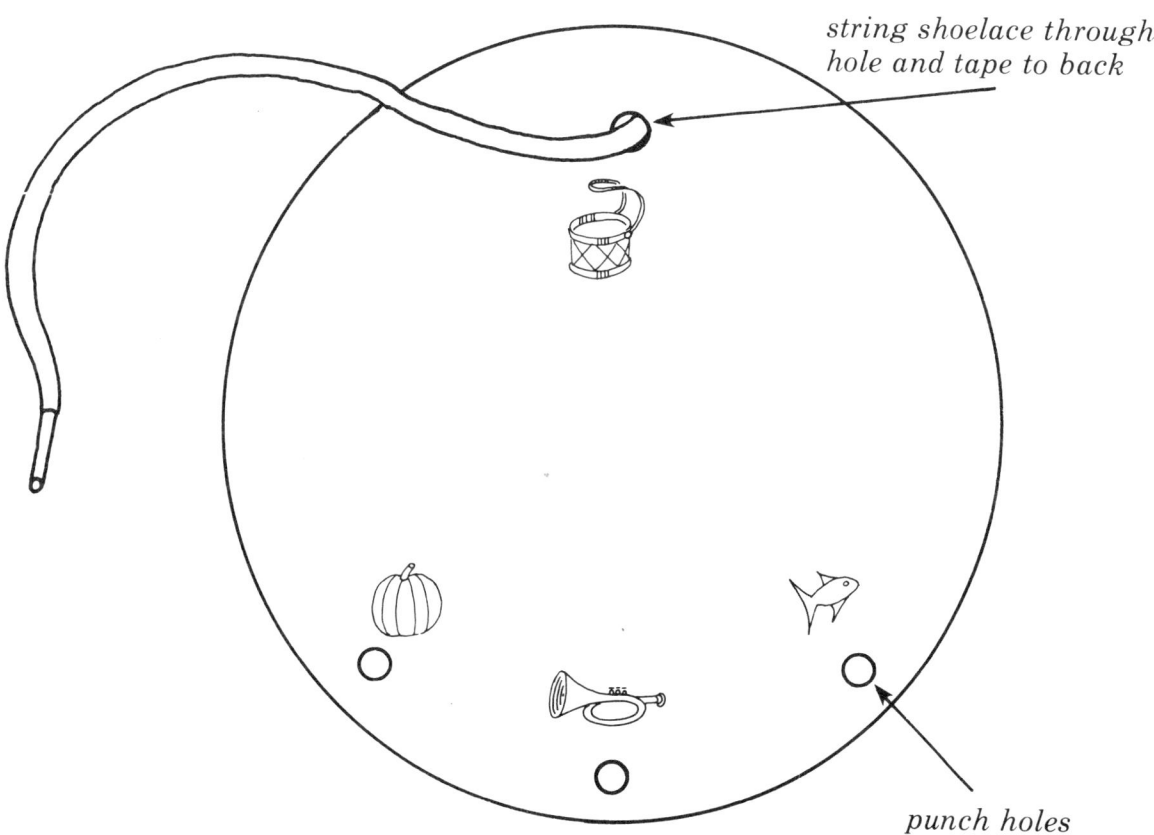

2. Mark each of the following picture groups on a different circle as shown in the illustration. Mark around the back of the hole under the correct item on each playing board.

Game Play:

1. Choose one of the game boards and look at the picture at the top.
2. Look at the other three drawings. Which one of these drawings has something to do with the one at the top? For example, are they both animals? Are they both toys? Try to find the one that has something in common with the top drawing.
3. When you think you know, place the shoelace through the hole under that drawing. Turn it over. If the shoelace is through the marked hole, you are correct.

Word Fit

Skill Reinforced: sight word knowledge

Grade Level: primary

Materials Needed:

    5 sheets of 8½" × 11" colored posterboard, 1 yellow,
       1 orange, 1 red, 1 green, 1 blue

    5 pictures from old basal readers (about 7" × 7")

    scissors

    glue

    ruler

    felt-tipped pen

Construction Directions:

1. Select a picture showing various objects and glue the picture to one of the posterboard pieces as shown below.
2. Print the names of five items in the picture on the right side of the posterboard. Draw arrows from each word to the item in the picture. Cut out the words as shown in the illustration. Do this with each of the posterboard pieces.

Game Play:

1. Separate the large picture cards and the word cards according to color.
2. Choose one of the colors to begin. Place the large picture in front of you. Notice that arrows have been drawn to parts of the picture. These objects have names and you are to try to find the names on the word cards.
3. When you think you have found them, place them next to the large card at the end of the arrow. If they fit, you are correct. Continue to do the same with the rest of the picture cards.

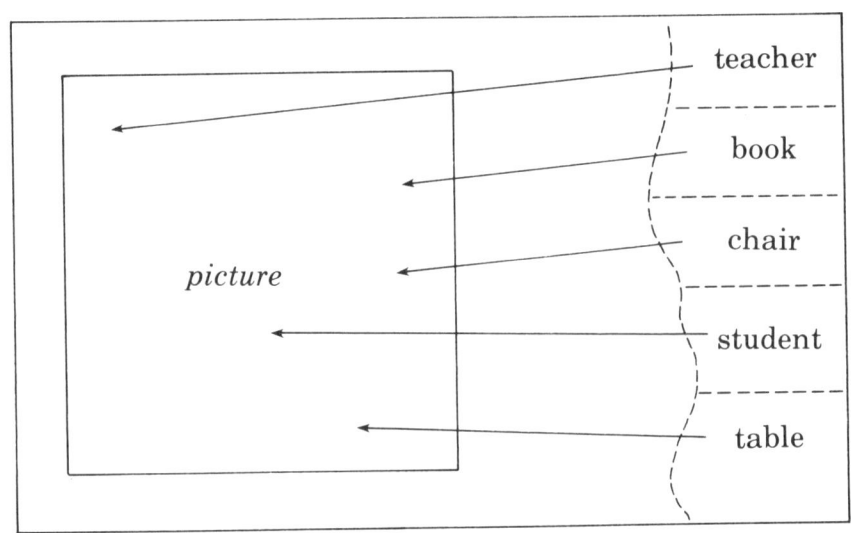

Stop and Go

Skill Reinforced: sight word knowledge
Grade Level: primary
Materials Needed:

    14 sheets of 4" × 11" dark blue posterboard
    14 green posterboard circles with 3" diameters
    14 yellow posterboard circles with 3" diameters
    14 red posterboard circles with 3" diameters
    glue
    felt-tipped pen

Construction Directions:

1. Glue the red and yellow circles to the dark blue posterboard pieces as shown on the following page.
2. Draw the following pictures on the red posterboard circles. Mark the corresponding numerals on the backs of the blue posterboard pieces.

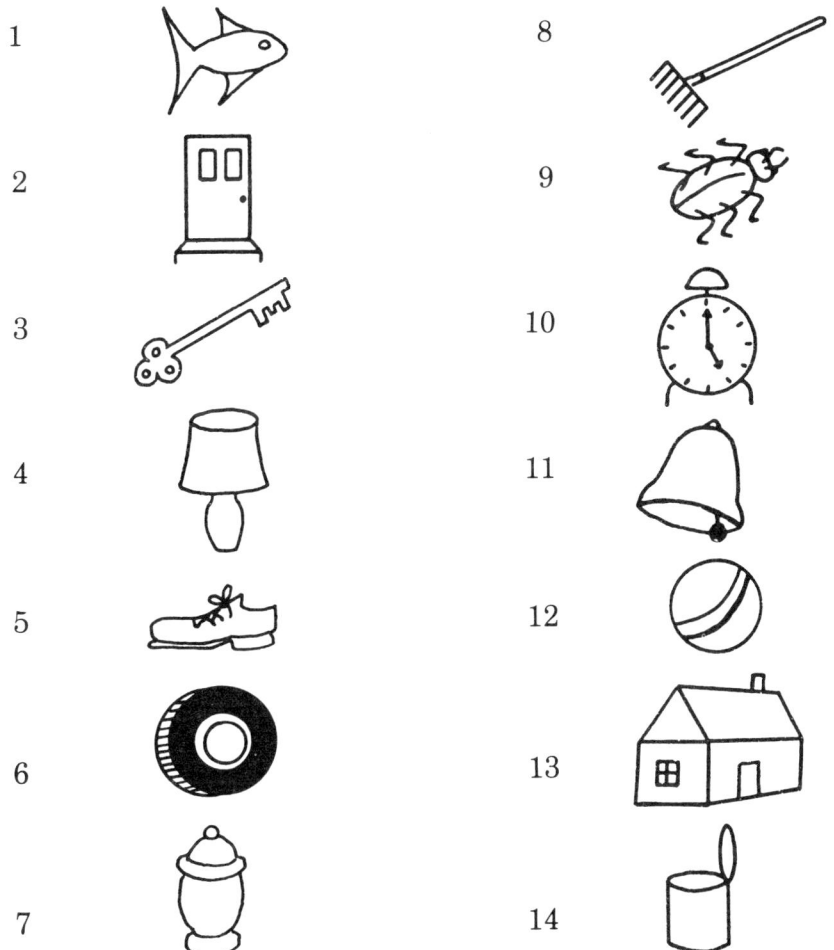

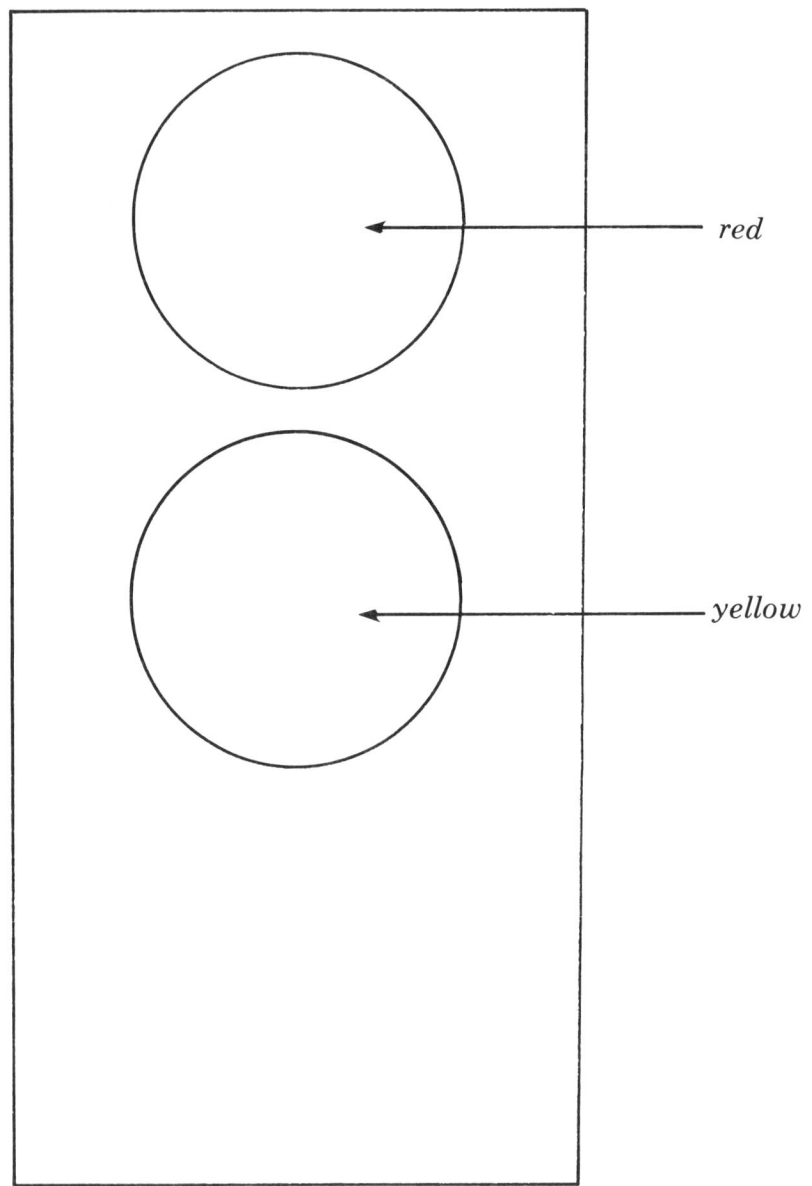

3. Print each of the following words on a different green circle. Mark the corresponding numerals on the backs.

1	fish
2	door
3	key
4	lamp
5	shoe
6	wheel
7	shell
8	rake
9	bug
10	clock
11	bell
12	ball
13	house
14	can

Game Play:

1. Make two piles, one with the traffic lights and one with the green lights.
2. Choose one of the traffic lights. Look at the picture on the red light. Look through the green light in order to find the name of the picture.
3. When you think you have found it, turn both pieces over. If the numerals are the same, you are right.

Swimmy Flips His Fins

Skill Reinforced: sight word knowledge
Grade Level: primary
Materials Needed:
   10 sheets of 7" × 10" orange posterboard
   scissors
   felt-tipped pen

Construction Directions:
1. Cut and mark the posterboard pieces using the fish pattern on the next page.
2. Copy each of the following groups of words and numerals on a different fish as shown in the illustration.

one	ten	five
1	2	3
six	two	three
four	five	two
4	5	6
five	seven	six
seven	three	nine
7	8	9
one	eight	seven
two		
10		
ten		

3. Fold the fins of all of the fish as shown in the illustration.
4. Mark a star on the backs of all of the fins that contain a correct answer.

Game Play:
1. Look at the numeral on Swimmy. Say the word for this number quietly to yourself.
2. Now, look at both of his fins. Which word do you think is the word for this numeral?
3. When you think you know, flip that fin. If you find a star on it, you are correct.

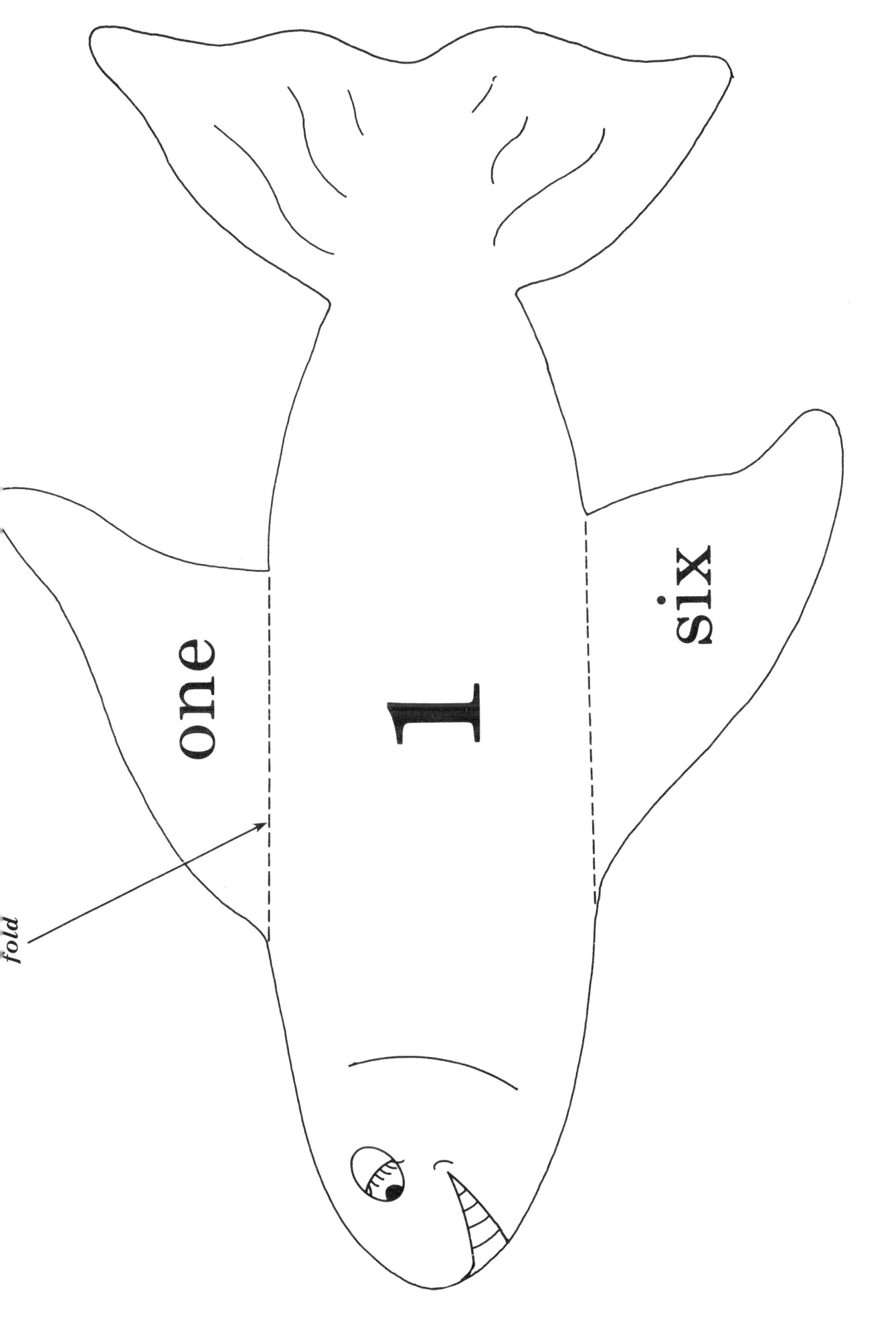

Inside—Outside

Skill Reinforced: sight word knowledge
Grade Level: primary
Materials Needed:

    1 sheet of 6″ × 9″ green posterboard
    1 yellow posterboard circle with 8½″ diameter
    2 sheets of 2″ × 8″ white posterboard
    20 sheets of 1½″ × 2½″ white posterboard
    scissors
    tape
    felt-tipped pen
    color markers

Construction Directions:

1. Print the following words on ten of the 1½″ × 2½″ posterboard pieces. Place green markers on the backs of these cards.

    bed
    desk
    stove
    mirror
    hall
    sink
    carpet
    kitchen
    television
    lamp

2. Print the following words on the remaining ten small white posterboard cards. Place yellow markers on the backs of these cards.

    wind
    hike
    tree
    grass
    fence
    football
    rake
    rain
    snow
    tractor

3. Cut and mark the large green posterboard piece using the house pattern on page 44.
4. Cut and mark the large yellow posterboard circle using the sun pattern on page 45.

5. Attach the white strips of posterboard to the backs of these pieces as shown here.

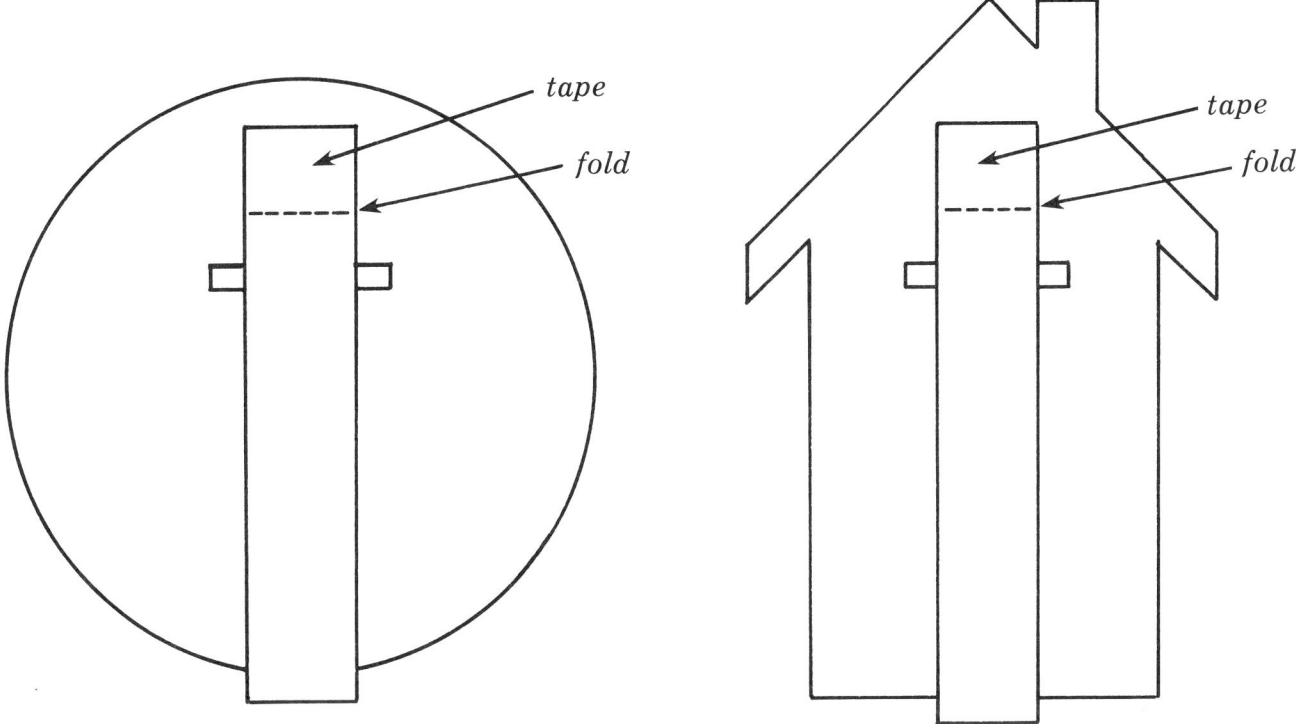

Game Play:

1. Stand up the house and the sun on a flat surface.
2. Look at one of the word cards. Do you think you would normally find this item inside or outside a house? When you think you know, push the card through the slot in either the house or the sun. Use the house if you think it is an "inside" word and the sun if you think it is an "outside" word.
3. When you finish with all of the word cards, turn them over to see if you are correct. The green color means that the item is found inside. The yellow color means that it is found outside.

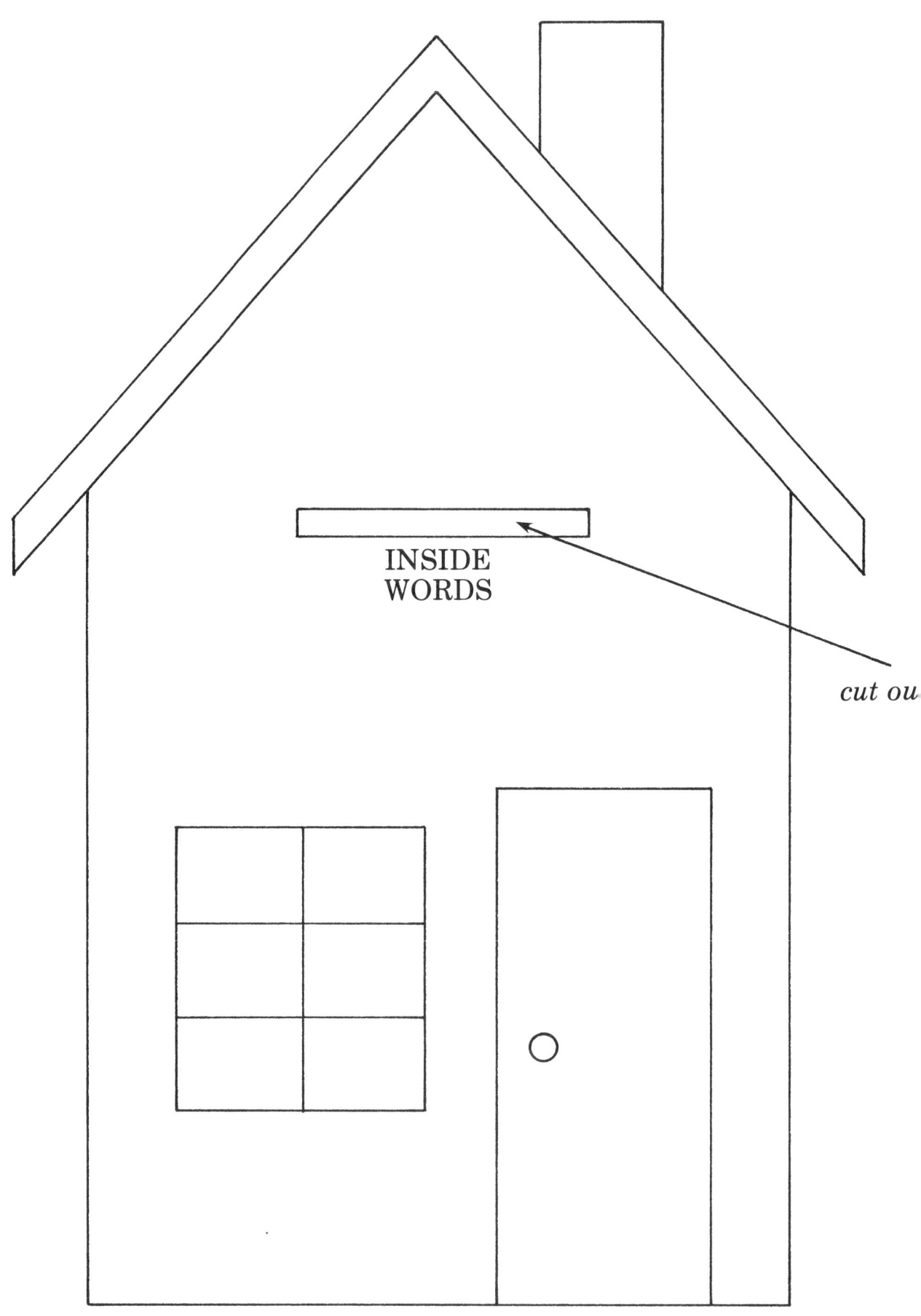

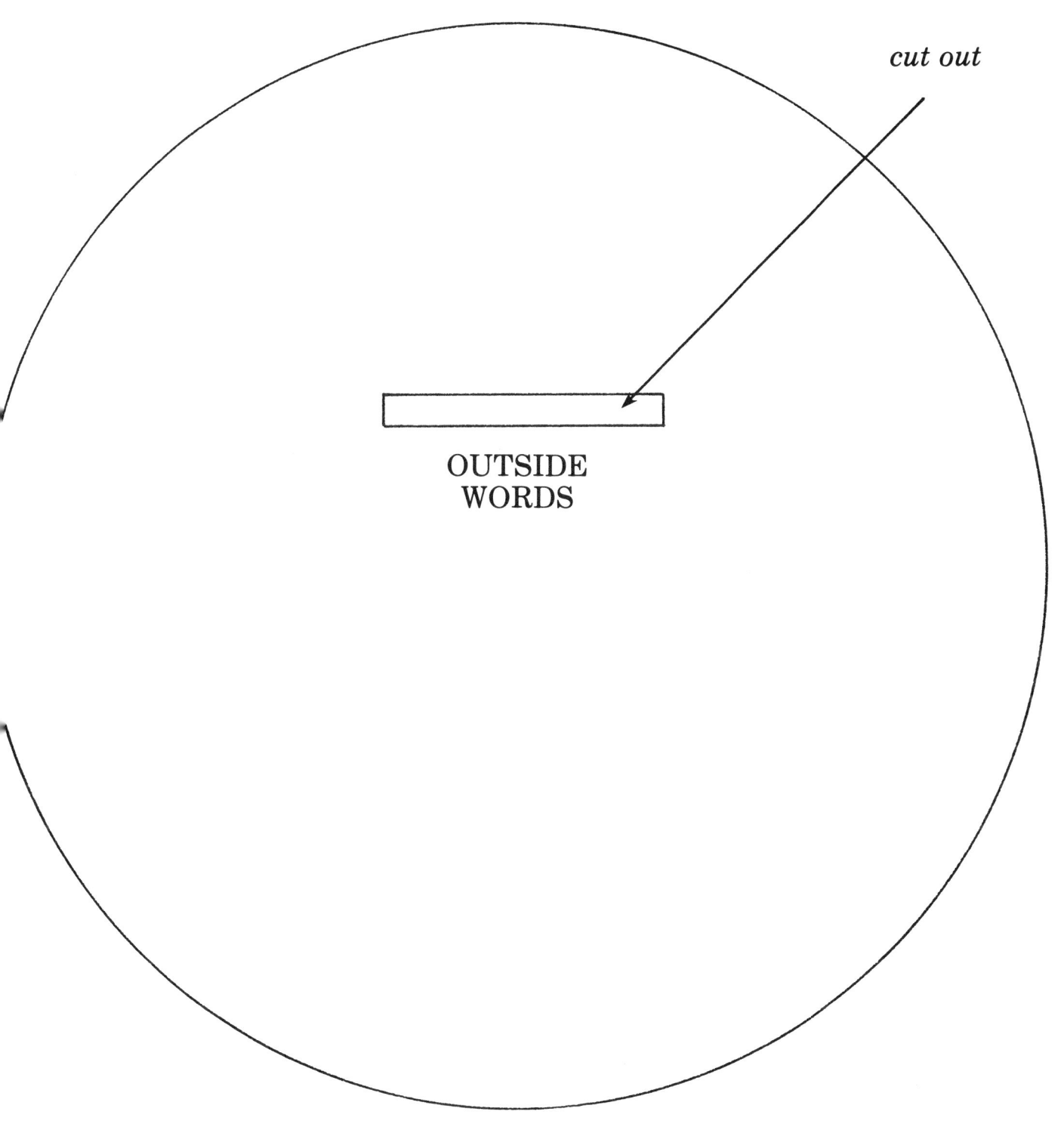

Busy As a Bee

Skill Reinforced: sight word knowledge
Grade Level: primary
Materials Needed:

    12 sheets of 5″ × 8″ orange posterboard
    4 sheets of 6″ × 6″ red posterboard
    4 sheets of 6″ × 6″ blue posterboard
    4 sheets of 6″ × 6″ yellow posterboard
    scissors
    felt-tipped pen
    pictures from a catalog or readiness book
    glue

Construction Directions:

1. Cut and mark the orange posterboard pieces as shown here.

2. Cut and mark the red, blue, and yellow posterboard pieces using the flower pattern shown here.

3. Glue a picture onto the body of each bee. Then, print each of these picture words in the center of a flower. Put self-checking numerals on the backs of both.

Game Play:

1. Make two piles, one with the bees and one with the flowers.
2. Choose one of the bees and look at the picture on its body. Look through the flowers and find the name of this object.
3. When you think you have found it, turn over the two pieces. If the numerals are the same, you are correct. Continue to match the bees with the flowers.

Turn On the Light

Skill Reinforced: sight word knowledge
Grade Level: primary
Materials Needed:

    10 sheets of 6" × 10" white posterboard
    10 sheets of 1½" × 11" yellow posterboard
    scissors
    felt-tipped pen
    pictures from a catalog or readiness book
    glue

Construction Directions:

1. Cut and mark the white posterboard pieces using the light bulb pattern on the following page.
2. Insert the yellow posterboard strips as shown in the illustration.
3. Glue a small picture of an item onto the top of each light bulb. Print this picture word along with two other words on the yellow strips so that they can be read by pulling the strip through the light bulb.
4. Print the correct word on the back of the light bulb.

Game Play:

1. Place the light bulbs on a flat surface.
2. Look at the picture on one of the light bulbs. Do you know what it is?
3. See if you can find the word on the yellow strip by moving it up and down.
4. When you think you have found the correct word, turn over the light bulb and check your answer.

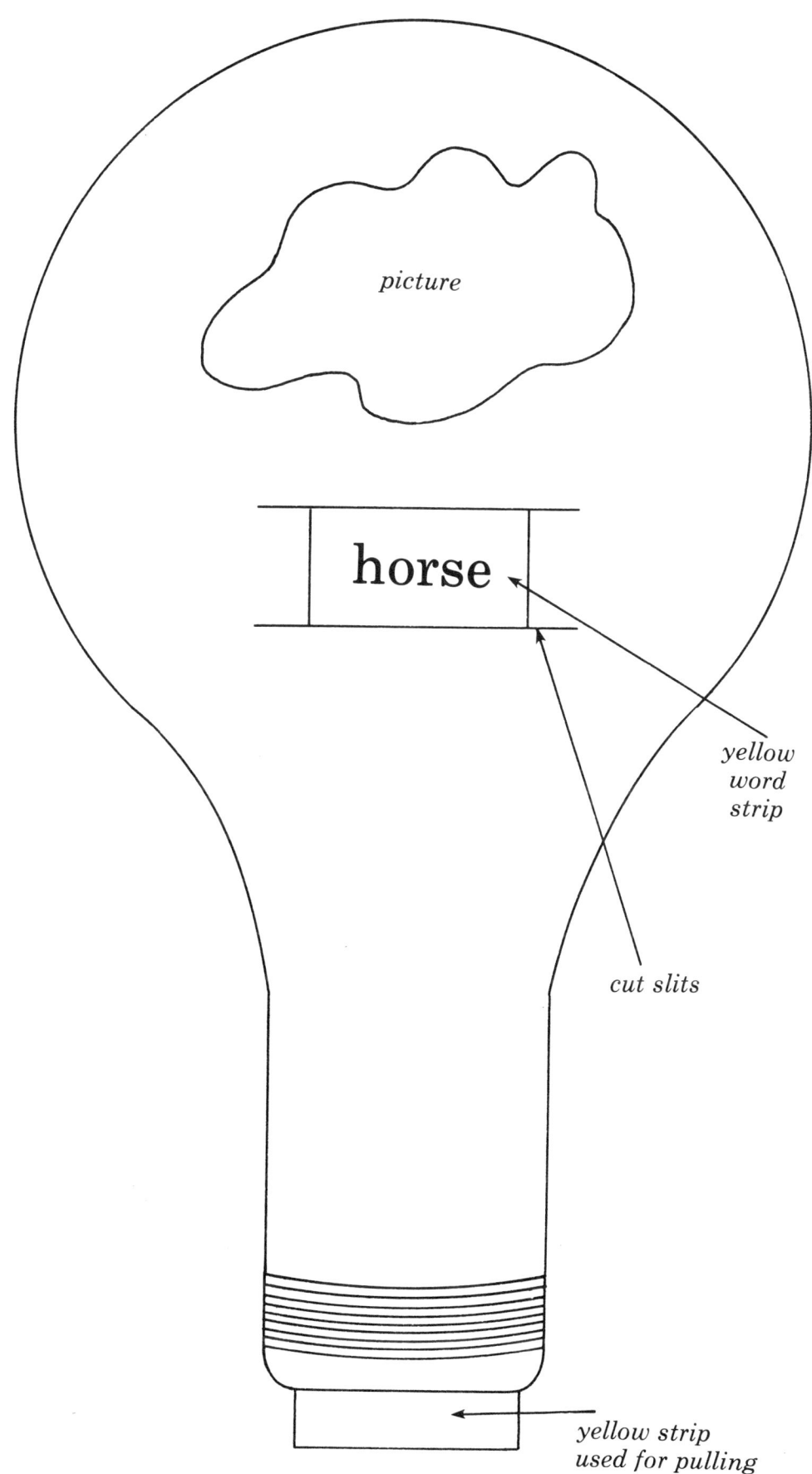

Let Toby Help

Skill Reinforced: initial consonants
Grade Level: primary
Materials Needed:
   8 sheets of 5" × 9" green posterboard
   scissors
   felt-tipped pen
   paper hole punch
   8 shoelaces
   tape

Construction Directions:
1. Cut and mark the posterboard pieces using the turtle pattern on the following page.
2. Attach the shoelaces by putting them through the hole as shown in the illustration and then taping one end to the back of Toby.
3. Mark each of the following picture and letter combinations on a turtle as shown in the illustration. Make a mark around the back of the correct hole.

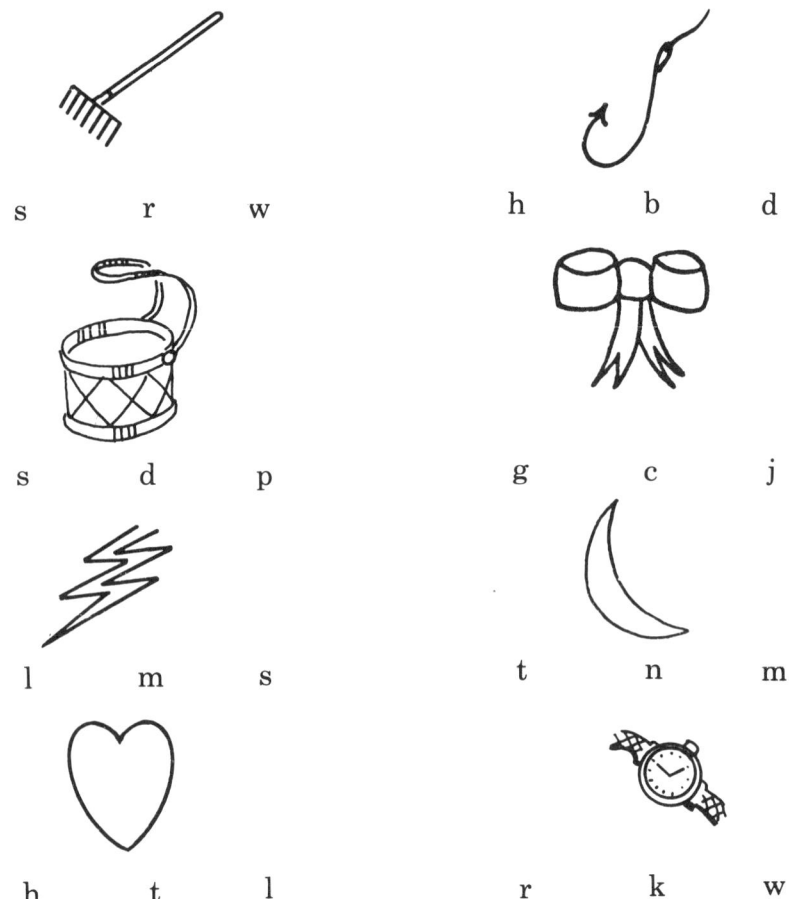

s   r   w   h   b   d

s   d   p   g   c   j

l   m   s   t   n   m

h   t   l   r   k   w

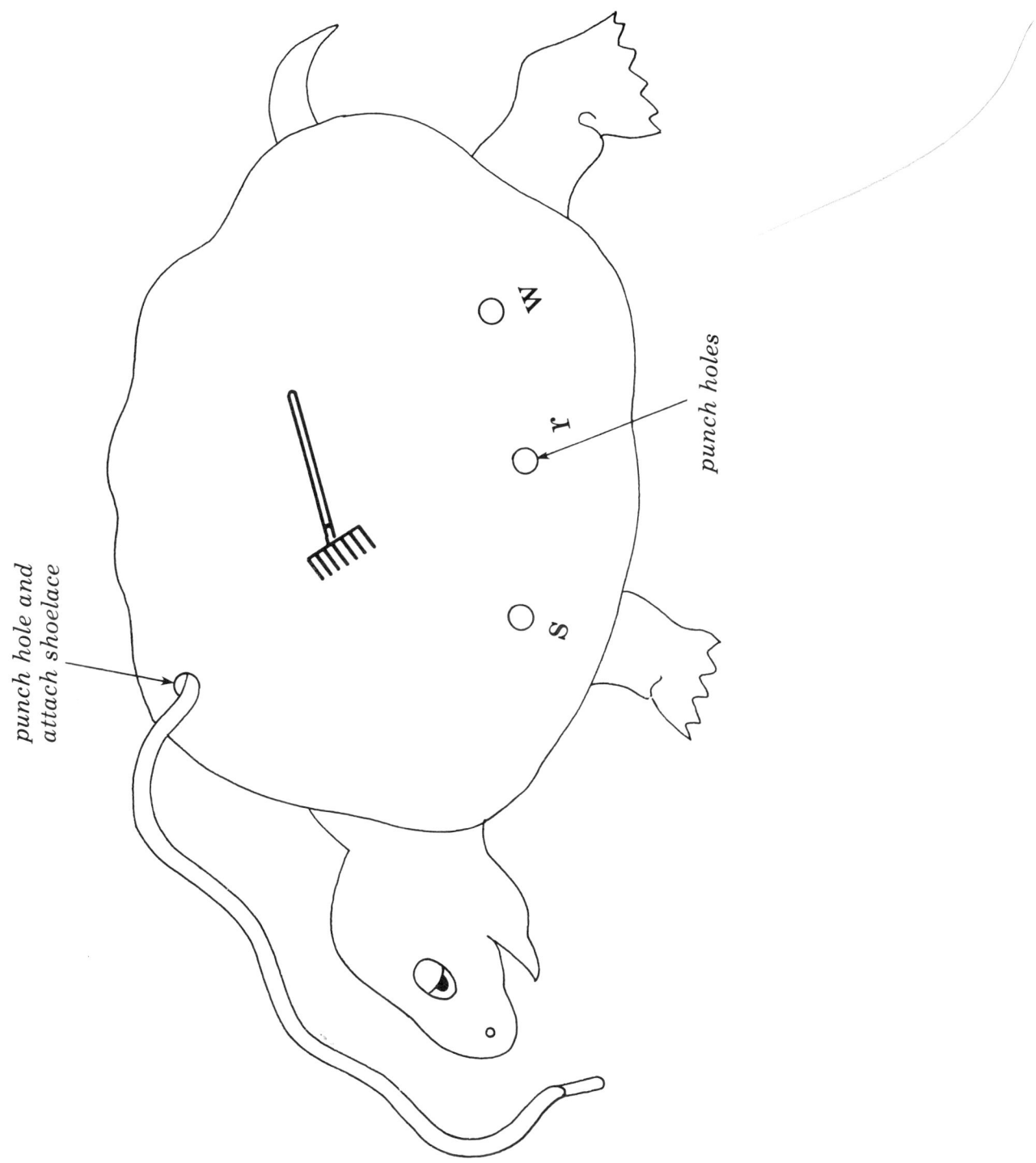

Game Play:
1. Look at one of the turtles. There is a drawing of something on Toby's back. Do you know what it is? Say the word quietly to yourself. Say it again and listen for the beginning sound.
2. Now, look at the letters under the drawing on Toby's back. One of these letters represents the beginning sound you have just said. Say the word again and see if you can find the correct letter.
3. Put the shoelace through the hole above the letter you think is correct. Now turn over the turtle. If you put the shoelace through the hole that is marked, you are correct.

Do a Daisy

Skill Reinforced: initial consonants
Grade Level: primary
Materials Needed:
    6 sheets of 5" × 7" orange posterboard
    6 sheets of 4" × 9" green posterboard
    24 sheets of 2½" × 5" pink posterboard
    scissors
    felt-tipped pen
    pictures from a catalog or readiness book
    glue

Construction Directions:
1. Cut the orange posterboard pieces using the pot pattern shown here.

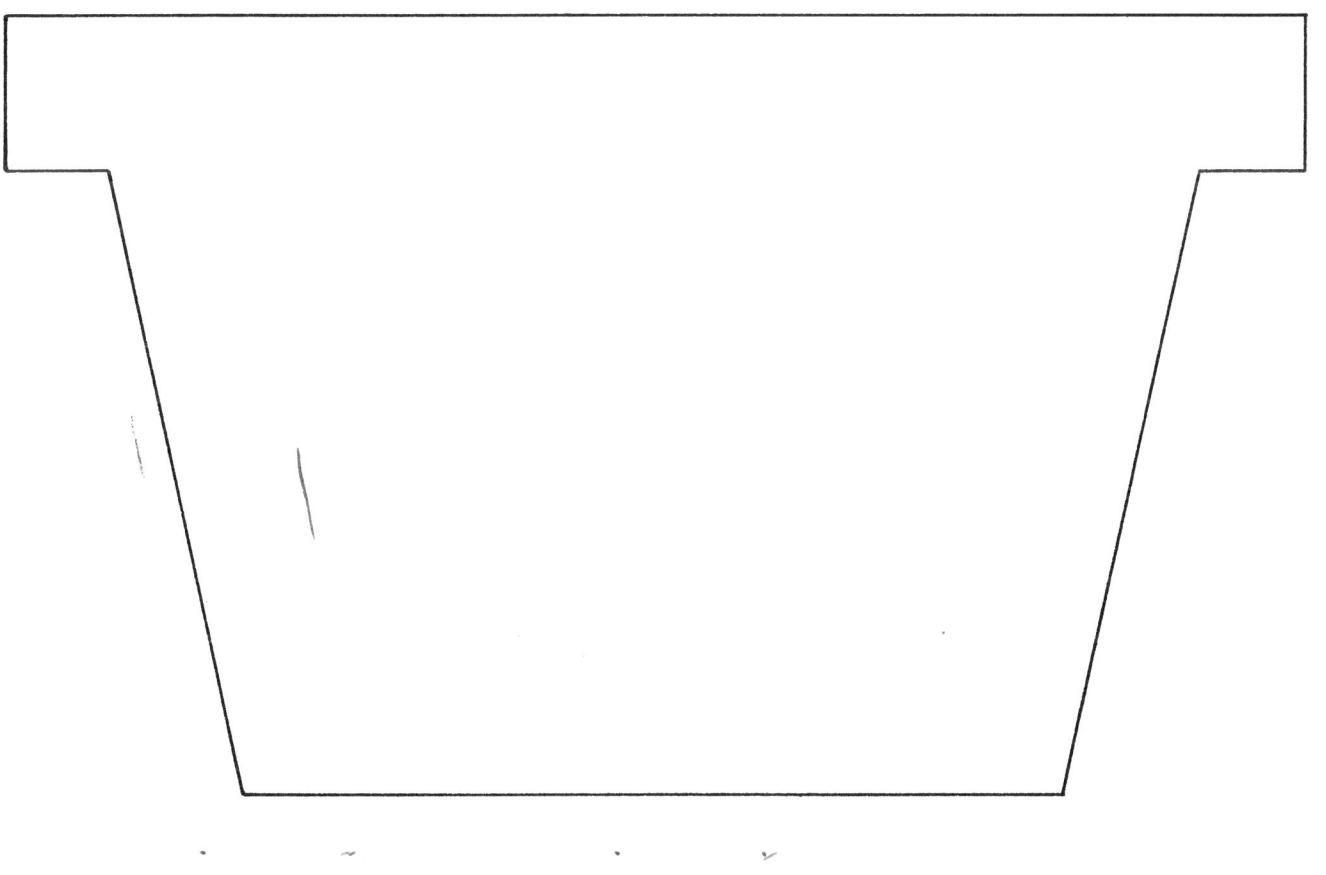

2. Cut and mark the green posterboard pieces using the stem pattern shown here.

3. Glue or tape the green stem and leaf to the back of the pot. Use the bottom two inches of each stem for this purpose.
4. Print each of the following letters on the top of the stems as shown in the illustration: l d c s j m
5. Cut the pink posterboard pieces using the petal pattern shown here.

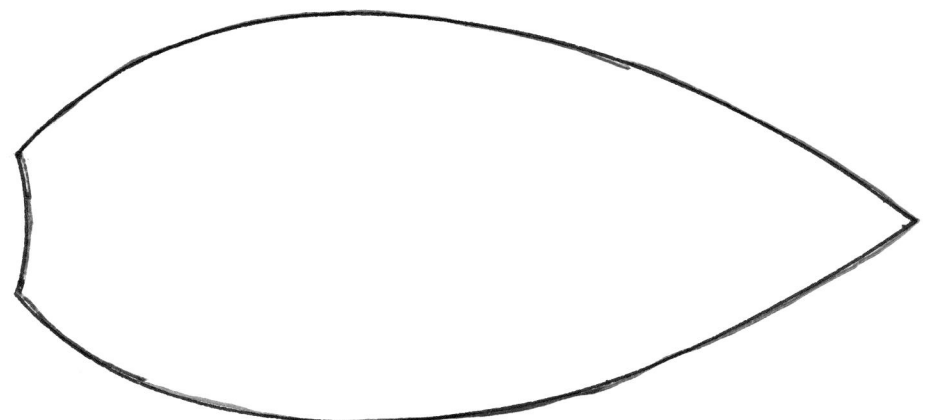

6. Find four small pictures of objects whose names begin with each of the letters listed above. The best place to find these is in a reading readiness workbook. Glue each of these pictures to a different pink petal. Number the backs of the petals with corresponding numerals on the backs of the pots for a self-check.

Game Play:

1. Make two piles, one with the flower pots and stems and the other with the pink petals.
2. Choose a flower pot and stem to begin. Place it in front of you. Look at the letter at the top of the stem. Look through all of the pictures on the petals and find four that begin with this letter.
3. Place them around the top of the stem to form a flower.
4. Continue to do the same with the rest of the flower pieces. When you are finished, you can turn over the pieces. If the numerals are the same, you are right.

Mail the Letters

Skill Reinforced: final consonants
Grade Level: primary
Materials Needed:

    5 sheets of 7″ × 10″ red posterboard
    5 sheets of 1½″ × 10″ white posterboard
    20 sheets of 3″ × 4½″ white posterboard
    scissors
    felt-tipped pen
    tape
    small pictures from a catalog or readiness workbook
    glue

Construction Directions:

1. Cut and mark the red posterboard pieces using the mailbox pattern on the following page.
2. Print each of the following final consonants on a separate mailbox as shown in the illustration: d l p k t
3. Attach each of the white posterboard strips to a mailbox with tape as shown here.

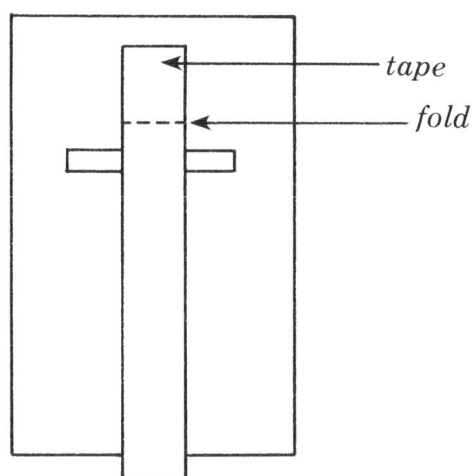

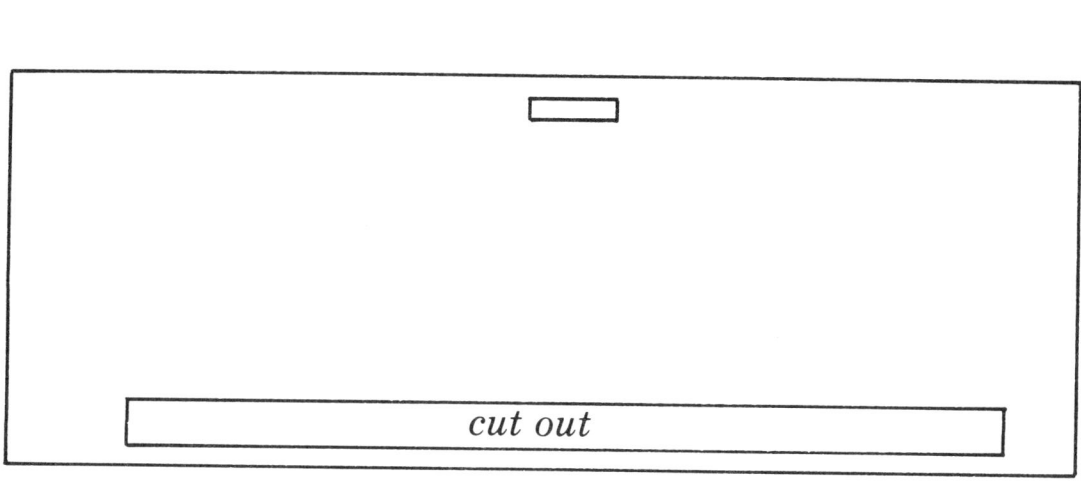
cut out

U.S. Mail

4. Mark the 3″ × 4½″ posterboard pieces as shown here.

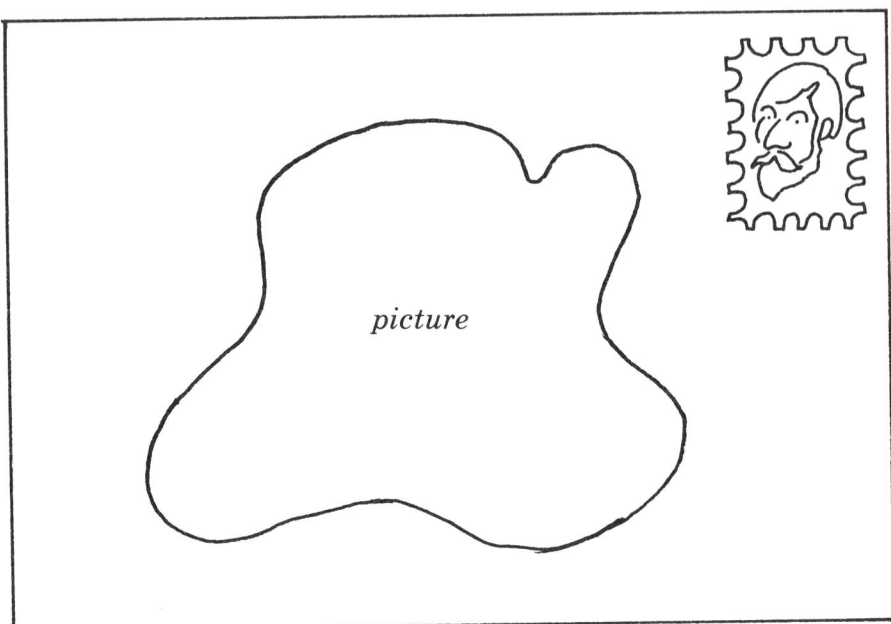

5. Find four small pictures of things whose names end with each of the consonants on the mailboxes. Glue each one to a letter as shown in the illustration.
6. Mark self-checking numerals on the backs of the letters and mailboxes.

Game Play:

1. Stand the mailboxes up on a flat surface.
2. Look at one of the pictures on a letter. Say the word for this picture quietly to yourself. What sound is at the end of this word? Look at the letters on each of the mailboxes and see if you can find the one that comes at the end of the picture word.
3. When you think you have found the correct mailbox, mail the letter! Now, take another letter and try mailing it the same way. Mail all of the letters.
4. When you are finished, turn the letters and mailboxes over to see if you are correct. The numerals should be the same.

Meet the Frog Family

Skill Reinforced: final consonants
Grade Level: primary
Materials Needed:
  10 sheets of 8″ × 9″ green posterboard
  scissors
  felt-tipped pen

Construction Directions:
  1. Cut and mark the posterboard pieces using the frog pattern on page 61.
  2. Copy each of the following drawings and final consonant combinations on a frog as shown in the frog pattern illustration. Cut each frog apart, using a different pattern, so that the drawing is on one half and the letter is on the other half. The dotted line in the illustration shows how the frogs are to be cut.

Game Play:

1. Make two piles, one with the pieces that have pictures on them and one with the pieces that have letters on them.
2. Now, take one of the pieces that has a picture on it. Say the word for this picture quietly to yourself. Say it again, but this time listen carefully to how the word ends. Look through the letter pieces to find a letter that represents that sound.
3. When you think you have found it, place the pieces next to one another. If they fit to form a frog, you are correct. Continue to do the same with all of the pieces.

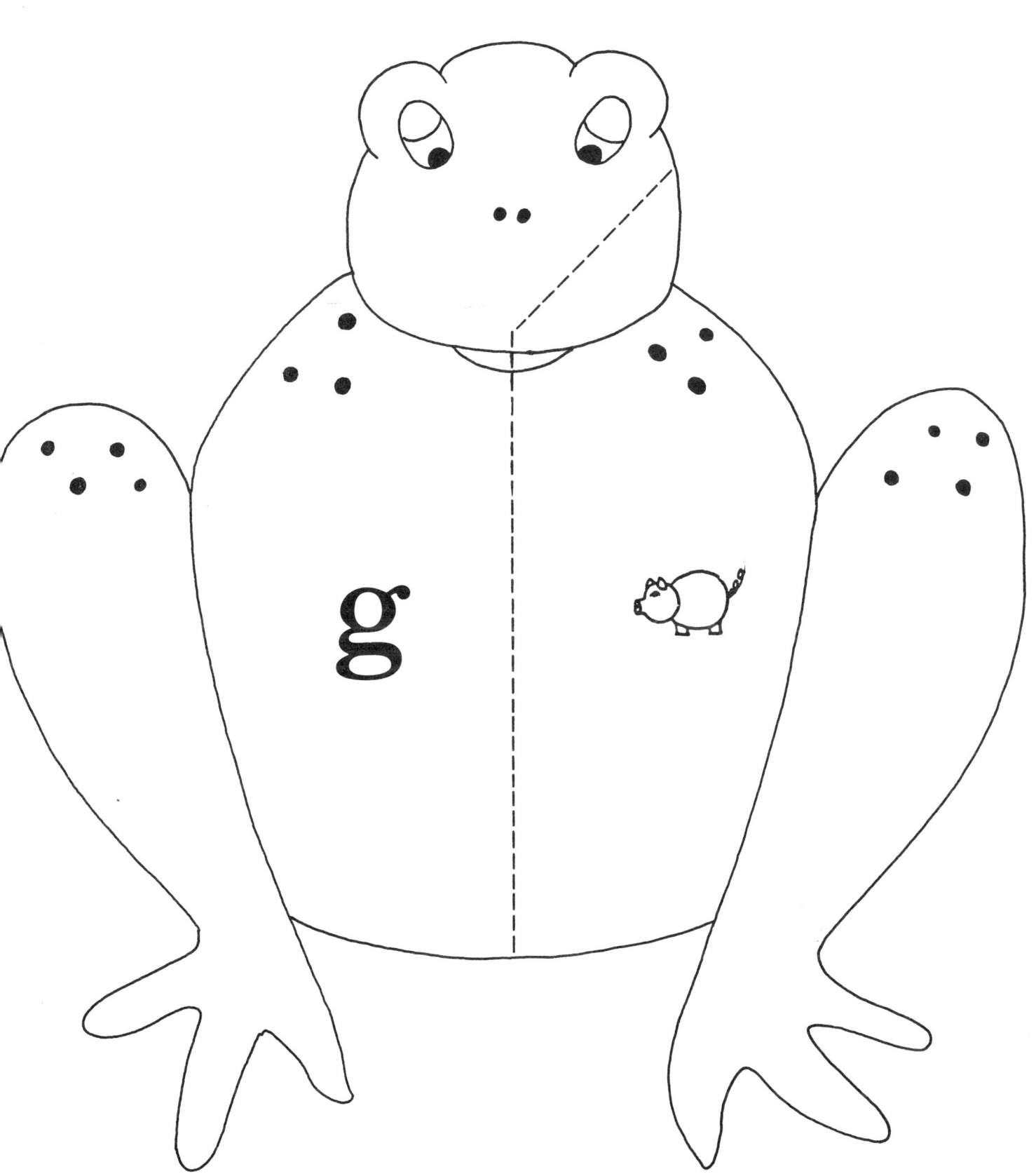

Polly Wants a Cracker

Skill Reinforced: medial vowels
Grade Level: primary
Materials Needed:
  10 sheets of 4″ × 10″ red posterboard
  10 sheets of 3″ × 3″ yellow posterboard
  scissors
  felt-tipped pen
  color markers

Construction Directions:

1. Mark the yellow posterboard pieces using the cracker pattern shown here.

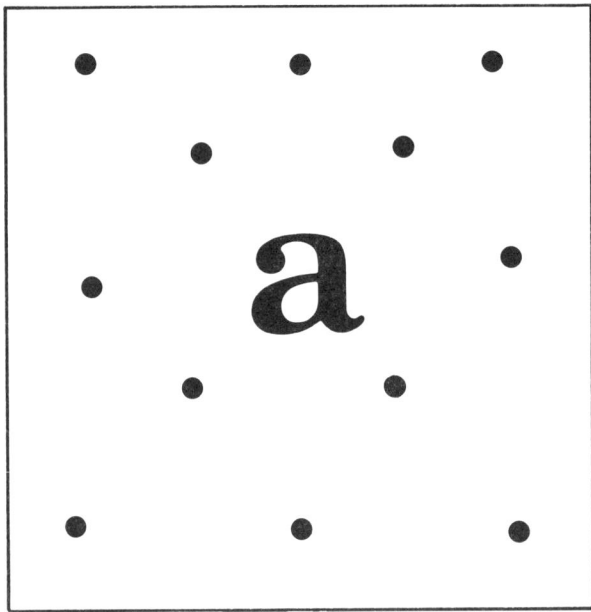

2. Print each of the five vowels on two of the crackers as shown in the illustration.
3. Cut and mark the red posterboard pieces using the parrot pattern on page 64. Copy each of the following drawings on a parrot as shown in the illustration.

4. Place the same color markers on the backs of the parrots and crackers that have the same vowel sounds.

Game Play:

1. Make two piles, one with the parrots and one with the yellow crackers.
2. Choose one of the parrots and say the word for the picture that is drawn on it. Say it again, and this time listen to the vowel sound that is in the middle of the word.
3. Now, look through the crackers until you find that vowel. When you think you have found it, turn the pieces over. If the markers are the same color, you are right. Continue to do this with all of the pieces.

Take Daffy Swimming

Skill Reinforced: consonant blends
Grade Level: primary
Materials Needed:

10 sheets of 7" × 9" blue posterboard
10 sheets of 4½" × 7" yellow posterboard
scissors
felt-tipped pen

Construction Directions:

1. Cut and mark the yellow posterboard pieces using the duck pattern shown here.

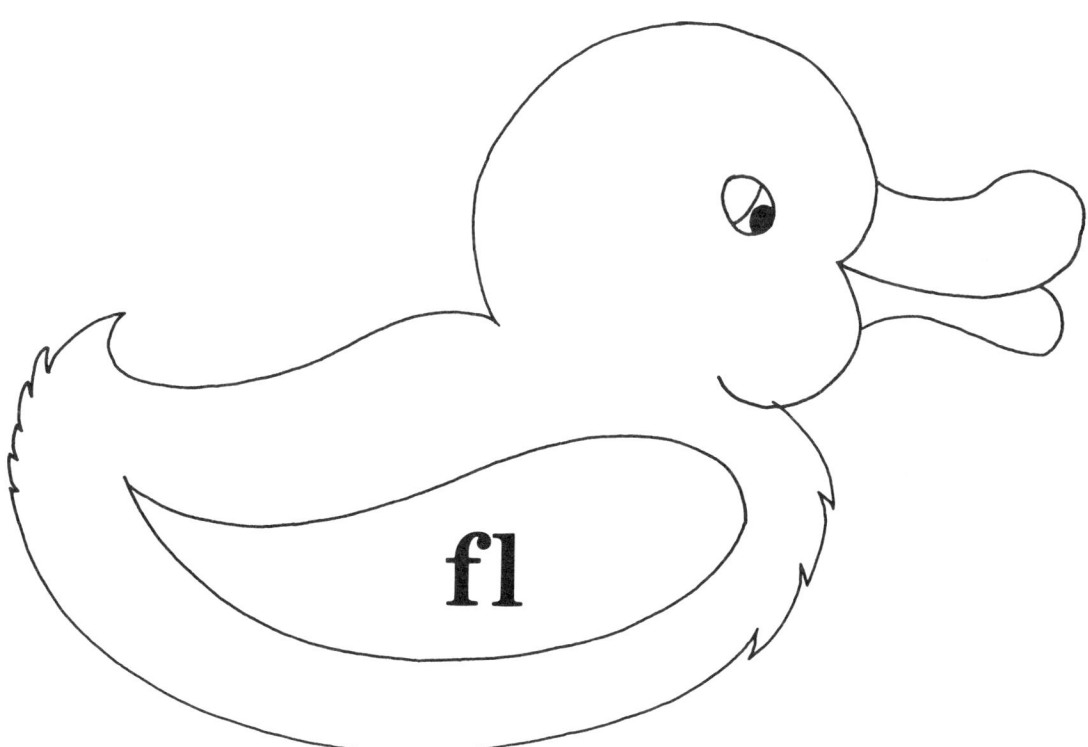

2. Print each of the following blends on a duck as shown in the illustration. Mark the corresponding numerals on the back of each duck.

1	fl	6	gl
2	st	7	cr
3	sp	8	br
4	sn	9	tr
5	cl	10	sl

3. Cut and mark the blue posterboard pieces using the pond pattern on the following page.
4. Draw each of the following on a pond as shown in the illustration. Mark the corresponding numerals on the back of each pond.

Game Play:

1. Make two piles, one with the yellow ducks and one with the blue ponds.
2. Spread the ducks out on a flat surface. Now, take one of the ponds and say the word for the drawing on it. Say it again and listen to the beginning of the word.
3. Look through the ducks and find the letters that represent this beginning sound. When you do, let Daffy go swimming by slipping him into the slit in the pond.
4. After you have finished with all of the ducks, you may turn them over. If the numerals match, you are correct.

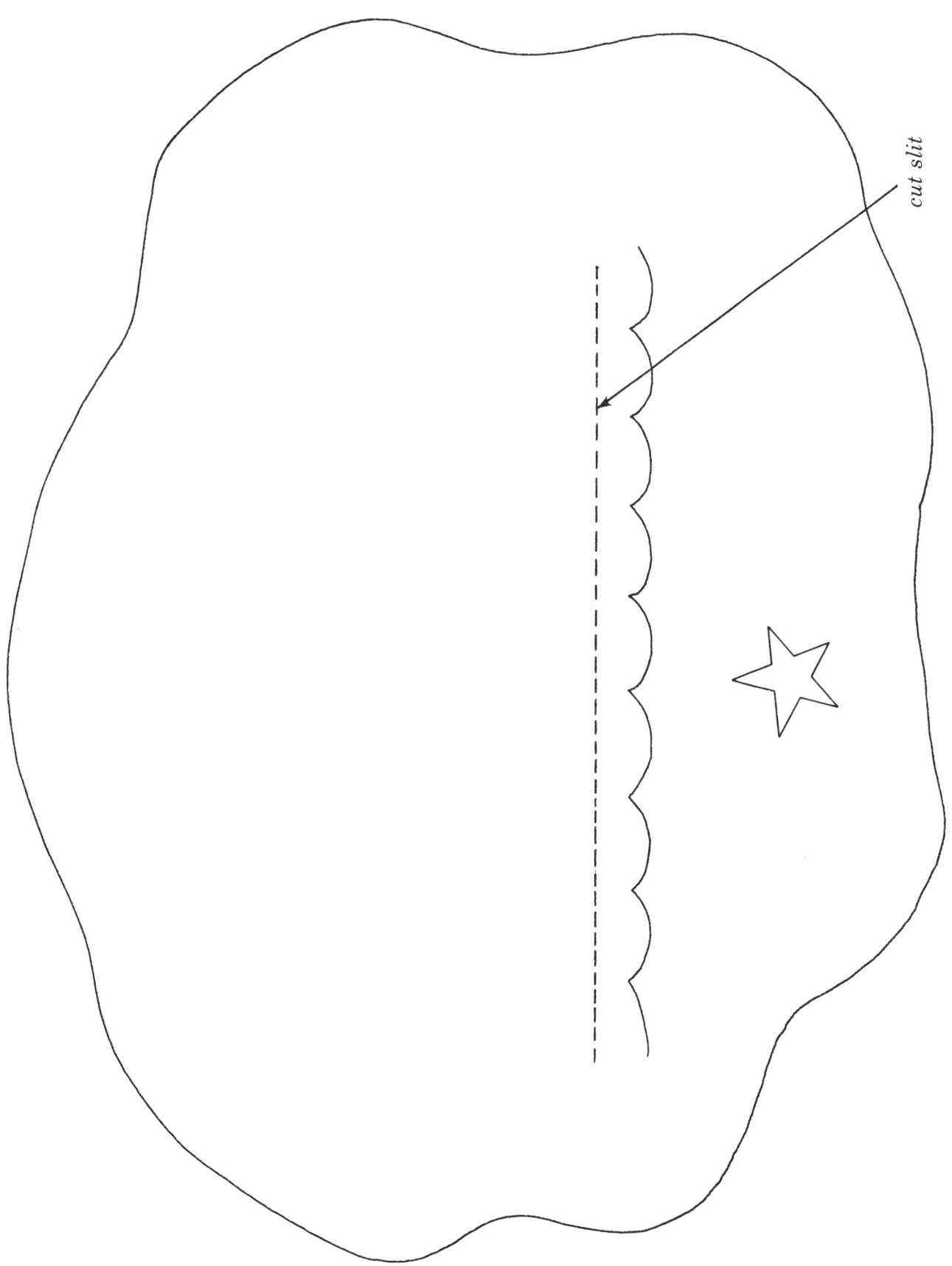

Time for Baseball

Skill Reinforced: word meaning
Grade Level: primary
Materials Needed:
    10 sheets of 6" × 7" tan posterboard
    scissors
    felt-tipped pen
Construction Directions:
  1. Cut and mark the posterboard pieces using the mitt pattern shown here.

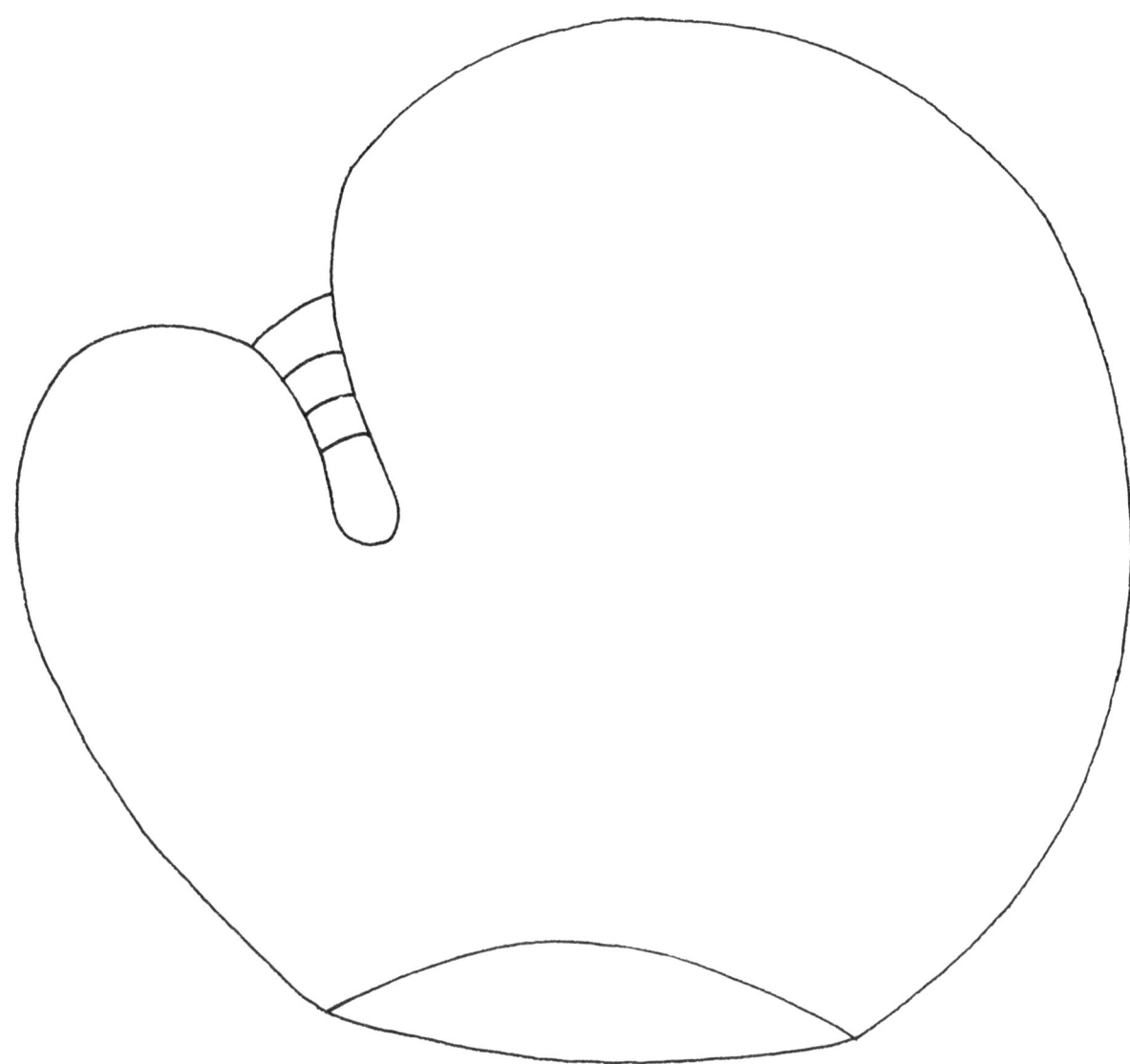

2. Print the following words on the mitts. Cut each one on the dotted line.

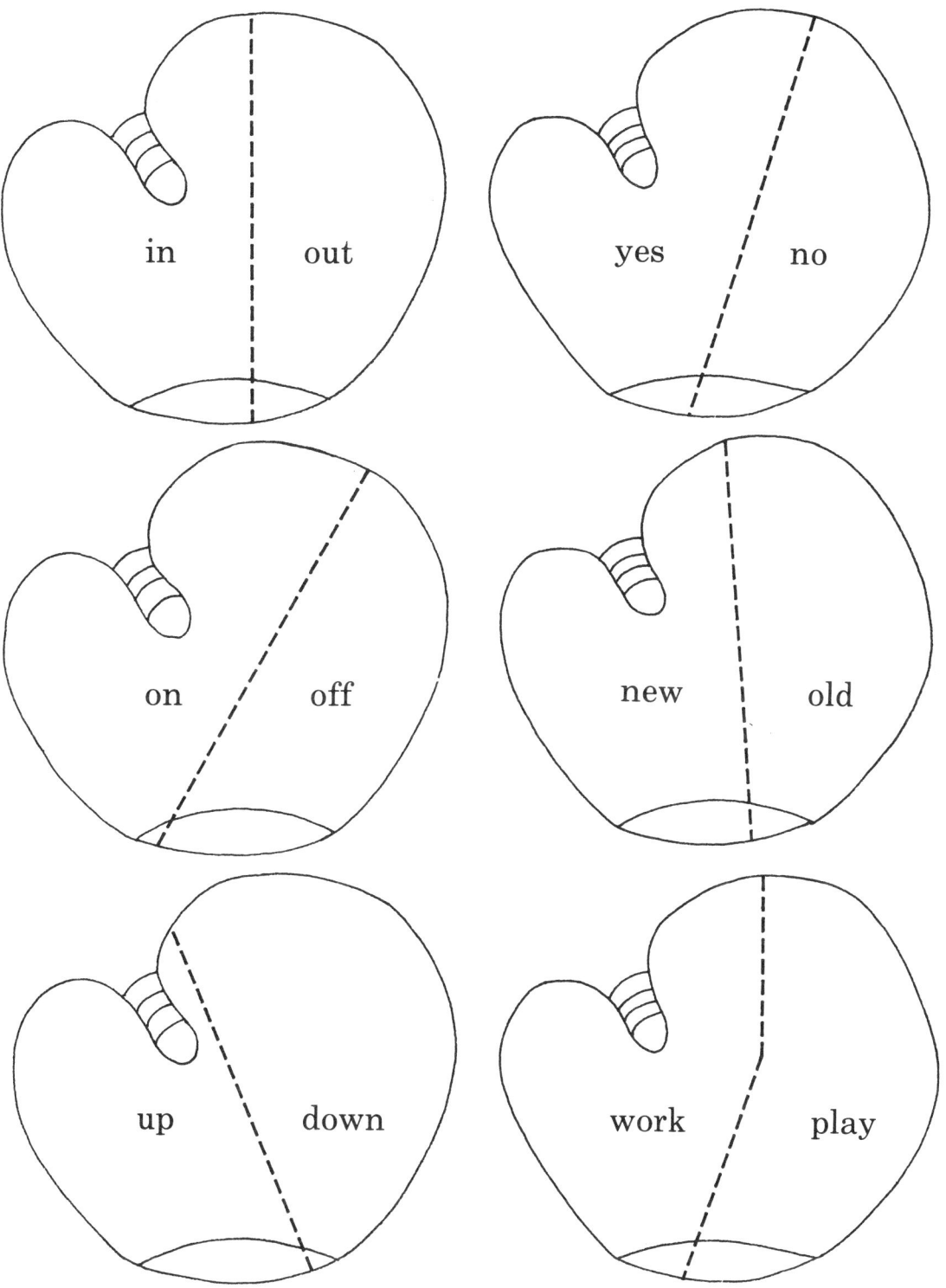

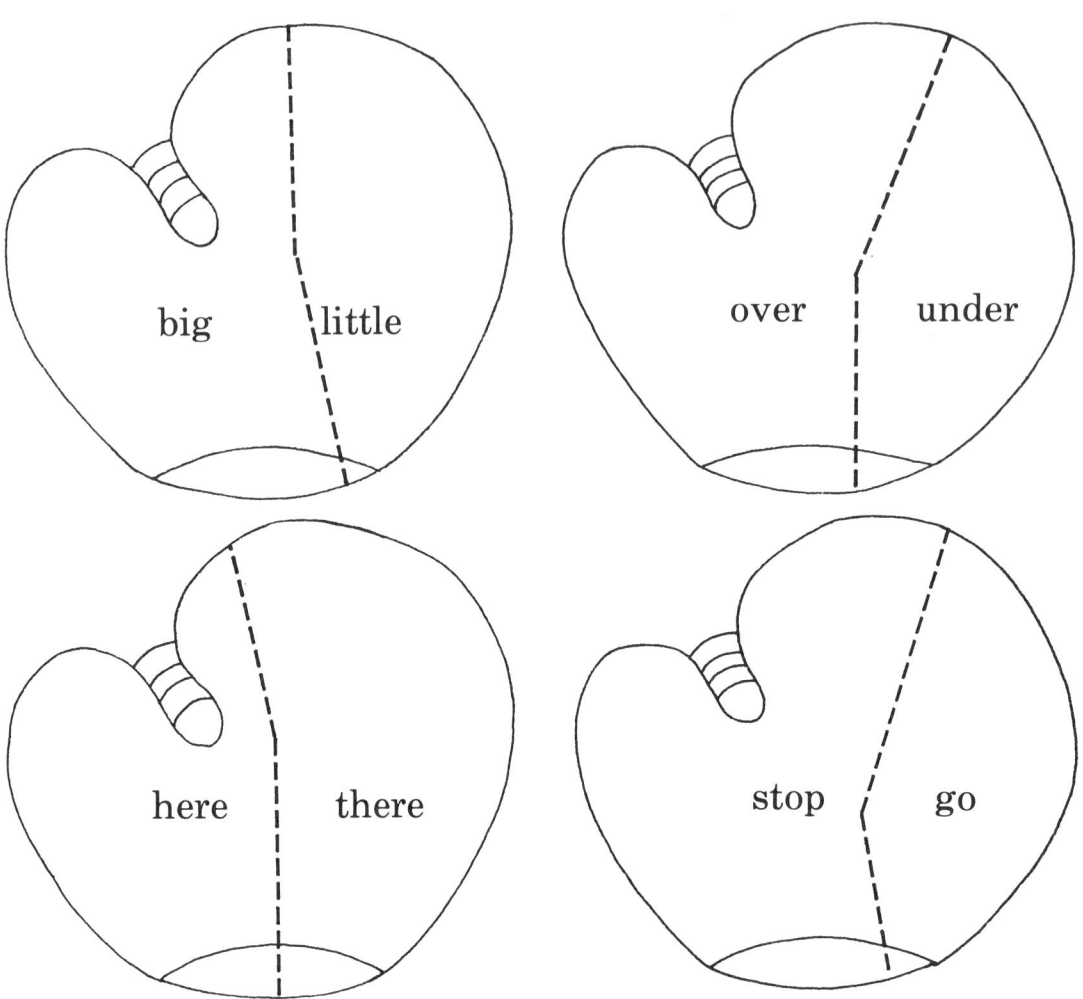

Game Play:

1. Place the game pieces on a flat surface. You will try to fit these pieces together to form many baseball mitts.
2. In order to do this, choose one of the pieces. Read the word that is on this piece. Now, look through the rest of the pieces and find a piece with a word on it that means the opposite.
3. When you think you have found it, place the two pieces together. If they form a baseball mitt, you are correct. Continue to do the same with all of the pieces.

Form a Picture

Skill Reinforced: word sequence
Grade Level: primary
Materials Needed:

    5 sheets of 10″ × 12″ posterboard (each of a different color)
    5 large magazine pictures
    scissors
    felt-tipped pen
    glue

Construction Directions:

1. Glue a different picture to each of the posterboard pieces as shown here.

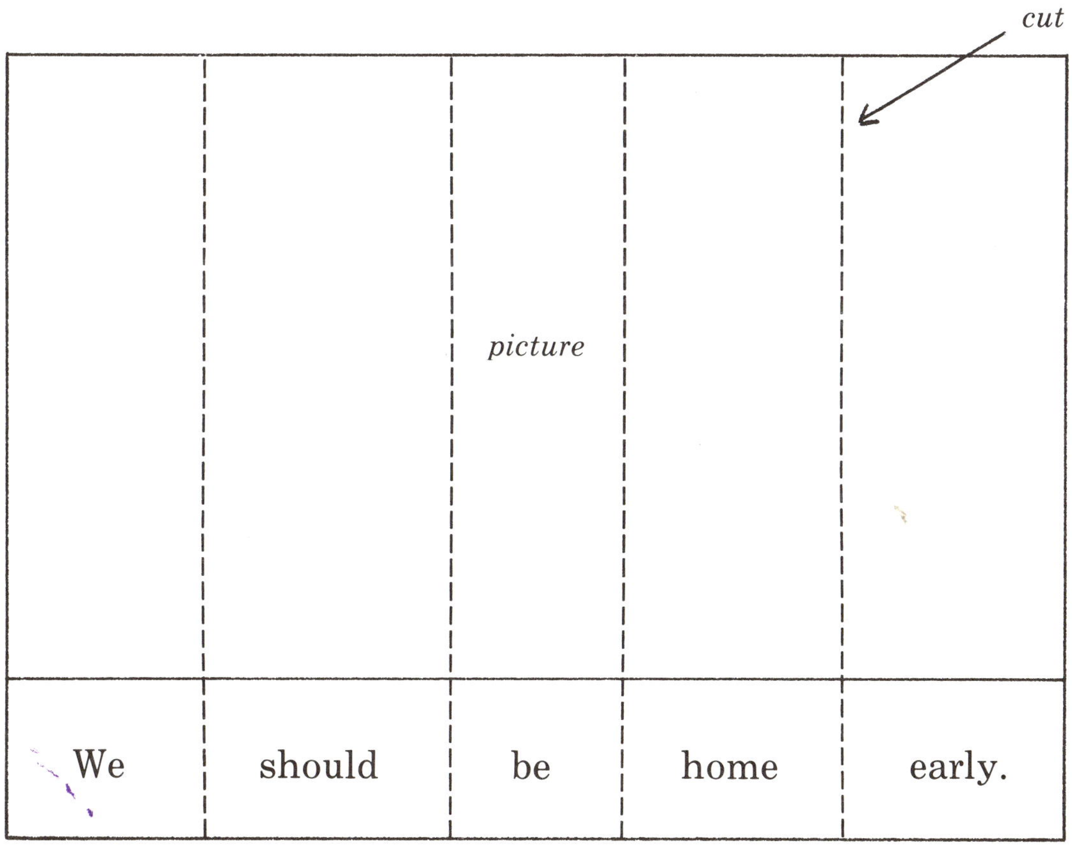

				cut
		picture		
We	should	be	home	early.

2. Leave an inch of the posterboard exposed on the bottom on which to write a sentence. You may use the following five sentences or use some from your basal reader.

> We should be home early.
> Do you remember that surprise party?
> I cannot go to school today.
> Look at the two kittens.
> Is that your teacher?

3. Cut the sentence and picture apart as indicated in the illustration.

Game Play:

1. Separate the picture pieces according to the colors at the bottoms of the pieces.
2. Choose a color to begin. Look at the words at the bottom of the picture pieces. If you put these words in the right order, they will form a sentence. If you are correct in forming the sentence, a complete picture will form above the sentence.

Marching Toy Soldiers

Skill Reinforced: word sequence

Grade Level: primary

Materials Needed:

    5 sheets of 5″ × 8″ green posterboard

    5 sheets of 5″ × 8″ red posterboard

    5 sheets of 5″ × 8″ blue posterboard

    scissors

    felt-tipped pen

Construction Directions:

1. Cut and mark all of the posterboard pieces using the toy soldier pattern on the following page.
2. Print the following sentence on the red soldiers, one word per soldier as shown in the illustration. Number the backs of these soldiers in the correct order.

    The boys made another trade.

3. Print the following sentence on the green soldiers and number the backs as you did before.

    I have work to do.

4. Print the following sentence on the blue soldiers and number the backs as as you did before.

    This is not good enough.

Game Play:

1. Separate the toy soldiers according to color.
2. Choose one of the colors and spread them out on a flat surface. If you put these toy soldiers in the correct order, the words on them will form a sentence.
3. When you think you have formed a complete sentence, turn over the toy soldiers. The numerals should be in order.

Ride the Streetcar

Skill Reinforced: context clue usage
Grade Level: high primary
Materials Needed:

    9 sheets of 8" × 8" yellow posterboard
    9 shoelaces
    scissors
    felt-tipped pen
    paper hole punch

Construction Directions:

1. Cut and mark the posterboard pieces using the streetcar pattern on the next page.
2. Print each of the following sentences and word groups on a streetcar as shown in the illustration. Mark the back of the correct hole using a felt-tipped pen.

I want to _____ in the boat.
    road
    ripe
    ride

May I have _____ donuts?
    the
    that
    this

Can you _____ me?
    how
    here
    help

Here is something _____ you.
    far
    for
    fat

I _____ to ride.
    when
    where
    want

_____ out of here.
    Is
    Get
    The

_____ do you want?
    When
    What
    Where

This is what I _____ .
    want
    why
    who

_____ is fun.
    That
    Then
    The

Game Play:

1. Read the sentence on one of the streetcars. You will see that one of the words is missing.
2. Now, look down on the running board of the streetcar and you will see three words. Can you find the missing word?
3. If you think you can find it, put the shoelace through the hole above the word. Now, turn the streetcar over in order to see if you are correct. If the shoelace is through the marked hole, you are correct.

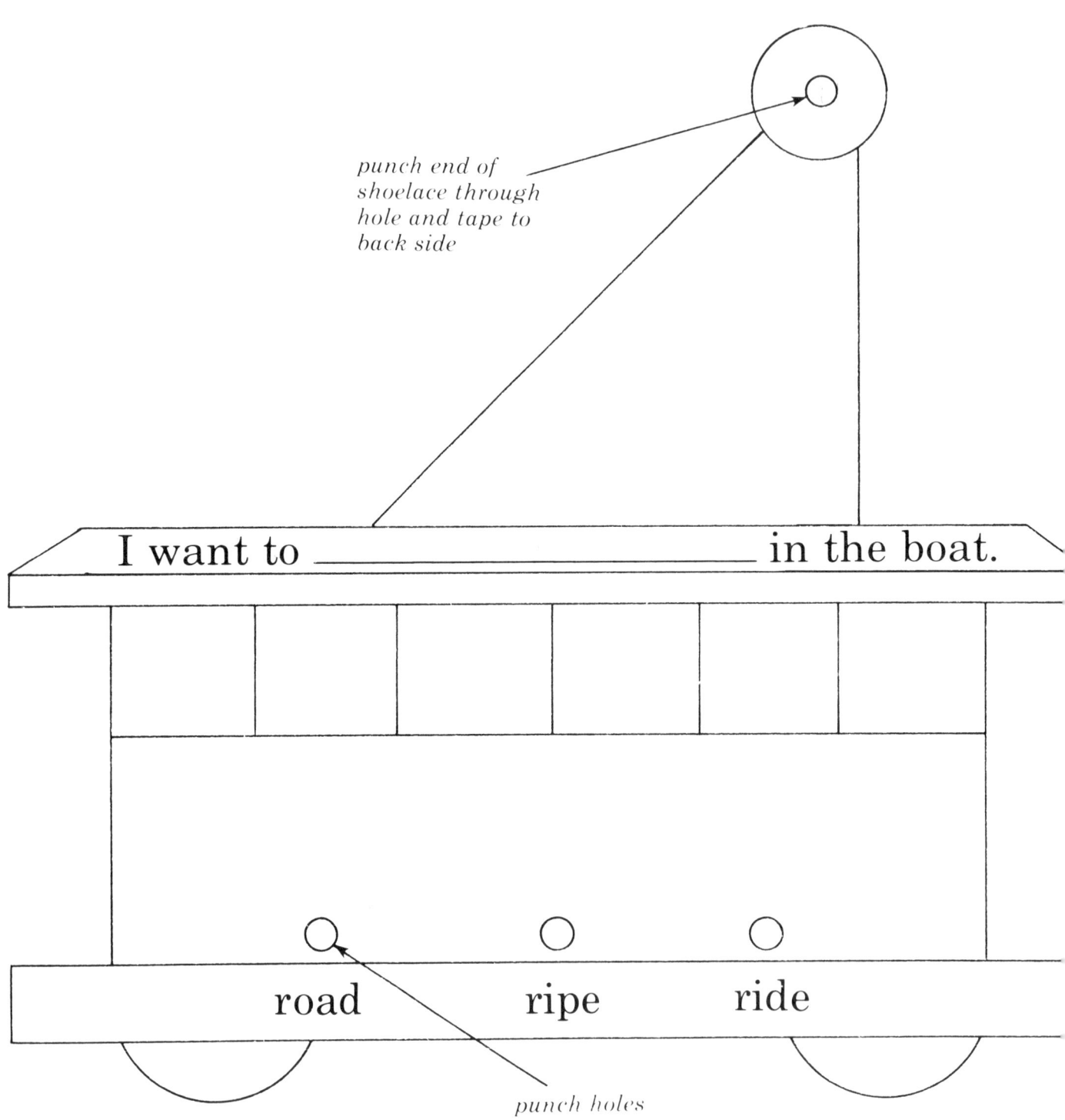

Help the Bluebird

Skill Reinforced: context clue usage
Grade Level: high primary
Materials Needed:
   8 sheets of 5″ × 9″ blue posterboard
   8 sheets of 4″ × 10″ brown posterboard
   scissors
   felt-tipped pen

Construction Directions:
   1. Cut and mark the blue posterboard pieces using the bluebird pattern shown here.

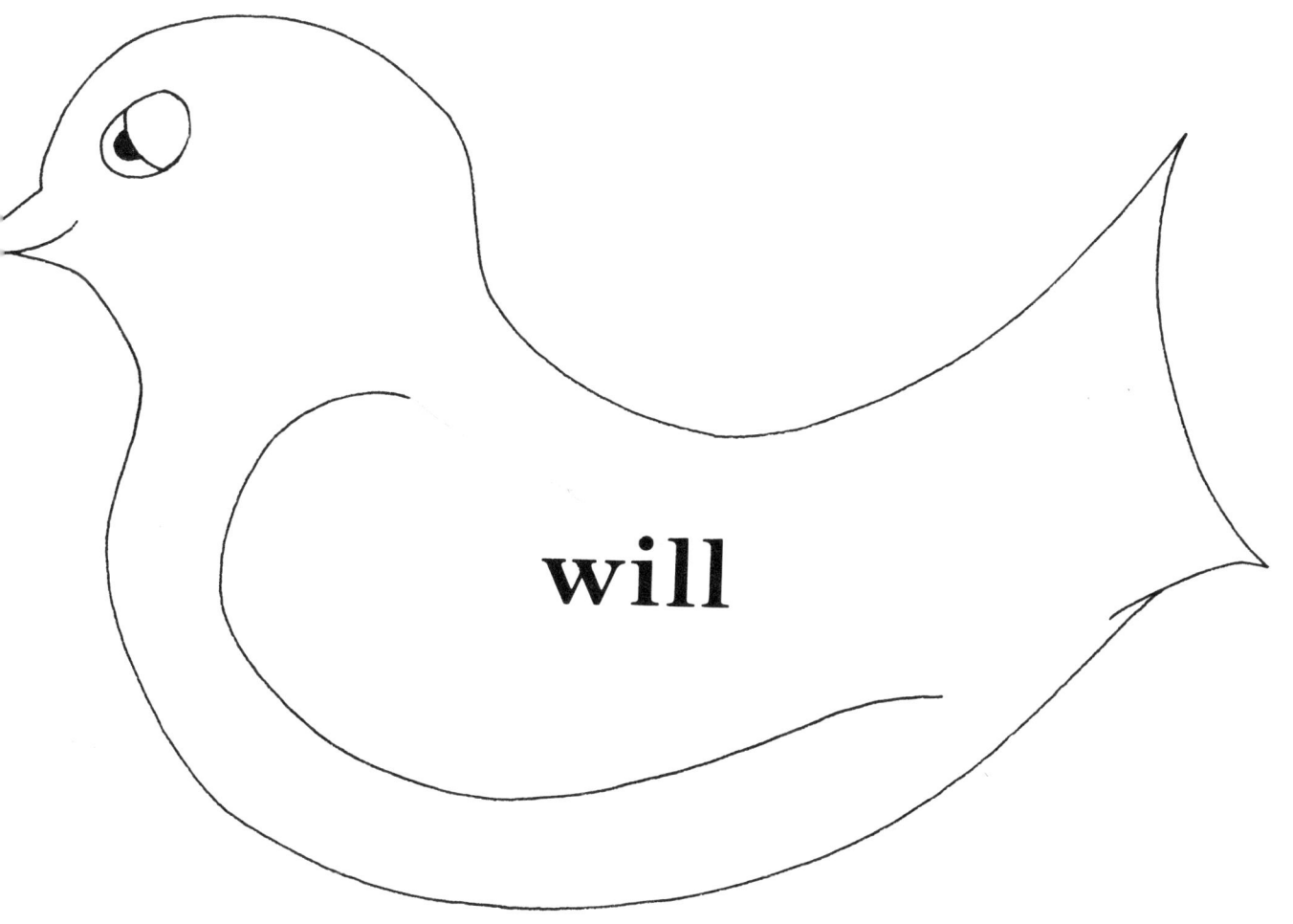

2. Cut and mark the brown posterboard pieces using the branch pattern shown here.

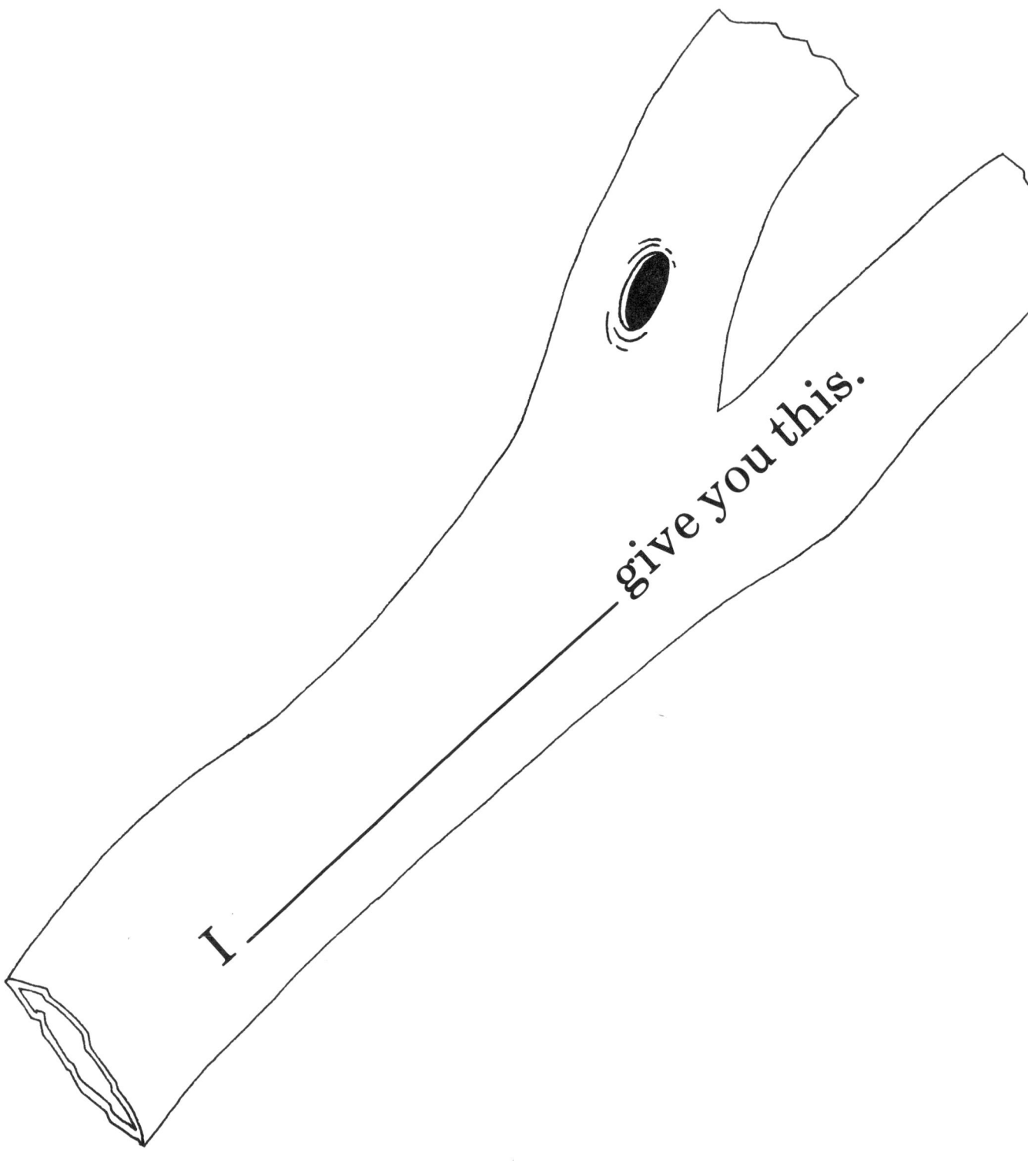

3. Print each of the following sentences on a different branch. Mark the corresponding numerals on the backs.

    May I _____ in your new car? (1)
    Do we have to stay at _____? (2)
    I want to go _____ the new boy. (3)
    I _____ give you this. (4)
    My _____ is my best pet. (5)
    The dog went _____ his doghouse. (6)
    My hair is very _____ . (7)
    _____ cat is outside. (8)

4. Print each of the following words on a different branch. Mark the corresponding numerals on the backs.

    ride   (1)
    home   (2)
    see   (3)
    will   (4)
    dog   (5)
    into   (6)
    long   (7)
    The   (8)

Game Play:

1. Place one of the branches on a flat surface.
2. Read the sentence. One of the words is missing.
3. Look at the words on the bluebirds and see if you can find the missing word.
4. When you think you have found it, set the bird on the branch.
5. Now, take another branch and do the same thing.
6. When you are finished, you can turn the birds and branches over for a self-check.

Silly Seal

Skill Reinforced: sentence structure

Grade Level: high primary

Materials Needed:

    7 sheets of 7" × 9" gray posterboard

    7 red posterboard circles with 4" diameters

    scissors

    felt-tipped pen

Construction Directions:

1. Print the following sentence endings on the red circles. Mark the corresponding numerals on the backs of each.
   - (1) down the path.
   - (2) the baby cry.
   - (3) all day.
   - (4) have a sled?
   - (5) six white kittens.
   - (6) going to school?
   - (7) come home now?
2. Cut out and mark the gray posterboard pieces using the seal pattern on the following page.
3. Print the following sentence beginnings on the seals. Mark the corresponding numerals on the backs of each.
   - (1) The rabbit hopped
   - (2) I can hear
   - (3) We worked
   - (4) Do you
   - (5) They have
   - (6) Are you
   - (7) Can you

Game Play:

1. Make two piles, one with the seals and one with the red balls.
2. Choose one of the seals and read the words written on it. This is the beginning of a sentence. See if you can find the ending of this sentence on one of the red balls.
3. When you think you have found the right ending, turn over the pieces. If the numerals are the same, you are correct. Continue to do the same with the rest of the seals and balls.

II
Games for Group Instruction

Reading group time often becomes a routine and consequently boring event for both students and teacher. This section presents group game activities that are designed to add a spark to your reading skills development program. These games have been designed so that they may be used with your reading groups.

The only materials necessary for most of the games are lightweight posterboard, scissors, and a felt-tipped pen. Several of the games require easily found items such as small pictures, glue, shoelaces, potato chip cans, and egg cartons. In order to help you reproduce these games quickly and easily, this aid offers you detailed instructions concerning game construction. You will also notice that most of the game directions include actual-size patterns for simple copying.

The following readiness and reading skills are reinforced by the designated games.

Game	Reading Skill	Grade Level
Eggs in the Basket	alphabet knowledge	low primary
Sew an Alphabet	alphabet knowledge	low primary
Bunch of Balloons	auditory discrimination	low primary
Birds in the Tree	visual discrimination	low primary
Build a Ship	visual discrimination	low primary
Elmo's Peanut Game	categorization	low primary
The Magic Hat	initial consonants	primary
Roll a Blend	consonant blends	primary
Road Signs	medial vowels	primary
Flying High	final consonants	primary
Magic Pictures	word meaning	primary
A Flock of Birds	word meaning	primary
Egg Carton Picture Game	sight word knowledge	primary
Toby's Problem	contractions	primary
Watch the Forest Grow	compound words	primary

Game	Reading Skill	Grade Level
The Long Train	word sequence	primary
Crossing the Ocean	context clue usage	high primary
Picture Plus	main idea	high primary
Old Oak Tree	making inferences	high primary
Going Fishing	fact from fantasy	high primary

Eggs in the Basket

Skill Reinforced: alphabet knowledge
Grade Level: low primary
Materials Needed:
    26 sheets of 2″ × 3″ yellow posterboard
    26 sheets of 6″ × 8″ brown posterboard
    scissors
    felt-tipped pen

Construction Directions:

1. Cut the yellow posterboard pieces using the egg pattern shown here. Print one of the lower-case letters of the alphabet on each of the eggs.

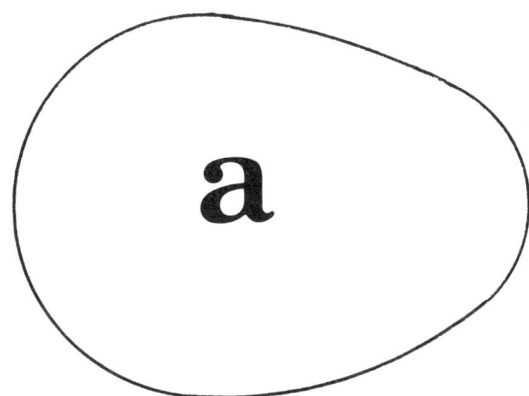

2. Cut and mark the brown posterboard pieces using the basket pattern on the following page. Print one of the upper-case letters of the alphabet on each of the baskets.

Game Play: This game is for two to six players.

1. Have the students sit in a circle around a table or on the floor. In the center of the playing area, spread out the eggs so that the children can see the letters on them.
2. Hold up several of the baskets and allow the first player to choose one. This child must try to find the egg with the matching lower-case letter.
3. If the game pieces are matched correctly, the child keeps the basket and the egg. If not, the pieces are returned to their places.
4. The players take turns choosing baskets and eggs until all of the pieces have been matched correctly. The player who has the most baskets and eggs at the end of the game is the winner.

Sew an Alphabet

Skill Reinforced: alphabet knowledge
Grade Level: low primary
Materials Needed:

    3 one-gallon cardboard milk containers
    paper hole punch
    21 sheets of 1″ × 2″ white posterboard
    3 long shoelaces
    1 posterboard circle with 7″ diameter
    1 paper fastener
    1 sheet of 1″ × 6″ black posterboard
    3 sheets of Con-Tact paper (1 red, 1 blue, 1 yellow)
    scissors
    felt-tipped pen

Construction Directions:

1. Cut and mount the Con-Tact paper on the posterboard circle as shown on page 88. Cut and attach the black posterboard piece as shown in the illustration.
2. Cut the milk cartons and cover each with a different color of Con-Tact paper. Punch holes and attach a shoelace to each as shown on page 88.
3. Copy each of the following letters of the alphabet onto three of the small posterboard cards. Punch a hole in each as shown in the illustration.   a   b   c   d   e   f   g

Game Play: This game is for two or three players.

1. Each player places a game box in front of him or her. The letter cards are spread out, letter side up, in the center of the playing area.
2. A player spins the arrow (players may take turns spinning). The player who has the game box with the color that the arrow points to looks for a card with the letter "a." The player "sews" the card to the first hole in his or her game box.
3. The players continue to "sew" letters, in the correct alphabetical order, as their colors are indicated on the spinner.
4. The first player to correctly "sew" all seven letters to his or her game box is the winner.

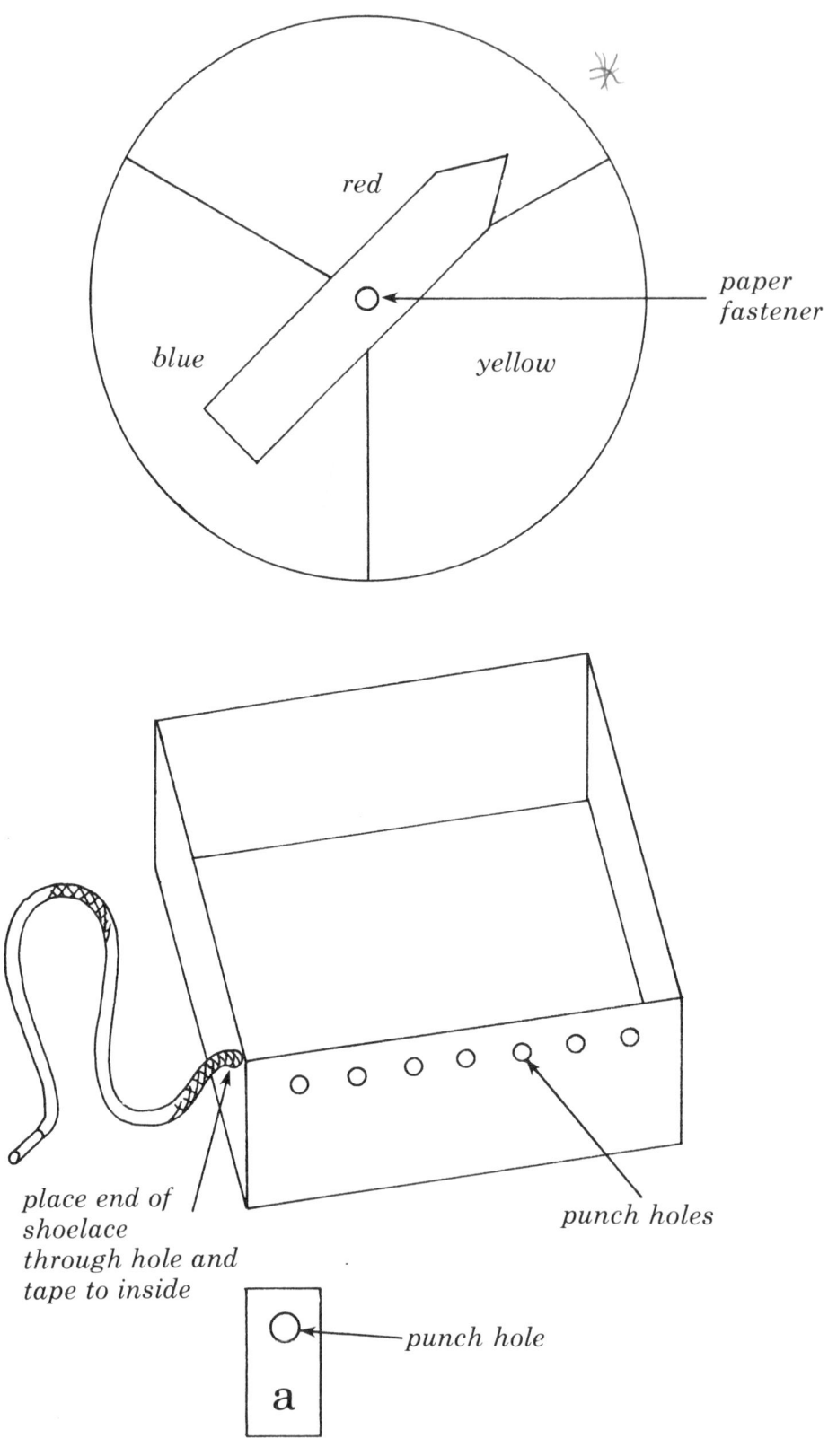

Bunch of Balloons

Skill Reinforced: auditory discrimination
Grade Level: low primary
Materials Needed:
   3 sheets of 12″ × 12″ white posterboard
   12 sheets of 3″ × 3″ assorted color posterboard
   scissors
   felt-tipped pen
Construction Directions:
   1. Mark and cut 1½″ slits in the three large posterboard pieces, using an enlargement of the game board pattern shown here.

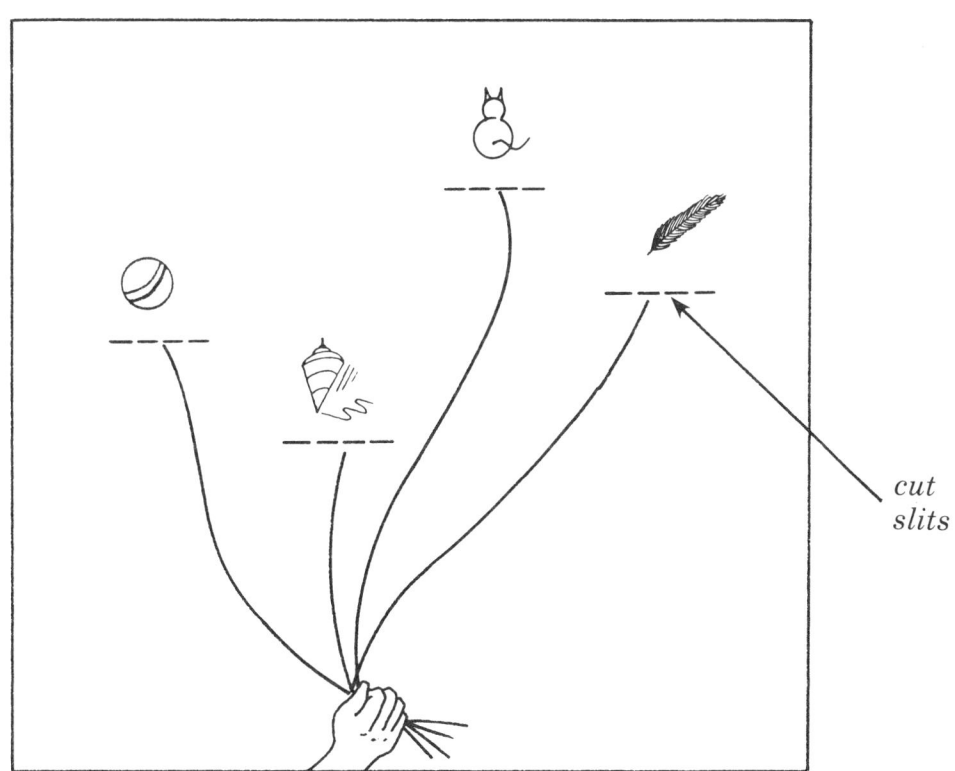

cut slits

2. On each of the game boards, draw one of the following picture groups. Each picture should be drawn above a slit as shown in the illustration.

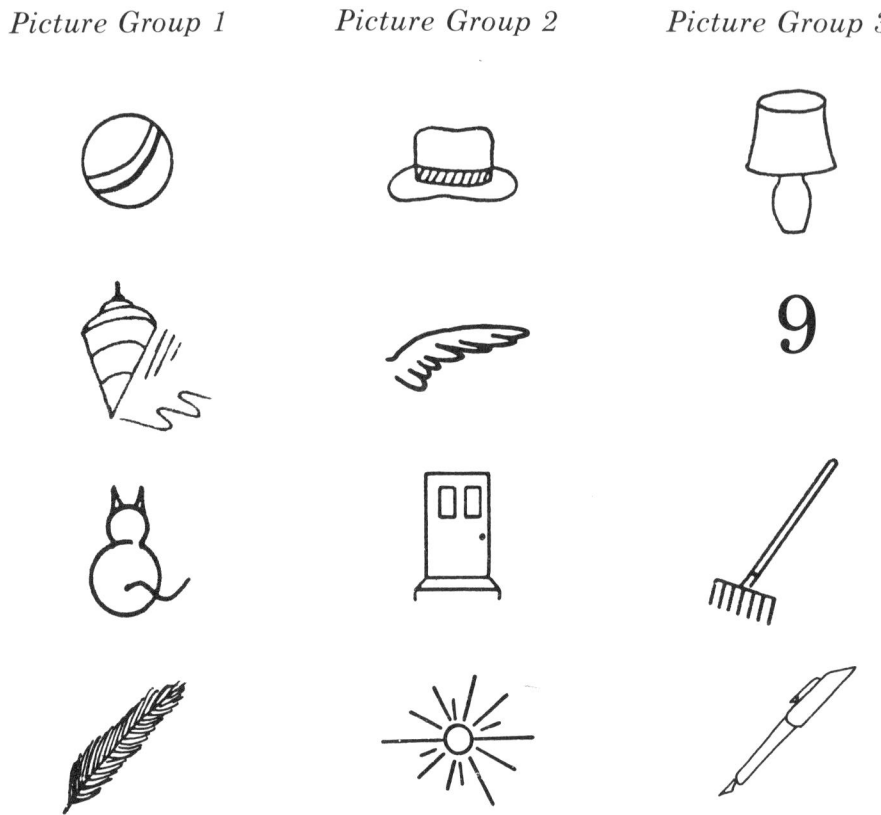

3. Cut the small posterboard pieces using the balloon pattern shown here.

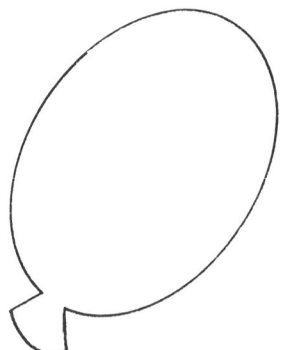

4. Draw each of the following pictures on a different balloon.

Game Play: This game is for two or three players.

1. Each player chooses a game board. The balloons are placed, word side down, in the center of the playing area.
2. The first player takes a balloon and looks at the picture on it. If the beginning sound matches the beginning sound of a drawing on that player's game board, he or she slips it into the slit under the appropriate picture. If it does not match, the balloon is placed on the bottom of the stack from which it came.
3. The next player continues the game in the same manner.
4. The first player to place four balloons correctly on his or her game board is the winner.

Birds in the Tree

Skill Reinforced: visual discrimination
Grade Level: low primary
Materials Needed:
   8 sheets of 7" × 5" green posterboard
   16 sheets of 2½" × 2½" yellow posterboard
   scissors
   felt-tipped pen

Construction Directions:

1. Cut four of the green posterboard sheets using an enlargement of the tree pattern shown here.

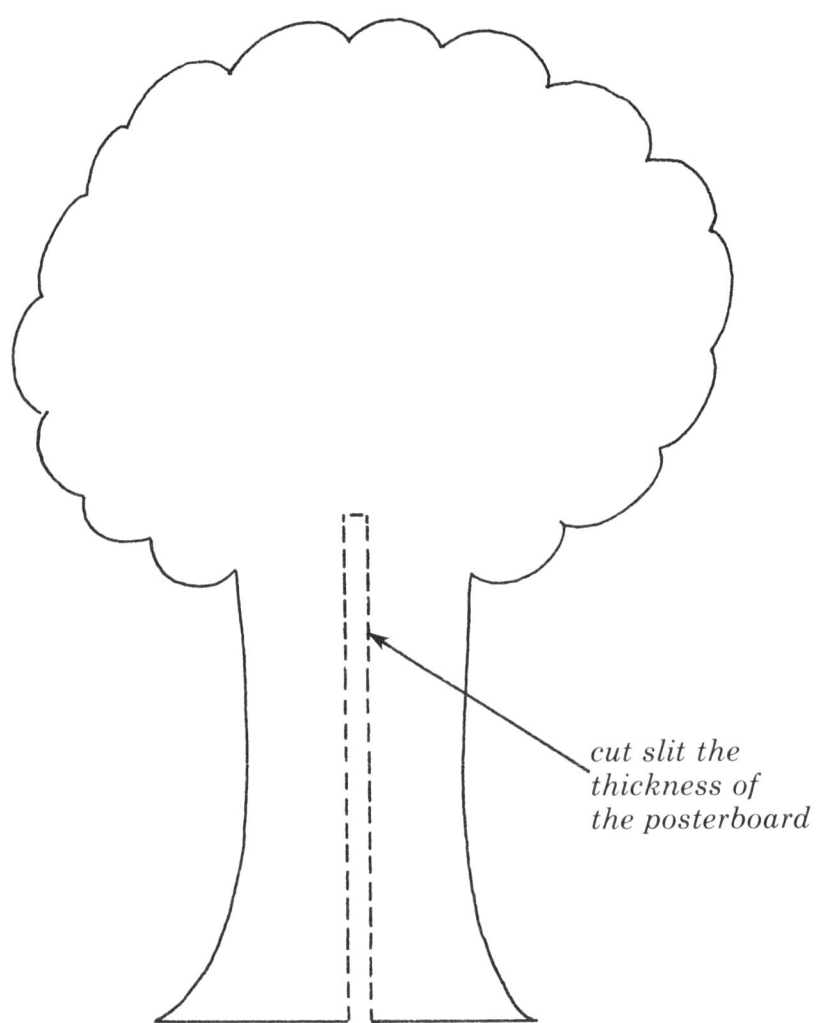

cut slit the thickness of the posterboard

2. Cut the remaining four of the green posterboard sheets using an enlargement of the tree pattern shown here.

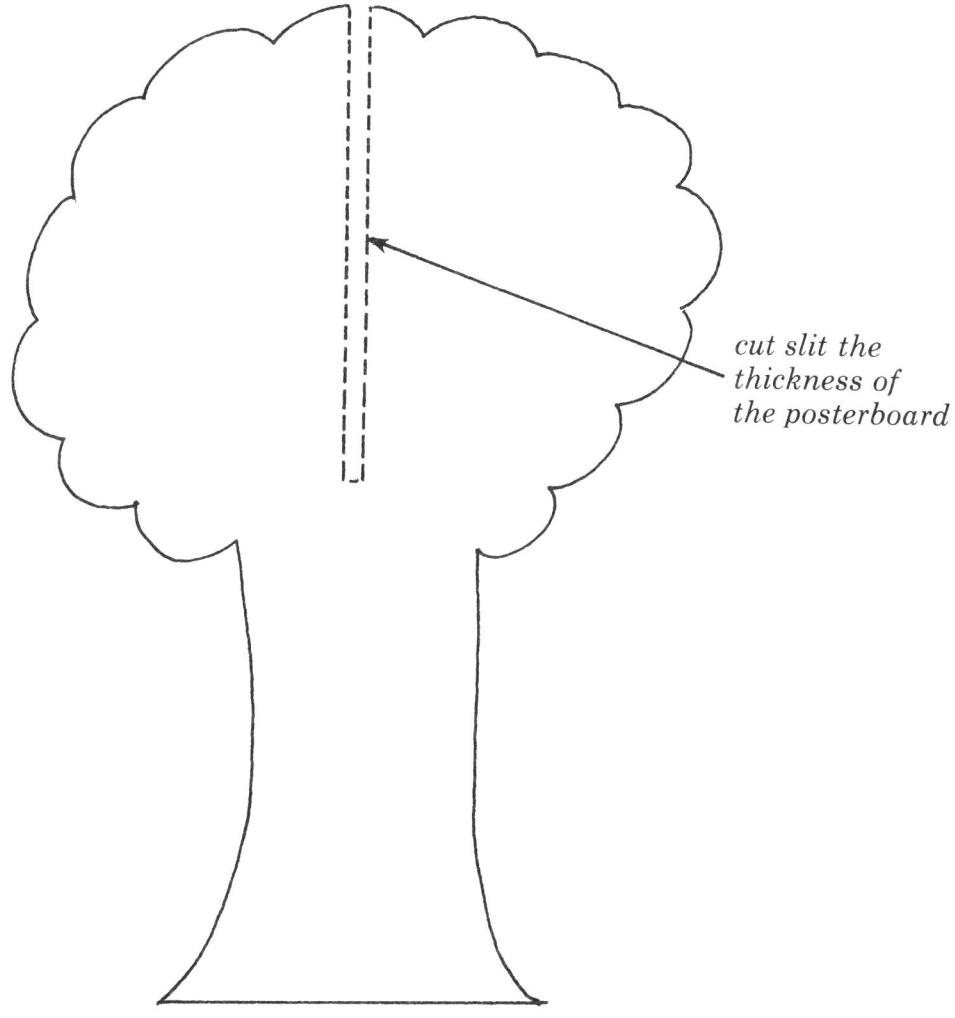

cut slit the thickness of the posterboard

3. Slide the tree pieces together. You should now have four standing trees.
4. Copy each of the following words onto a different tree.
           that   than   this   then
5. Cut and mark the yellow posterboard sheets using the bird pattern on the following page.
6. Copy each of the following words onto four birds as shown in the illustration.
           that   than   this   then

Game Play: This game is for two to four players.

1. Each player chooses a tree and stands it up in front of him or her. The birds are placed, face down, in a stack in the center of the playing area.
2. The first player takes the top bird and looks at the word on it. If it matches the word on the player's tree, he or she places it on the tree. If not, the bird is placed on the bottom of the stack from which it was taken.
3. The next player continues the game in the same manner.
4. The first player to put four birds on his or her tree is the winner.

Build a Ship

Skill Reinforced: visual discrimination
Grade Level: low primary
Materials Needed:
   5 sheets of 4″ × 6″ gray posterboard
   5 sheets of 1″ × 4″ gray posterboard
   10 sheets of 1″ × 1″ gray posterboard
   10 white posterboard circles with 1″ diameters
   scissors
   felt-tipped pen

Construction Directions:
   1. Cut and mark the large posterboard pieces using the ship pattern shown here.

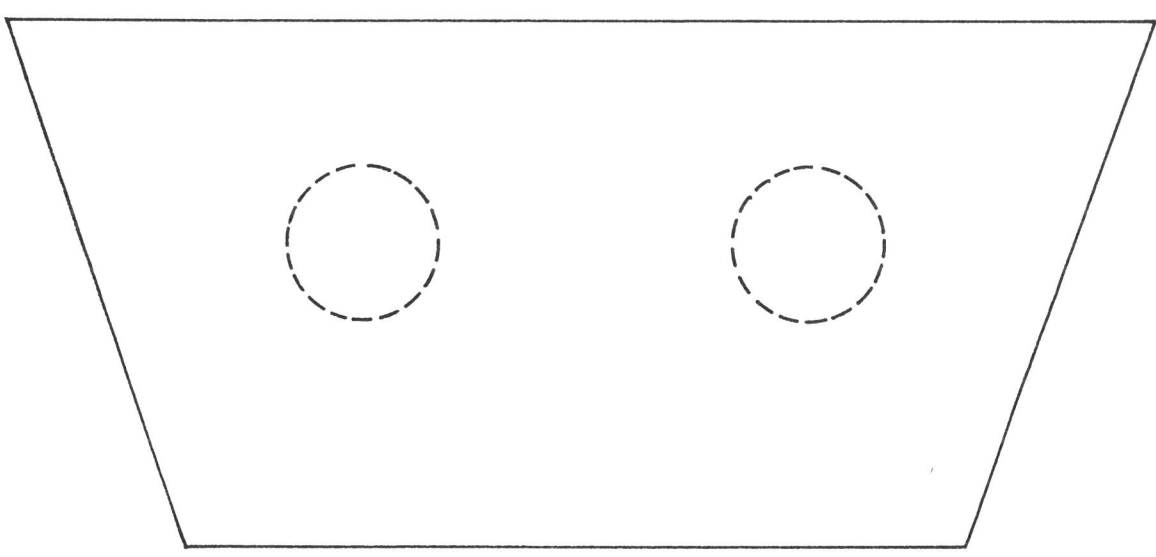

   2. Print each of the following letters on a different boat.
          b   d   t   l   k
   3. Print each of the same letters on two of the circle pieces.
   4. Print the same letters on one of the 1″ × 4″ pieces.
   5. Print the same letters on two of the 1″ × 1″ pieces.

Game Play: This game is for two to five players.

1. Each player chooses a ship. The other pieces are placed in three separate stacks, word side down, in the center of the playing area.
2. The first player takes a game piece from one of the three stacks and looks at the letter on it. If it matches the letter on the player's ship, he or she places it on the appropriate part of the ship. If it does not match, the piece is placed on the bottom of the stack from which it came.
3. The next player continues the game in the same manner.
4. The first player to put two portholes, one deck, and two smokestacks on a ship is the winner.

Elmo's Peanut Game

Skill Reinforced: categorization
Grade Level: low primary
Materials Needed:
   3 sheets of 9" × 9" gray posterboard
   9 sheets of 3" × 4" yellow posterboard
   scissors
   felt-tipped pen

Construction Directions:
   1. Cut and mark the gray posterboard pieces using an enlargement of the elephant pattern shown here.

   2. Copy each of the following drawing and word pairs onto a different elephant.

animals   toys   clothing

3. Cut the yellow posterboard pieces using the peanut pattern shown here.

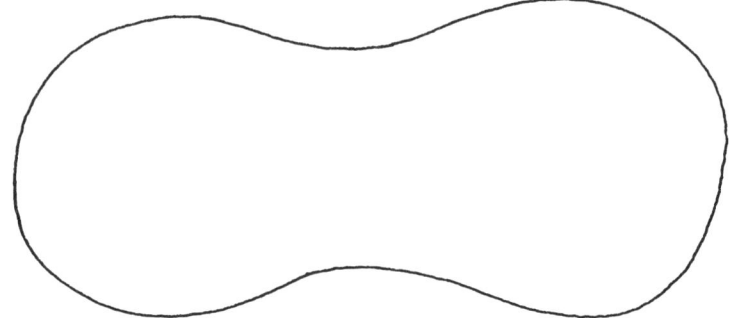

4. Copy each of the following drawings onto a different peanut.

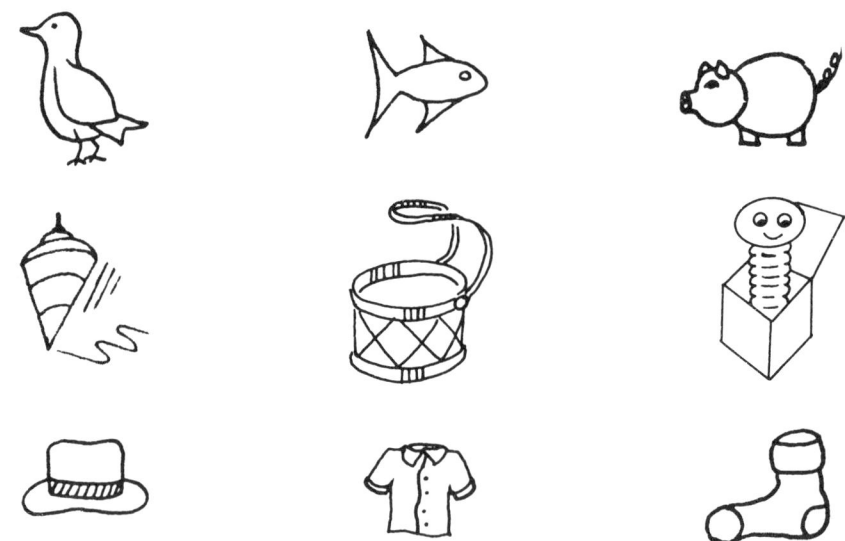

Game Play: This game is for two or three players.

1. Each player chooses an elephant game board. The peanuts are placed face down in front of the players.
2. The first player draws a peanut. If the picture fits the category on his or her elephant, it is placed on his or her game board. If not, the player puts the peanut back into the pile and the next player takes a turn.
3. The first player to find three correct peanuts is the winner.

The Magic Hat

Skill Reinforced: initial consonants
Grade Level: primary
Materials Needed:
 4 sheets of 6″ × 8″ gray posterboard
 12 sheets of 2″ × 4″ white posterboard
 scissors
 felt-tipped pen

Construction Directions:
1. Cut the gray posterboard pieces using the top hat pattern on the following page.
2. Mark each of the following consonants on a different hat as shown in the illustration.

    b   c   s   t

3. Cut the white posterboard pieces using the bunny pattern shown here.

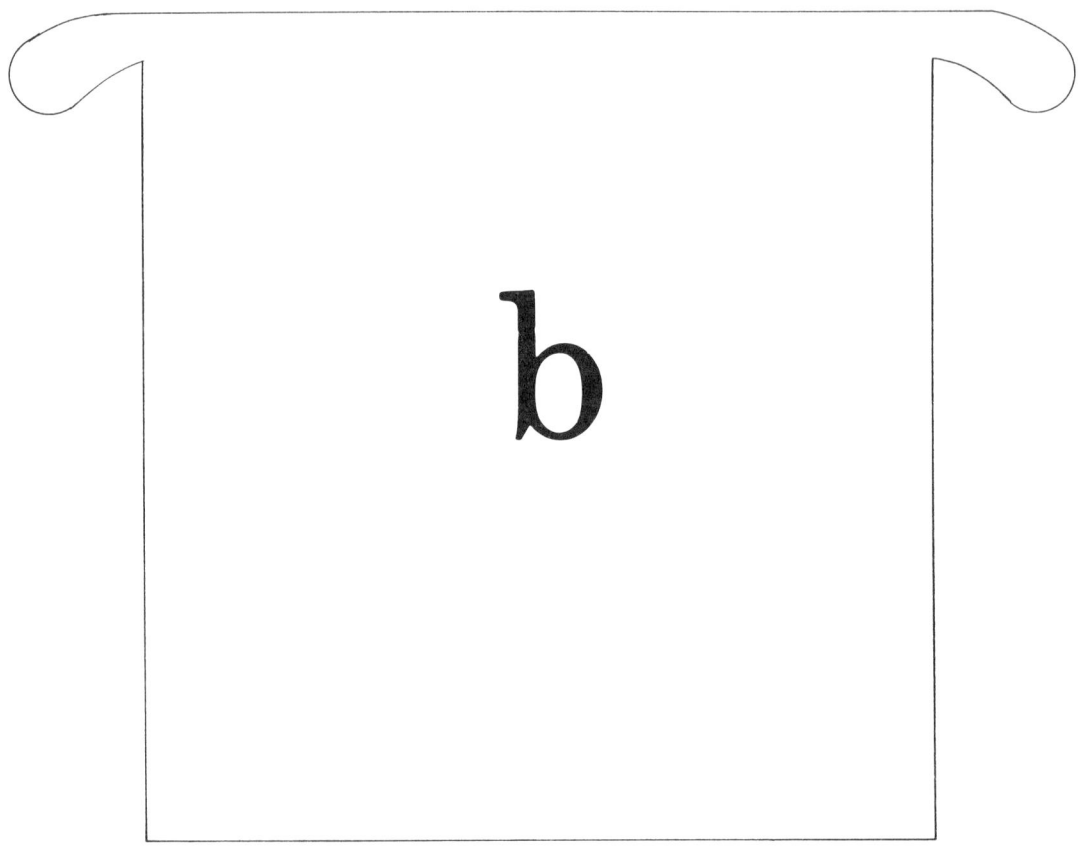

4. Copy each of the following drawings onto a different bunny as shown in the illustration.

Game Play: This game is for two to four players.

1. Each player chooses a hat game board. The bunnies are placed face down in front of the players.
2. The first player draws a bunny. If the picture begins with the letter on his or her hat, the player places it at the top of the hat. If not, the bunny is put back in the center of the playing area and the next player takes a turn.
3. The first player to find three correct bunnies is the winner.

Roll a Blend

Skill Reinforced: consonant blends
Grade Level: primary
Materials Needed:
   8 shoe boxes or boxes of similar size
   1 ping-pong ball
   19 sheets of 4" × 4" white posterboard
   felt-tipped pen
   scissors
   tape

Construction Directions:
   1. Cut off the ends of the boxes and tape them together as shown here. Print the blends on the boxes as shown in the illustration.

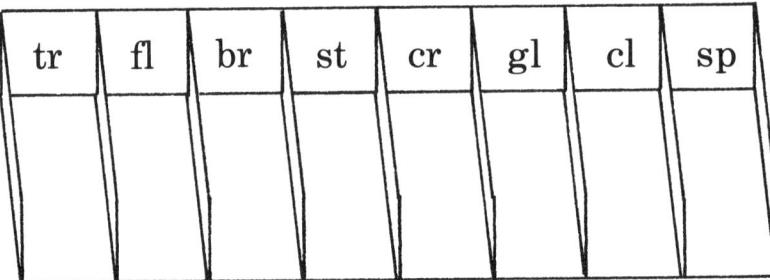

   2. Draw each of the following pictures on a different posterboard card.

Game Play: This game is for two to five players.

1. The players sit in a semicircle with the line of boxes placed about five feet in front of them. The picture cards are placed on the floor, picture side up, in the center of the playing area.

2. The players choose someone to go first. This player takes the ball and attempts to roll it into one of the boxes. If he or she fails, the ball goes to the next player. If the player succeeds, he or she then has a chance to find a picture card that begins with the same sound that is on the box. If the choice is correct, the player can keep the card. If it is incorrect, the card is put back on the floor. Either way, the next player takes a turn.

3. The game is over when the last picture card has been picked up. The winner is the child who has collected the most cards.

Road Signs

Skill Reinforced: medial vowels
Grade Level: primary
Materials Needed:
  1 sheet of 20″ × 20″ yellow posterboard
  20 sheets of 2½″ × 3″ red posterboard
  dice
  felt-tipped pen
  4 game markers

Construction Directions:
  1. Mark the yellow sheet of posterboard using an enlargement of the game board shown here.

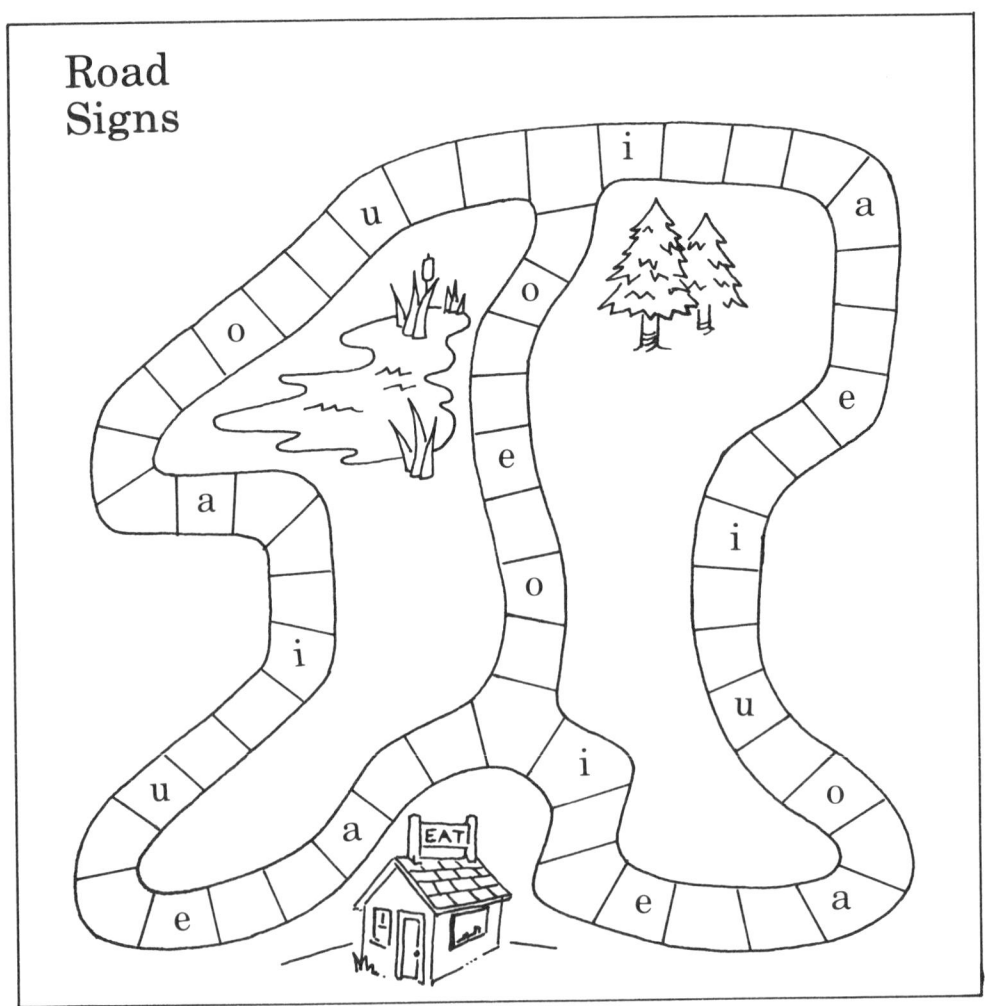

2. Copy each of the following drawings onto a different red card.

Game Play: This game is for two to four players.
1. Each player should be dealt five cards. Players should not show their cards to the other players. Each player chooses a marker and places it on any space on the game board that is not marked by a road sign (vowel).
2. The first player rolls the dice and moves his or her marker in any direction. If the player lands on a road sign (vowel), he or she may discard a card if it contains that vowel. The next player continues in the same manner.
3. The first player to discard all of his or her cards is the winner.

Flying High

Skill Reinforced: final consonants
Grade Level: primary
Materials Needed:
 50 pieces of 2″ × 6″ posterboard, 10 in each color:
 white, red, yellow, green, blue
 scissors
 felt-tipped pen

Construction Directions:

1. Cut and mark the posterboard sheets using the airplane pattern shown here.

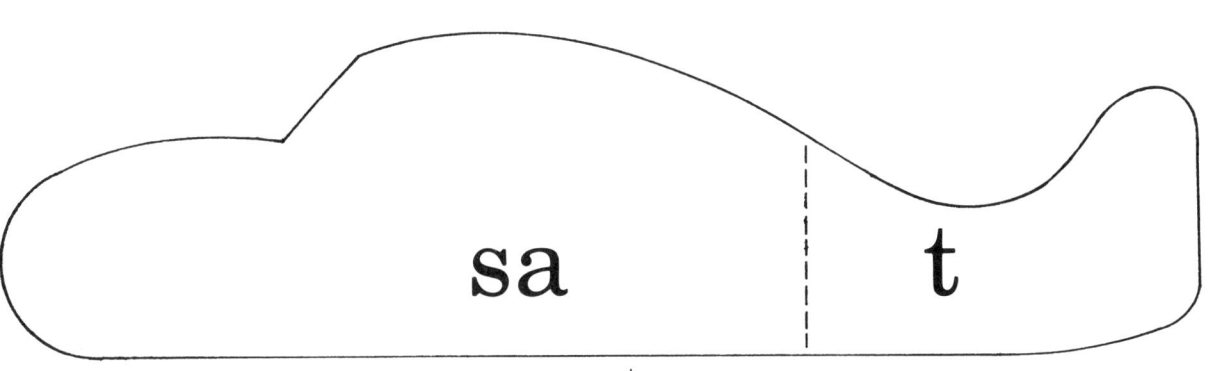

2. Copy each of the following words onto a different-colored airplane as shown in the illustration. Cut the pieces apart on the dotted line.

| sa/t | gu/n | li/p | hu/g | ne/t |
| roo/m | ro/b | si/x | sen/d | cal/f |

Game Play: This game is for two to five players.

1. The game pieces are separated according to color, face side down.
2. The players each choose a color and place those pieces, still face down, in front of them.
3. At a signal, all players turn over their pieces and make airplanes by forming words. The first one to complete ten airplanes correctly is the winner.

Magic Pictures

Skill Reinforced: word meaning
Grade Level: primary
Materials Needed:

    6 sheets of 6″ × 8″ white posterboard
    3 magazine pictures, about 6″ × 8″
    scissors
    glue
    felt-tipped pen
    ruler

Construction Directions:

1. Glue each of the three pictures onto a sheet of posterboard. Turn over the pictures and mark the lines using the ruler.

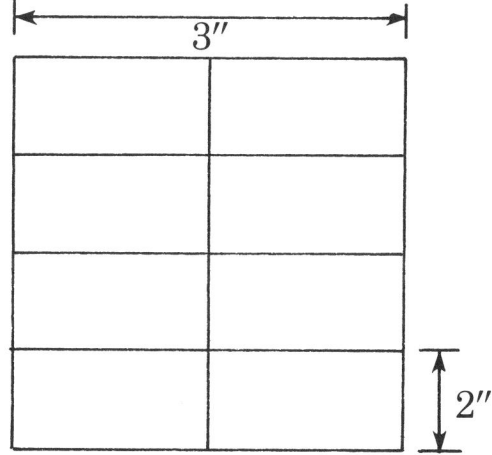

2. Mark the same lines on two other posterboard sheets. Pair each picture sheet with a plain sheet and place them next to each other, picture side down. Copy the following words onto the sheet pairs.

up	stop
yes	near
in	young
before	always

down	go
no	far
out	old
after	never

late	fat
short	dark
happy	take
black	first

early	thin
tall	light
sad	give
white	last

woman	run
stand	begin
easy	fast
won	push

man	walk
sit	end
hard	slow
lost	pull

3. Cut the picture sheets apart on the lines.

Game Play: This game is for two or three players.

1. The players each receive a game board and place it in front of them. The picture pieces are placed, word side down, in the center of the playing area.
2. The first player takes the top picture card and reads the word. He or she looks over the game board to find a word that means the opposite. If one is found, the picture card is placed on top of it, picture side up. If not, the player places the picture card at the bottom of the stack from which it came.
3. The next player continues the game in the same manner.
4. The first player to cover all of the words on his or her game board and form a complete picture is the winner.

A Flock of Birds

Skill Reinforced: word meaning
Grade Level: primary
Materials Needed:

    4 sheets of 12″ × 12″ brown posterboard
    4 sheets of 9″ × 12″ yellow posterboard
    scissors
    felt-tipped pen

Construction Directions:

1. Mark and cut three-inch slits in the brown sheets as shown here.

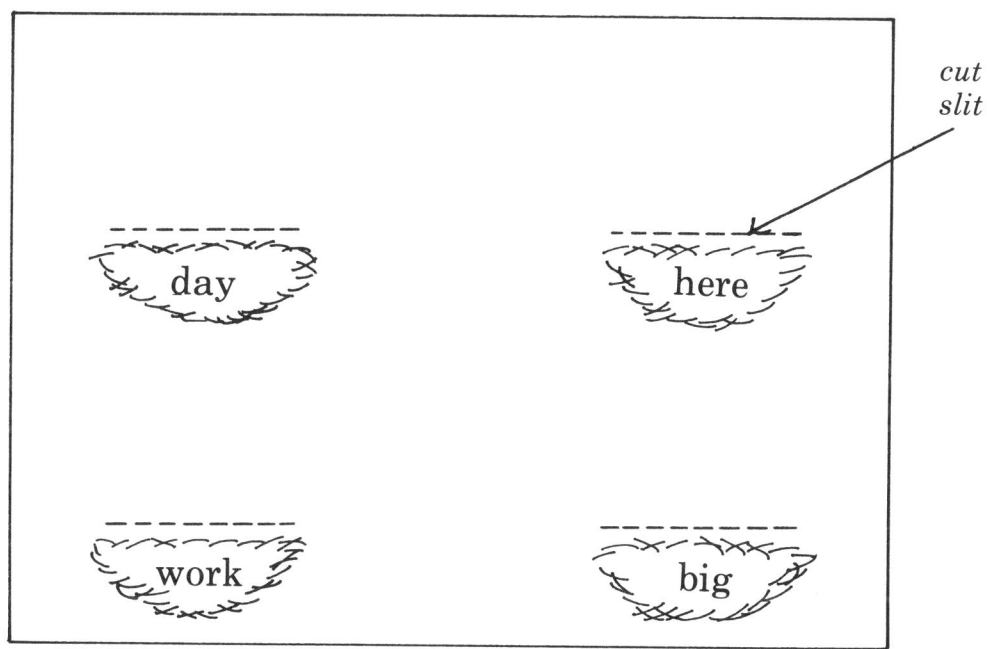

2. Print one of the following word groups on each of the brown game boards. Each word should go into a nest as shown in the illustration.

day here work big	under top back long
cool hard summer rich	wet off good all

3. Cut 16 birds from the yellow posterboard using the following pattern.

4. Print each of the following words on a different bird as shown in the illustration.

night	warm
there	soft
play	winter
little	poor
over	dry
bottom	on
front	bad
short	none

Game Play: This game is for two to four players.

1. Each player chooses a game board. The birds are placed, word side down, in the center of the playing area.
2. The first player takes the top bird and reads the word. He or she looks over the game board to find an antonym. If one is found, the bird is placed in the slot above the appropriate nest. If the player does not find one, he or she places the bird, word side up, next to the original bird stack.
3. The next player continues the game in the same manner. The first one to fill in all of his or her nests is the winner. If the players use all of the birds in the original stack and there is still not a winner, the birds that are not in the nests are turned over and the game continues.

Egg Carton Picture Game

Skill Reinforced: sight word knowledge
Grade Level: primary
Materials Needed:
- 3 egg cartons
- 18 sheets of 2" × 4" white posterboard
- 18 sheets of 2" × 2½" red posterboard
- scissors
- felt-tipped pen

Construction Directions:
1. Cut the egg cartons down the center so that you have six humps when they are turned over. Cut a slit crosswise in each of the humps.
2. Copy one of the following drawings onto each white card as shown here.

    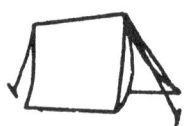

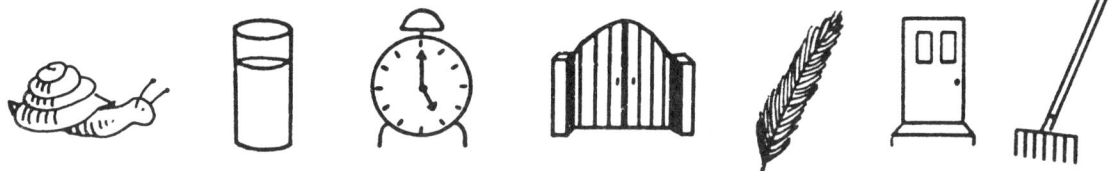

3. Print each of the following words on a different red card.

sun	fish
moon	house
star	snail
rain	glass
tent	clock
sock	gate
bird	feather
ghost	door
lamp	rake

Game Play: This game is for two or three players.

1. The players each place an egg carton (upside down) in front of them.
2. One player deals out six white cards to each of the other players. The players then place their cards in the egg carton holder, one card per slit. The red cards are placed face down in the center of the playing area.
3. The first player takes the top red card and reads the word on it. The player then looks to see if he or she has the matching picture card. If so, the red card is put in the same slit as the matching white card. If not, the red card is placed, word side up, next to the stack of red cards.
4. The next player continues the game in the same manner. The first player to match all six cards is the winner.
5. If all of the red cards in the original stack have been used and there is still no winner, the red cards that have not been matched are turned over and the game continues.

Toby's Problem

Skill Reinforced: contractions
Grade Level: primary
Materials Needed:
    25 sheets of 5" × 3" green posterboard
    25 sheets of 4" × 2" brown posterboard
    scissors
    felt-tipped pen

Construction Directions:

1. Cut and mark the green posterboard pieces using the turtle pattern shown here.

2. Copy the following words onto the green turtles as shown in the illustration.

do not	we will
I am	it is
is not	they are
I will	that is
we are	you have
you are	was not
there is	could not
let us	you did
can not	they will
she did	are not
have not	they have
has not	who will
you will	

3. Cut the brown posterboard sheets using the shell pattern shown here.

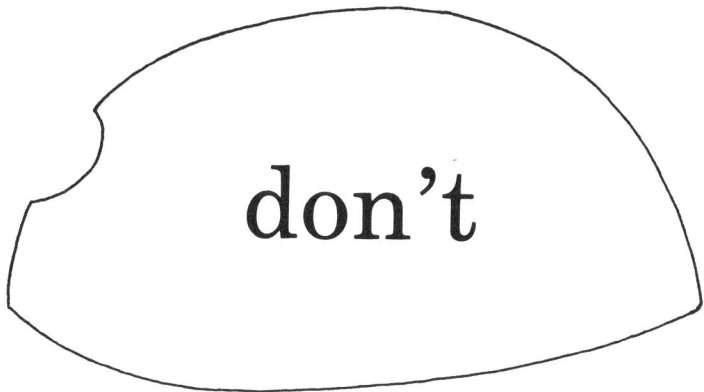

4. Copy each of the following contractions onto a different brown turtle shell.

don't	she'd
I'm	haven't
isn't	hasn't
I'll	you'll
we're	we'll
you're	it's
there's	they're
let's	that's
can't	you've
wasn't	couldn't
you'd	they'll
aren't	they've
who'll	

Game Play: This game is for two to five players.

1. Each player is dealt five turtles. The shells are placed face down in the center of the playing area.
2. The first player takes the top shell and reads the contraction. The player looks through his or her turtles to find the matching words. If one is found, the player puts the shell on the appropriate turtle. If not, the shell is placed, word side up, next to the stack of shells in the center of the playing area.
3. The next player continues the game in the same manner.
4. The first player to match five turtles is the winner. If all of the shells in the original stack have been used and there is still no winner, the shells that were not used are turned over and the game continues.

Watch the Forest Grow

Skill Reinforced: compound words
Grade Level: primary
Materials Needed:
  5 sheets of 8″ × 8″ corrugated cardboard
  25 sheets of 3″ × 6″ green posterboard
  scissors
  felt-tipped pen

Construction Directions:

1. Cut two-inch slits in the corrugated game boards as shown here.

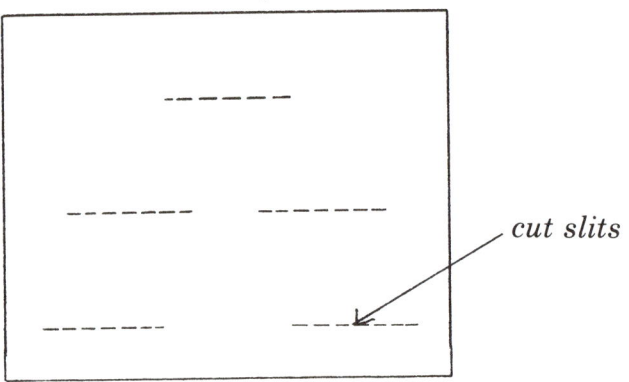

2. Cut and mark the green posterboard pieces using the tree pattern shown on page 118.
3. Print each of the following compound words on one of the trees. The base words that make up each compound word should be printed on separate parts of the tree as shown in the illustration.

snow/man	door/way
water/fall	down/town
blue/bird	shoe/lace
police/man	base/ball
note/book	sail/boat
him/self	door/mat
home/work	road/way
any/one	moon/light
sea/side	bath/room
turn/pike	tooth/brush
air/plane	bee/hive
some/thing	book/case

4. Divide each tree by cutting along the broken lines.

Game Play: This game is for two to five players.

1. Separate the tree pieces and place the right sides of the trees in one stack and the left sides of the trees in another. All playing pieces should be placed face down in the center of the playing area. Each player receives a heavy game board and then selects five left tree halves without looking at the words. These are placed in each of the five slots in the game boards. Players must not show their trees to one another.
2. All of the right tree halves are now dealt out to the players. Be sure that they are face down.
3. All players should look through the tree halves in their hands and try to match them with the halves in their game boards. If they are able to form any compound words, they should fit them together in their game boards.
4. The player who dealt out the tree halves begins the game by holding out his or her tree halves, word side down, to the player on his or her left. This player must take one of the pieces and should not show it to any other player. If it will form a compound word with any of the words in the player's game board, he or she places it in that slot. If not, it is simply added to the playing pieces already in the player's hand and he or she continues the game by holding out his or her tree halves, word side down, to the player on the left.
5. The game continues in this manner until one of the players has five correct trees. This player is the winner.

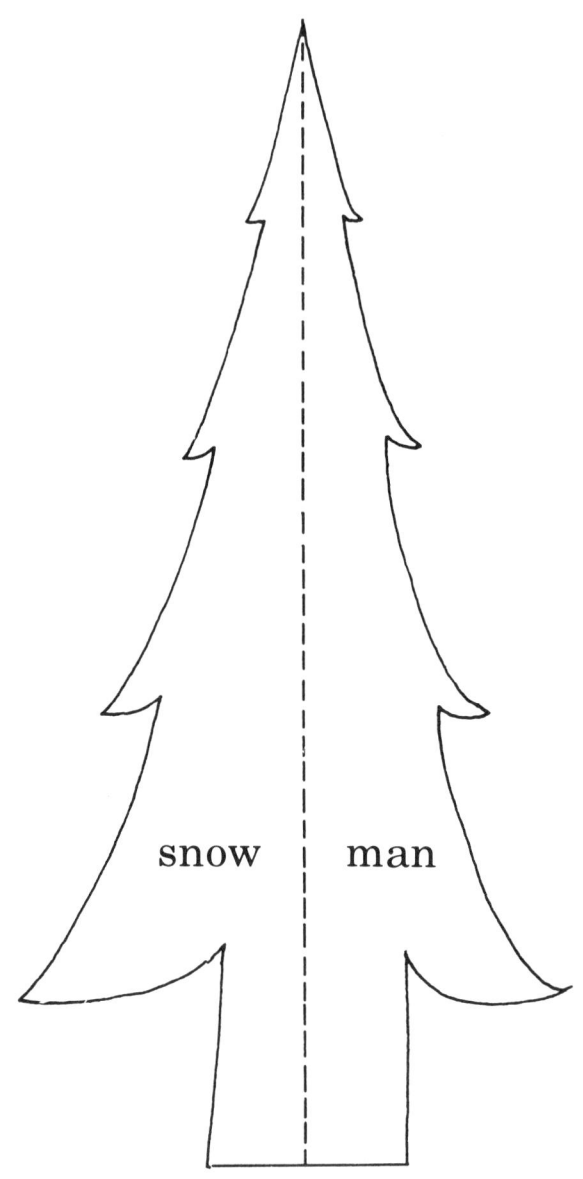

The Long Train

Skill Reinforced: sequence
Grade Level: primary
Materials Needed:

    2 sheets of 3″ × 3″ red posterboard
    2 sheets of 3″ × 3″ blue posterboard
    2 sheets of 3″ × 3″ green posterboard
    2 sheets of 3″ × 3″ yellow posterboard
    2 sheets of 3″ × 3″ gray posterboard
    20 sheets of 2″ × 3″ white posterboard
    scissors
    felt-tipped pen

Construction Directions:

1. Cut one of each color of the 3″ × 3″ posterboard pieces using the engine pattern shown here.

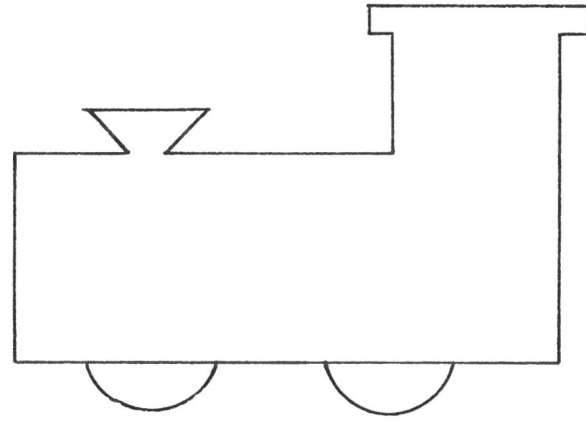

2. Cut the white posterboard pieces using the train car pattern shown here.

3. Cut one of each color of the 3″ × 3″ posterboard pieces using the caboose pattern shown here.

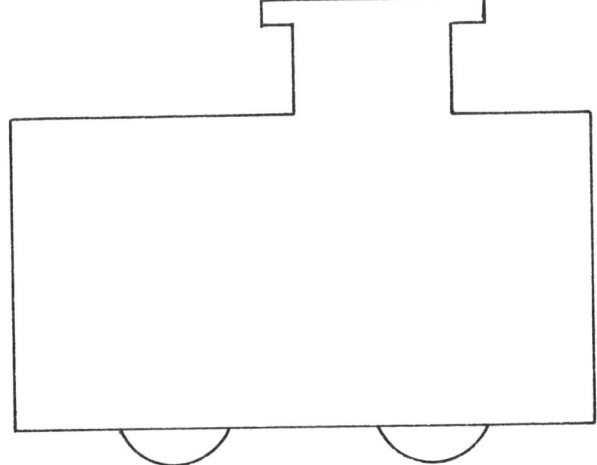

4. Copy each of the following words (capitalized) onto the appropriate engine.

    The (red)   A (blue)
    Father (green)   That (yellow)
    Nancy (gray)

5. Copy each of the following words onto a different train car.

    car   to
    is   the
    really   dog
    going   is
    kite   brown
    is   and
    flying   jumped
    very   over
    drove   that
    us   wide

6. Copy each of the following words (with periods) onto the appropriate caboose.

    fast. (red)   high. (blue)
    lake. (green)   white. (yellow)
    river. (gray)

Game Play: This game is for two to five players.

1. Each player chooses an engine and a caboose of the same color and places them in front of him or her.
2. All of the train cars are dealt to the players, face down. A player should not show the other players his or her cards.
3. Players should now look at the cars in their hands. Those that will help to form a sentence between their engine and caboose should be placed in the appropriate places.
4. The player who dealt the cars now begins the game by holding out the cars in his or her hand, word side down, to the player on his or her left. This player must take one of the cars. If it can be used in his or her sentence, it is placed down in the appropriate position. If not, it is simply added to the cars in his or her hand and the player continues the game by holding out his or her cars to the player on the left.
5. The game continues in this manner until one of the players is able to make a complete sentence with six words. This player is the winner.

Crossing the Ocean

Skill Reinforced: context clue usage
Grade Level: high primary
Materials Needed:

   1 sheet of 14″ × 20″ blue posterboard
   white and red gummed circles
   25 sheets of 3″ × 2½″ white posterboard
   felt-tipped pen
   7 sheets of 3″ × 2½″ red posterboard
   game markers

Construction Directions:

1. Mark the blue game board using an enlargement of the pattern shown here. Attach the gummed circles as indicated in the illustration (R = red; W = white).

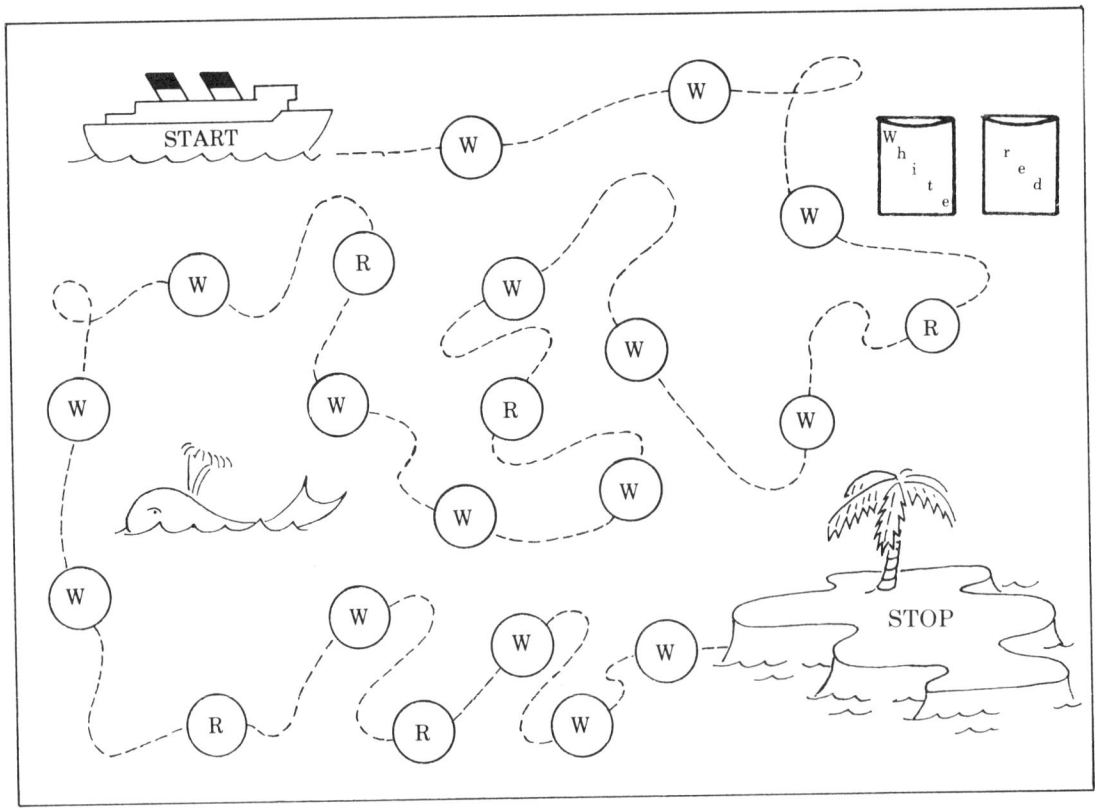

2. Copy each of the following sentences onto a different white card. Also, mark the numeral in parentheses on the lower right-hand corner of the card as shown on the following page.

122

> The dog began to
> d __ g deep down
> into the garden.
>
> 2

The dog began to d __ g deep down into the garden. (2)
It was a f ____ e day at the zoo. (1)
Bill was h _____ g his mother. (3)
They heard a n _____ e. (3)
There is something w _____ g here. (2)
He ate his b _____ t. (2)
We'll d _____ e the truck. (1)
What a beautiful f _____ r garden. (2)
Here comes the c _____ s parade. (3)
I think he l _____ s his bike. (2)
May I have a c _____ e to eat? (2)
She baked us fresh b _____ d. (1)
Don't get h ____ t. (1)
Sam owned t _____ e cats. (2)
Our f _____ y is going on a picnic. (1)
I like this ham s _____ h. (3)
At last all the w ___ k was done. (1)
He is e _____ g the best apples. (2)
I want to buy s _____ g. (2)
She made two p _____ n pies. (2)
The m _____ r is looking for her little boy. (1)
May I c ____ e to your party? (1)
There are many p _____ y trees in the schoolyard. (2)
One cold n _____ t it began to snow. (1)
They p _____ d on the swing. (2)

3. Copy each of the following sentences onto a different red card.
   Look out for sharks. Go back two circles.
   Boat has a leak. Go back one circle.
   Good weather. Go ahead one circle.
   Storm. Go back three circles.
   Stop at island. Go back two circles.
   Whale is in the way. Go back one circle.
   Calm sea. Go ahead one circle.

Game Play: This game is for two to four players.

1. Each player places his or her marker on START. The first player takes the top white card. If the player can *say and spell* the missing word, he or she moves the number of circles indicated on the card. If not, the player stays put and the next player takes a turn.
2. When a player lands on a red circle, he or she takes a red card and does what it says. This is part of the turn!
3. The first player to reach STOP is the winner.

Picture Plus

Skill Reinforced: main idea
Grade Level: high primary
Materials Needed:

    2 egg cartons

    scissors

    glue

    felt-tipped pen

    20 pictures from old basal readers

    20 sheets of 5" × 5" white posterboard

    20 sheets of 5" × 2" yellow posterboard

Construction Directions:

1. Cut the egg cartons apart. Turn them over and cut slits crosswise through each hump.
2. Glue each picture onto one of the white cards.
3. Write a sentence telling about each picture on the yellow cards. For example, if the picture is of children playing outside, you might write, "The children are having fun playing."

Game Play: This game is for two to four players.

1. The players each choose an egg carton game board and place it in front of them.
2. Each player is dealt five picture cards. They place them in the slits in their cartons. Now the sentence cards are dealt to the players. A player should not show the other players his or her sentence cards.
3. Players should now look at the sentence cards in their hands. Those who hold a sentence card that describes one of their pictures should place it in the same slot as the picture card.
4. The player who dealt the cards now begins by holding out his or her sentence cards, face down, to the player on the left. This player must take one of the cards and must not show it to the other players. If it describes one of his or her pictures, the player slides it into the appropriate slot. If not, it is added to the cards in the player's hand and he or she continues the game by holding out the cards to the player on the left.
5. The game continues in this manner until one of the players is able to match all of his or her pictures with sentence cards. This player is the winner.

Old Oak Tree

Skill Reinforced: making inferences
Grade Level: high primary
Materials Needed:

    10 toilet paper rolls
    20 sheets of 5″ × 5″ green posterboard
    scissors
    felt-tipped pen

Construction Directions:

1. Cut the toilet paper rolls in half and make slits as shown here.

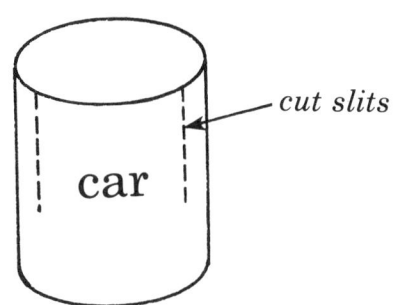

2. Copy each of the following words onto a different tree trunk (toilet paper roll) as shown in the illustration.

apple	tree	fish	pencil sharpener
grass	sun	paper	boat
bird	star	light	moon
clock	pumpkin	snow	bell
belt	book	car	ghost

3. Cut and mark the posterboard sheets using an enlargement of the treetop pattern shown here.

4. Copy each of the following riddles onto a different tree.

I am long and narrow.
I hold up your pants.
What am I?

I am usually white.
You write on me.
What am I?

I am on the wall.
I have two hands.
What am I?

I grow on a tree.
I am red.
You can eat me.
What am I?

I am green.
I grow in your yard.
What am I?

I can sit in a tree.
I like to sing.
What am I?

I hang on the wall.
I tell you what time it is.
What am I?

If you turn me on ...
you can see better.
What am I?

I am white and cold.
I fall from the clouds.
What am I?

I am metal.
You can ride in me.
What am I?

I grow very tall.
I have many leaves.
What am I?

I am bright.
I make things grow.
What am I?

You can see me at night.
I am white and twinkle.
What am I?

I am orange.
You like me at Halloween.
What am I?

I have a cover.
You can read me.
What am I?

I like to swim.
I don't like hooks.
What am I?

I float on water.
You can ride in me.
What am I?

You can see me at night.
I look like I change shape.
What am I?

I am metal.
I say, "Ding-dong."
What am I?

I am white.
I say, "Boo."
What am I?

Game Play: This game is for two to four players.

1. The players each choose five tree trunks and place them in front of them. The treetops are placed, face down, in the center of the playing area.
2. The first player takes the top treetop and reads the riddle. He or she looks at his or her tree trunks to find the answer. If one is found, the top is placed in the slits of the appropriate trunk. If the player does not find the answer, the treetop is placed next to the original stack.
3. The next player continues the game in the same manner. The first one to put treetops on all of his or her trunks is the winner. If the players use all of the treetops in the original stack and there is still not a winner, the trees that were not used are placed in the original stack and the game continues.

Going Fishing

Skill Reinforced: fact from fantasy
Grade Level: high primary
Materials Needed:
   8 sheets of 12″ × 12″ blue posterboard
   20 sheets of 4″ × 4″ yellow posterboard
   20 sheets of 4″ × 4″ red posterboard
   20 sheets of 4″ × 4″ green posterboard
   20 sheets of 4″ × 4″ orange posterboard
   scissors
   felt-tipped pen

Construction Directions:
   1. Cut the blue posterboard pieces using an enlargement of the pond pattern shown here. Write FACT on four of them and FANTASY on the other four.

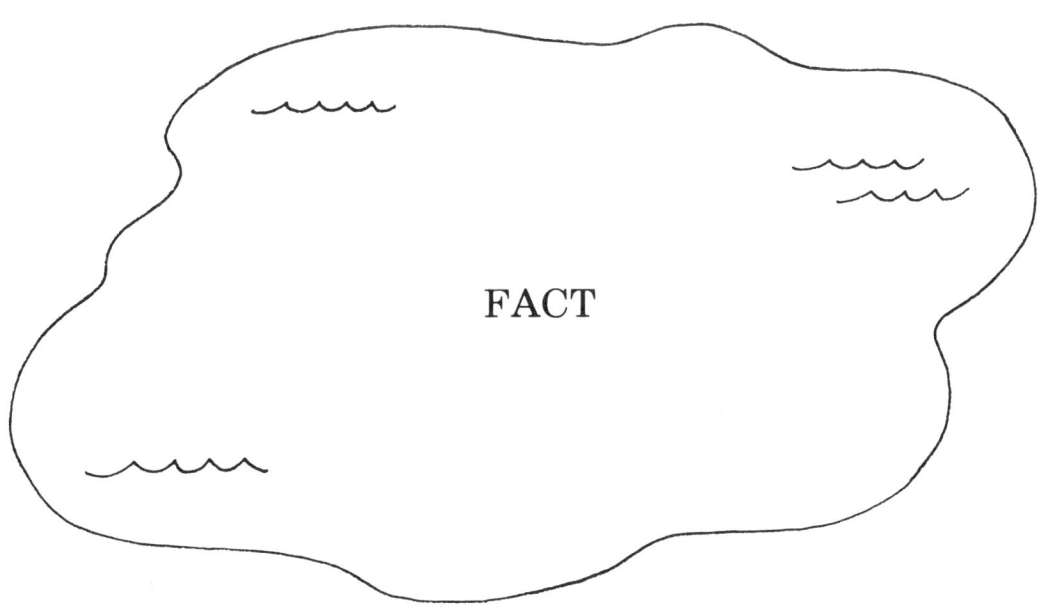

2. Cut and mark the 4″ × 4″ posterboard pieces using the fish pattern shown here.

3. Copy each of the following fact statements onto four different-colored fish.

> This bridge is the biggest in town.
> The truck could not pull the load.
> The wind blew down the tree.
> A bee flew into our school today.
> Chris has won over ten games.
> She swam across the pond.
> We went hiking through the woods.
> He flew his kite higher than mine.
> The boy ran around the track.
> Mike hit the ball into the road.

4. Copy each of the following fantasy statements onto four different-colored fish.

> The dragon frightened the princess.
> The cow jumped over the barn.
> The cabbage plant grew taller than the house.
> The car honked its own horn.
> The lady in the picture smiled at us.
> The knife and fork danced together.
> The little girl jumped from star to star.
> The house wished someone would buy it.
> The dog bowed and said goodbye.
> The turtle and the cow went to the movie.

Game Play: This game is for two to four players.
1. Separate the fish by color.
2. Give each player one FACT pond, one FANTASY pond, and all of the fish of one color.
3. Tell the players when to begin. Have them read their fish and place them on the appropriate ponds. The first child to successfully complete this task is the winner.

III
Puzzle Pages

The puzzle pages in this section may be duplicated and used directly with students to reinforce a variety of reading skills. A description and an answer key precede each puzzle.

The following reading skills are reinforced by the designated puzzle pages.

Puzzle Page	Reading Skill	Grade Level
Choo Choo!	alphabet knowledge	low primary
Colorful Garden	visual discrimination	low primary
The Island	alphabet knowledge	low primary
Wild Windows	auditory discrimination	low primary
Follow Suzy	fine motor skills	low primary
Can You See It?	initial consonants	low primary
All Aboard!	initial consonants	low primary
Rocket Puzzle	final consonants	low primary
Twirl a Vowel	medial vowels	low primary
Blend Box	consonant blends	primary
What Will We Ride Next?	sight word knowledge	primary
Into the Harbor	sight word knowledge	primary
What Do You Want to Play?	sight word knowledge	primary
Are You Hungry?	medial vowels	primary
Can You Find the Animals?	word meaning	primary
My Favorite Day	vowel digraphs	primary
Help Henry	making inferences	primary
Who Is Chickie Looking For?	context clue usage	primary
Flying High	story sequence	primary
Who Did It?	fact from fantasy	high primary
Going Swimming	mood of the story	high primary
What Happened at the Zoo?	main idea	high primary
Crazy Mixed-Up Words!	context clue usage	high primary
Let's Take a Walk	predicting outcomes	high primary
Compound Pictures	compound words	high primary
Our Picnic Mess	story sequence	high primary

Choo Choo!

Skill Reinforced: alphabet knowledge

Grade Level: low primary

Puzzle Description: The children begin at the star and draw a line to the letter "A." They continue drawing lines from letter to letter as they follow the sequence of the alphabet. If they complete the activity sheet correctly, the lines will form a picture.

Answer Key: The puzzle is self-correcting. As shown below, a picture of a train engine will be formed if the dots are connected in the correct order.

Choo Choo!

Begin at the star and draw a line to the letter "A."
Keep drawing lines following the alphabet.

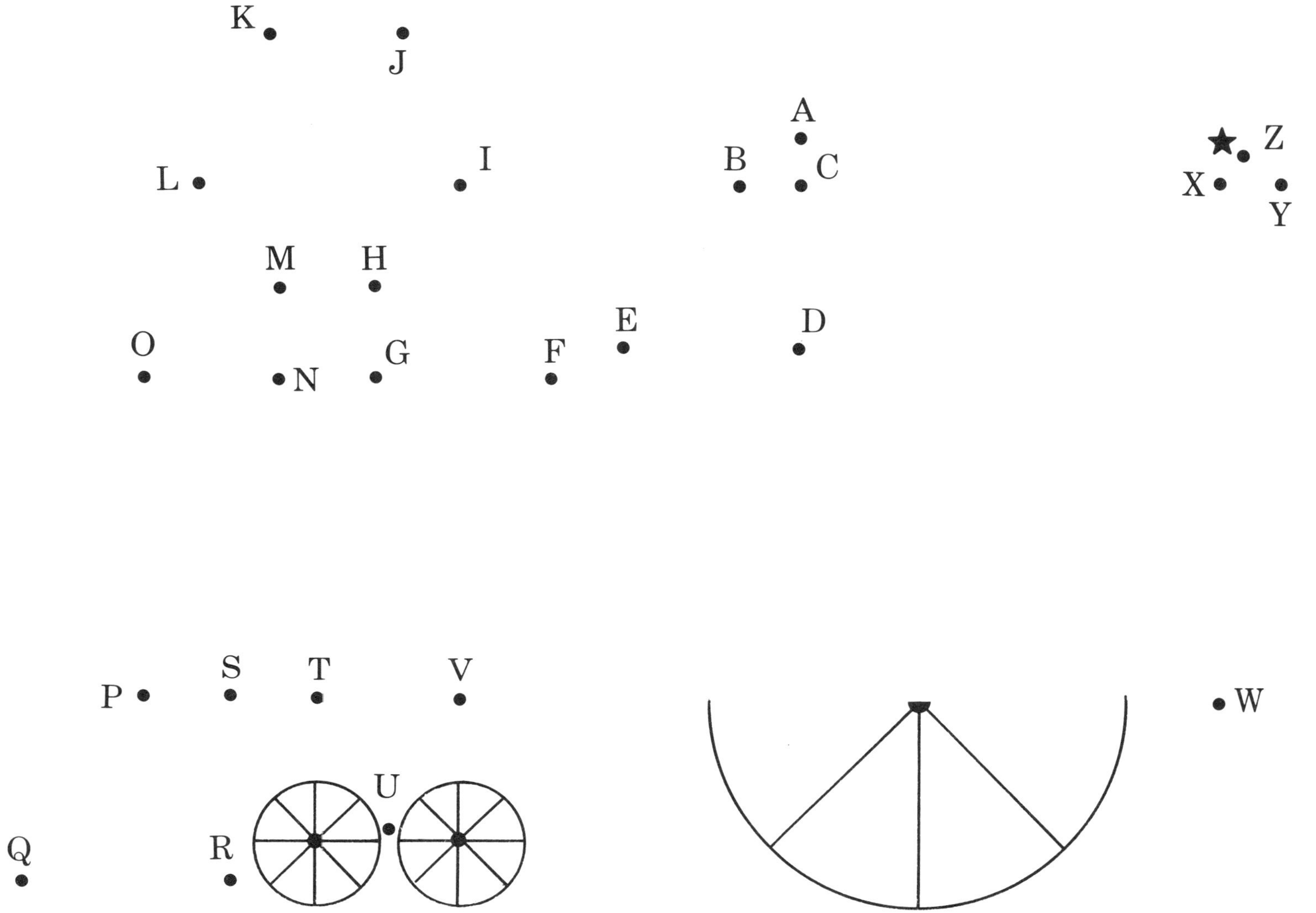

Name _____

Date _____

Colorful Garden

Skill Reinforced: visual discrimination

Grade Level: low primary

Puzzle Description: The puzzle includes a picture of a flower garden. Each flower has a word printed on it. The children color only the flowers that have the same word that is on the large bug. After completing the puzzle, the children should be allowed to color in the entire sheet.

Answer Key: This puzzle is easily evaluated. Simply check to see if each child has colored only those flowers containing the word "bug."

Name _____

Date _____

Colorful Garden

Look at the word on the bug. Color only those flowers on which you find the same word.

bug
bug
dug
big
bug
bug
bag
bug

137

The Island

Skill Reinforced: alphabet knowledge

Grade Level: low primary

Puzzle Description: The children cut the pages into strips along the broken lines. After this step, they place the strips in the correct alphabetical order. If they complete this task correctly, a picture of an island will be formed.

Answer Key: The puzzle is self-correcting. The following picture of an island will be formed if it is completed correctly.

Cut on the broken lines until you have 11 strips. Now, place the strips in the correct alphabetical order. If you are correct, a picture of an island will be formed.

Name _____
Date _____

jkl | abc | pqr | mno | vw | def | stu | xyz | ghi

THE ISLAND

139

Wild Windows

Skill Reinforced: auditory discrimination

Grade Level: low primary

Puzzle Description: This puzzle consists of a drawing of a house and includes the outlines of four windows. Inside each of these is a picture. Below the house are the "missing" windows which also have pictures on them. The children cut out the windows and paste them over the pictures of objects whose names begin with the same sound as those in the pictures on the windows. As an additional activity you might want your students to color the house.

Answer Key: The puzzle is easily corrected. Simply check for the following order of drawings on the house.

Name _____

Date _____

Wild Windows

Cut out the windows at the bottom of this sheet. Look at the picture on one of the windows. Can you find a picture on the house that begins with the same sound? If you do, paste the window over it. Do this with all of the windows.

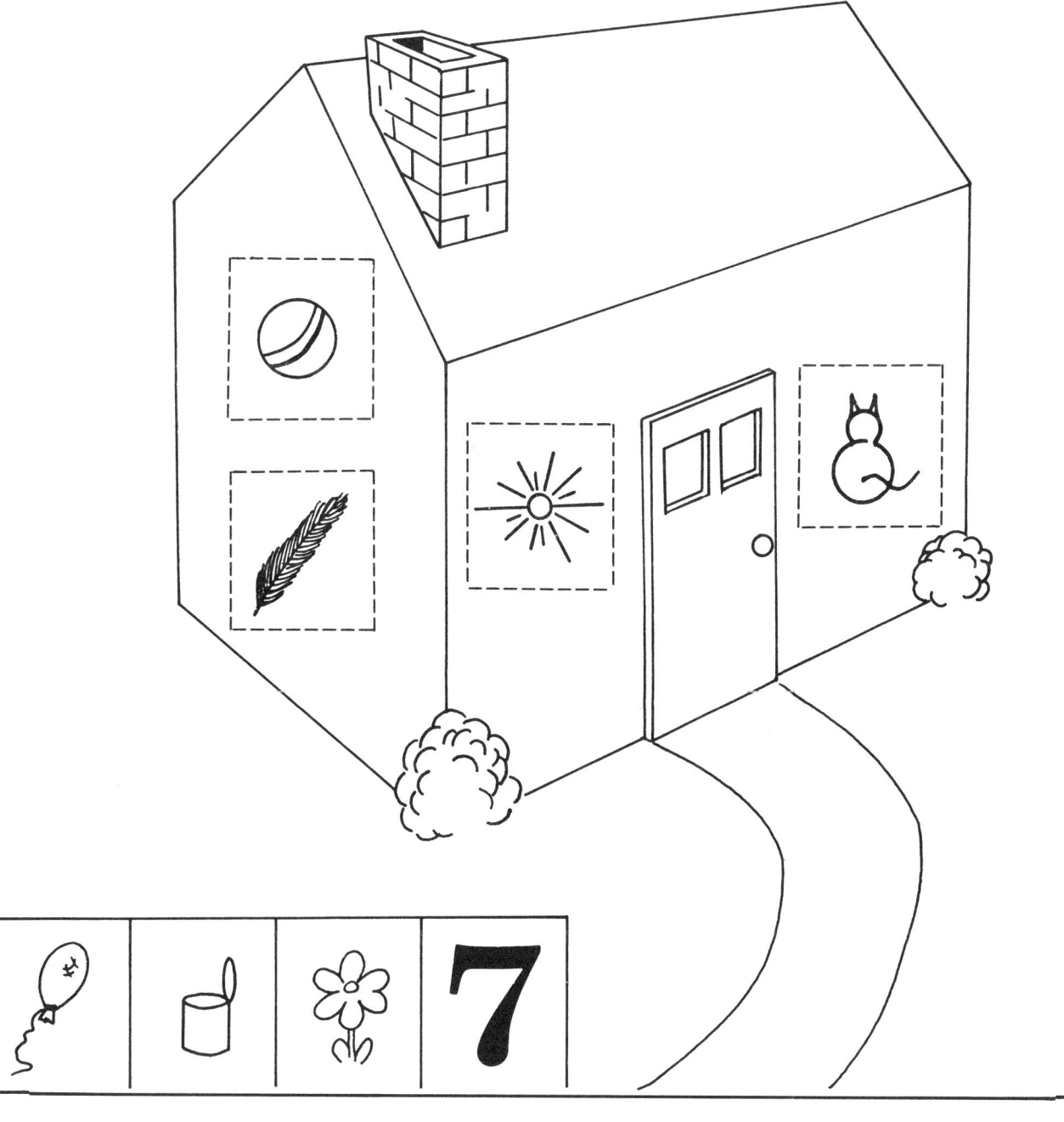

Follow Suzy

Skill Reinforced: fine motor skills

Grade Level: low primary

Puzzle Description: Beginning at the scissors drawing, the children cut along the broken line path.

Answer Key: The puzzle is easy to correct. Simply see if the children were able to cut along the broken line from the scissors to the star.

Name _____

Date _____

Follow Suzy

Suzy Scissors has to cut on the line. She's afraid she can't do it. Why don't you help her? Start where Suzy is and keep cutting on the line until you come to the star.

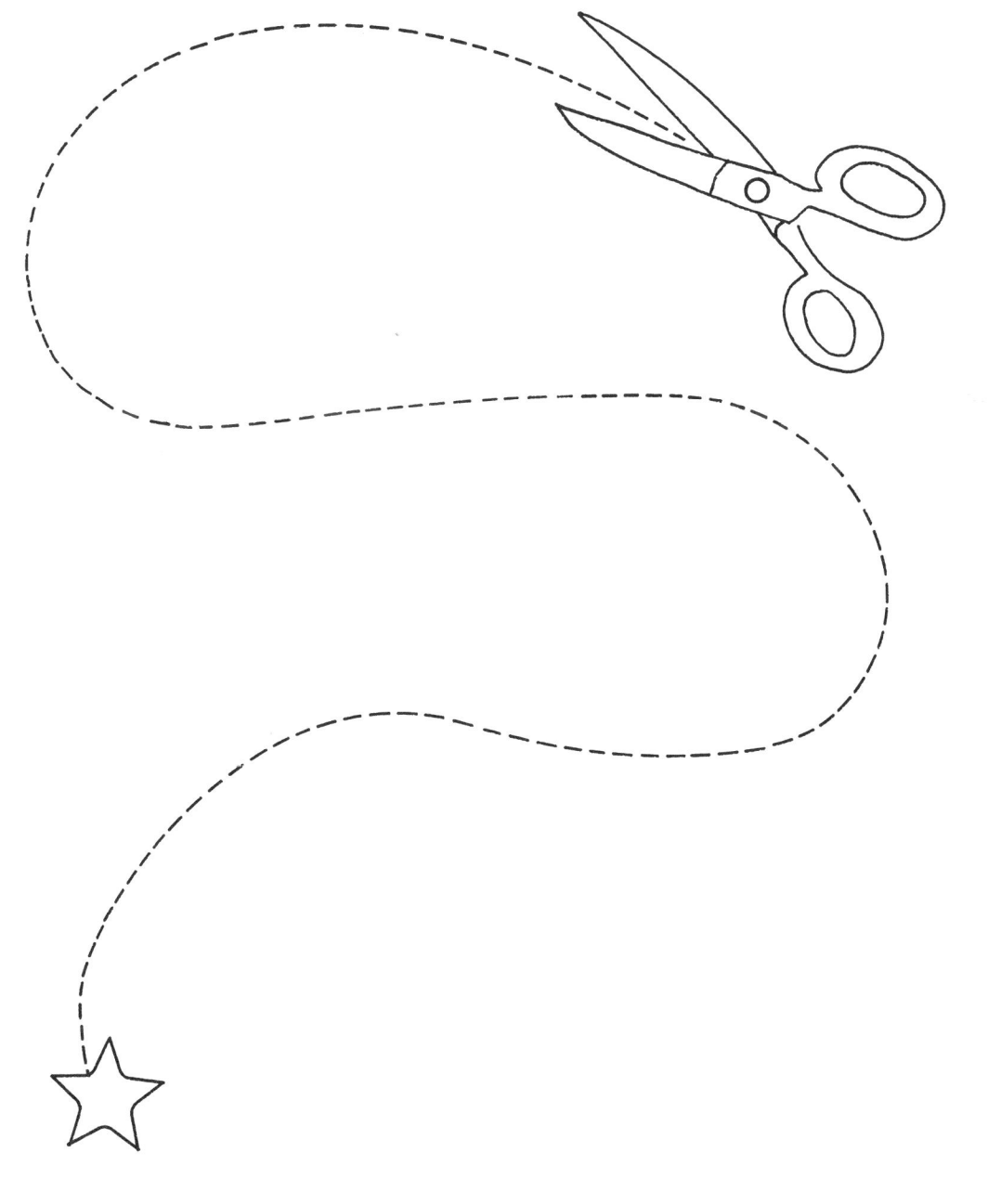

Can You See It?

Skill Reinforced: initial consonants

Grade Level: low primary

Puzzle Description: The children look at each picture and determine whether the illustrated object begins with the consonant "B." If the picture does begin with a "B," the children color the space. If it does not, they leave the space blank. If they complete the puzzle correctly, the colored spaces will form a sailboat.

Answer Key: The puzzle is self-correcting. As shown below, the colored spaces will form a sailboat if the puzzle is completed correctly.

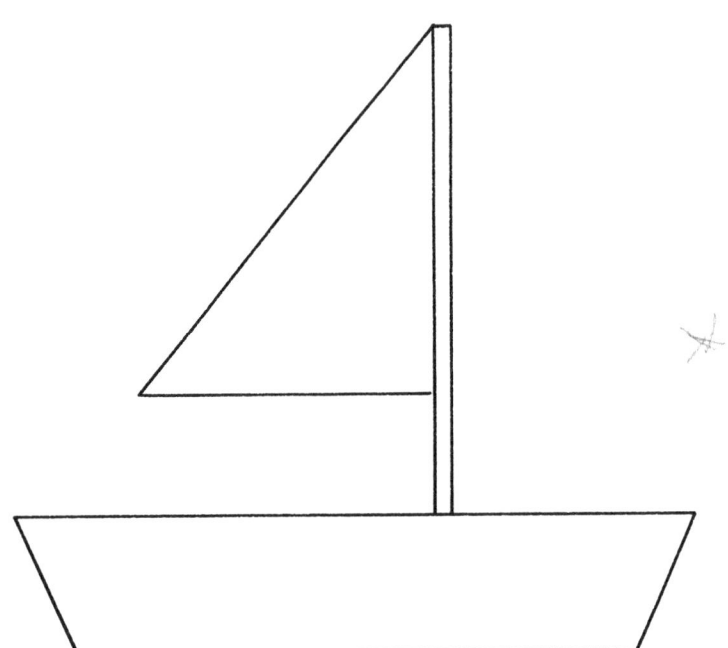

Can You See It?

Color in only those spaces that contain something beginning with the letter "B."

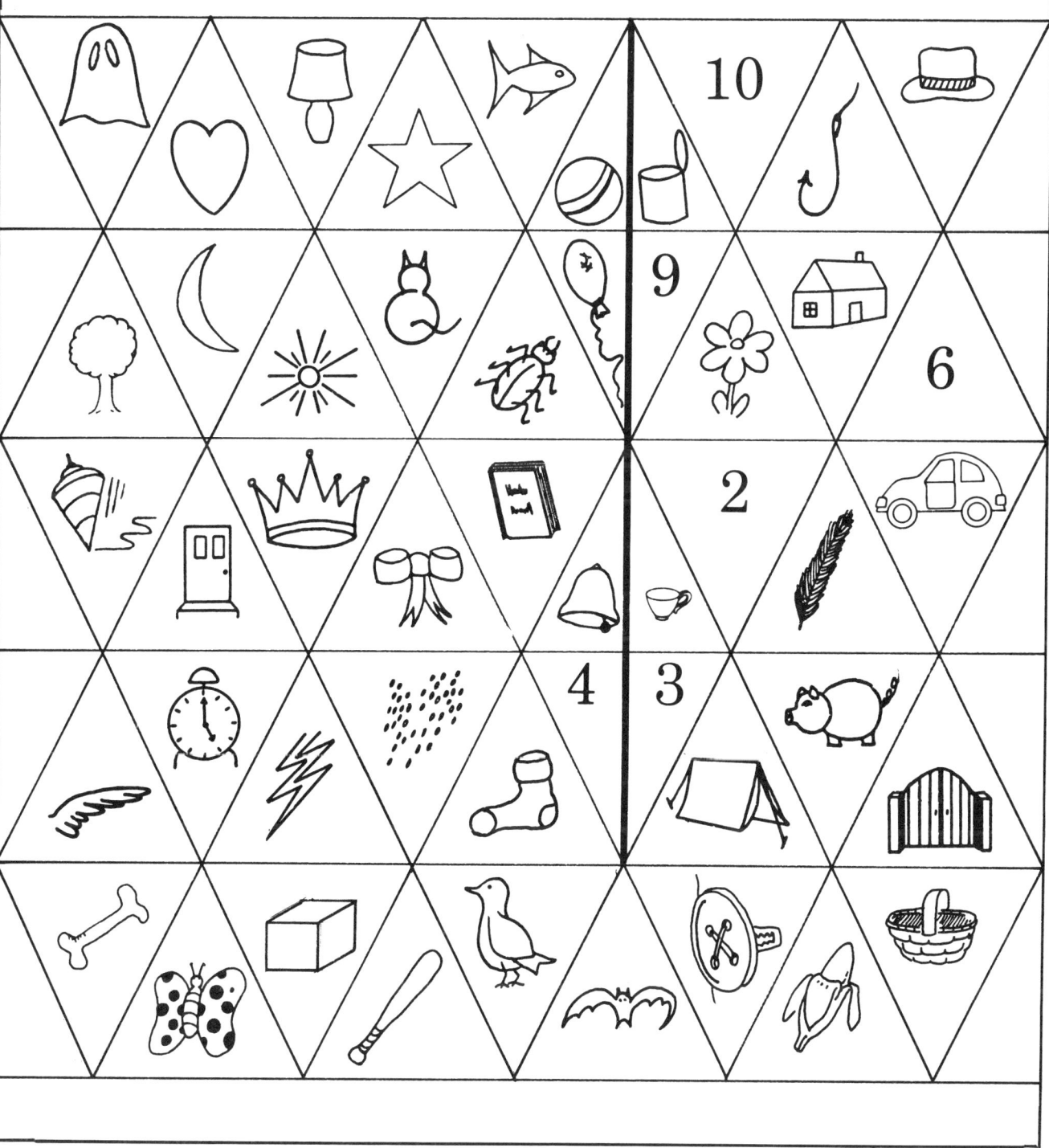

All Aboard!

Skill Reinforced: initial consonants

Grade Level: low primary

Puzzle Description: The puzzle consists of a drawing of a train and includes the outlines of eight train wheels. Inside each of these is a consonant. Below the train are the "missing" wheels which have pictures on them. Each picture is of an object whose name begins with one of the consonants on the train. The children cut out the wheels and paste them over the appropriate consonants. As an additional activity you might want your students to color the train.

Answer Key: The puzzle is easily corrected. Simply check for the following order of the drawings.

Name

Date

All Aboard!

This train is missing its wheels. There is a letter where each wheel should be. Below the train are the missing wheels which have drawings on them. The name of the object in each drawing begins with one of the letters. Cut out the wheels and paste them over the right letters. When you finish you may color the train.

Rocket Puzzle

Skill Reinforced: final consonants

Grade Level: low primary

Puzzle Description: The puzzle consists of a drawing of a rocket and its path to the moon. Along the way are outlines of ten planets. Inside each of these is a drawing. At the bottom of the page are the "missing" planets which have letters on them. Each drawing is of an object whose name ends with the letter on one of these planets. The children cut out the planets and paste them over the appropriate final consonants. As an additional activity you might want your students to color the sheet.

Answer Key: The puzzle is easily corrected. Simply check for the following order of the letters along the rocket's path.

1. g
2. t
3. k
4. s
5. n
6. d
7. p
8. r
9. m
10. l

Name

Rocket Puzzle

Date

Follow the rocket's path. Each time it comes to a planet outline, look at the picture inside. What letter do you think it ends with? Now, find that letter in the planets, cut it out, and paste it over the picture. Keep doing this until you have reached the moon!

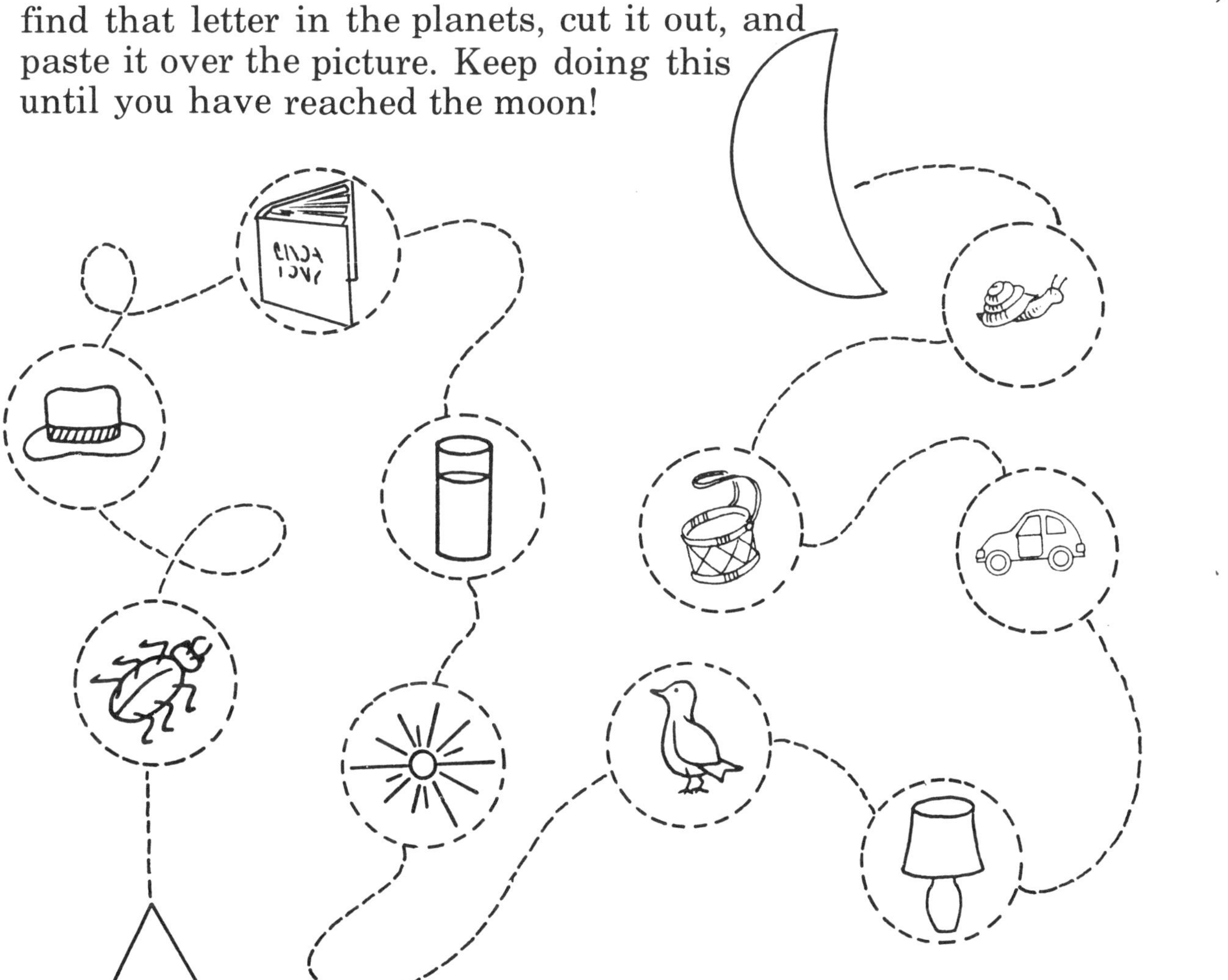

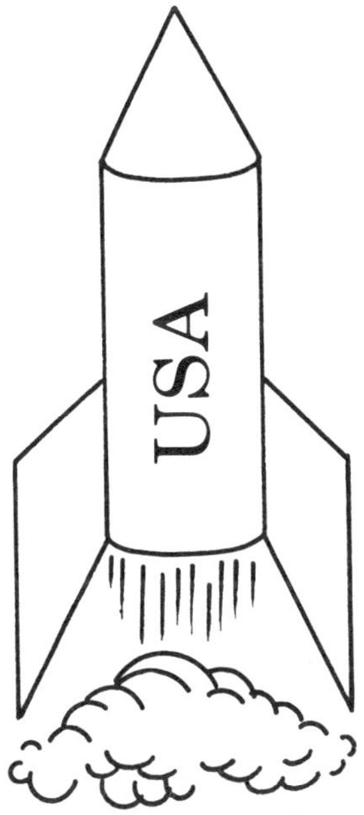

n l p d k

g s t m r

149

Twirl a Vowel

Skill Reinforced: medial vowels

Grade Level: low primary

Puzzle Description: The children cut out the middle vowel circle and then turn it until all vowels match drawings of objects whose names contain the appropriate vowels.

Answer Key: The puzzle is easy to correct. Simply check for the following corresponding letter and picture combinations.

Name _____

Twirl a Vowel

Date _____

Cut out the middle circle on the dotted line. Now, turn the letter wheel until each vowel is next to a drawing whose name has that sound in it.

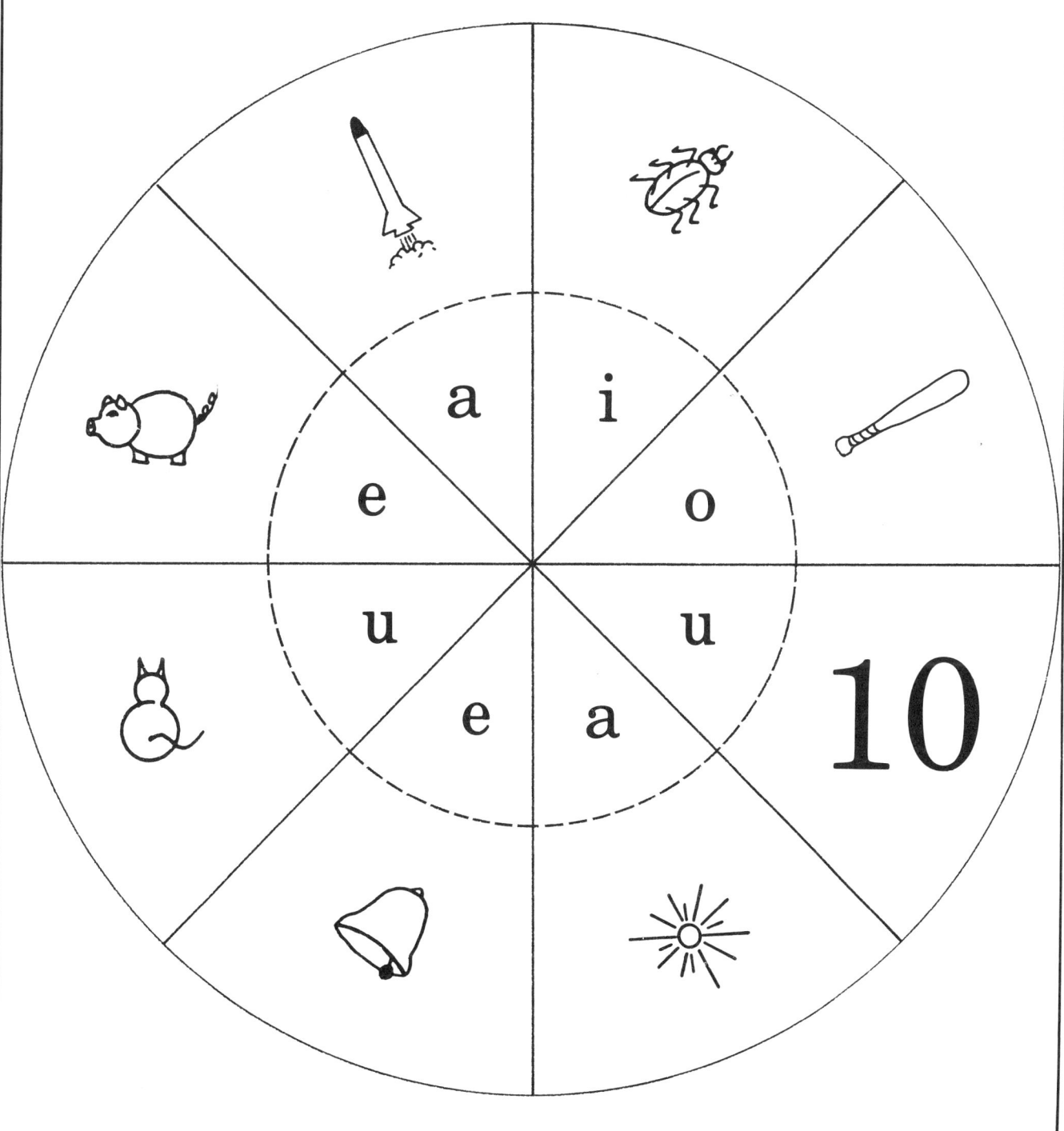

10

151

Blend Box

Skill Reinforced: consonant blends

Grade Level: primary

Puzzle Description: The puzzle consists of a row of pictures and a box containing the consonant blends with which the names of these objects begin. The children correctly match the blends with the pictures. They do this by writing a blend next to each picture in the row.

Answer Key: The puzzle is easily corrected. Simply check for the following picture-blend combinations.

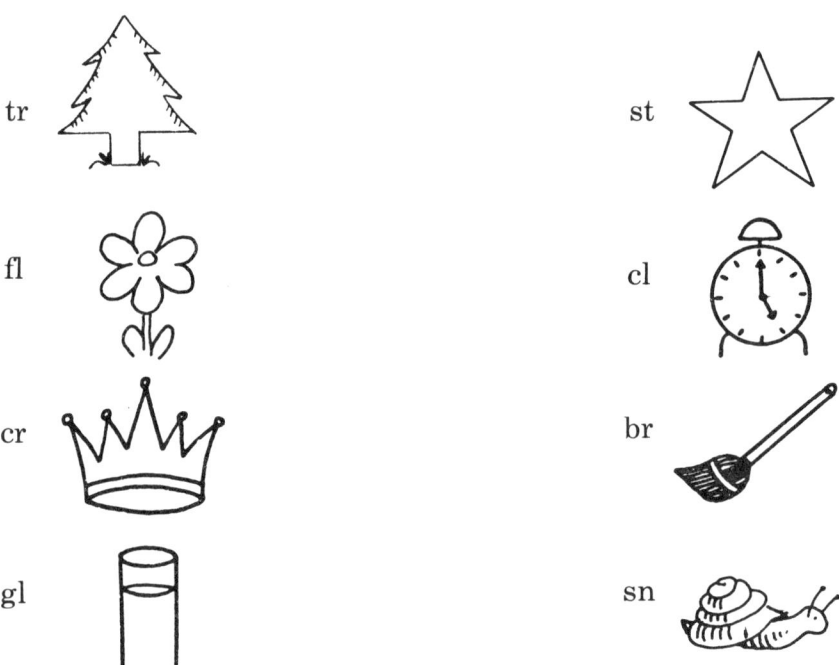

Blend Box

Name _____

Date _____

Below is a list of pictures. Look through the Blend Box and find the blend with which the name of each object begins. Write the blends in the space next to each picture.

 _____   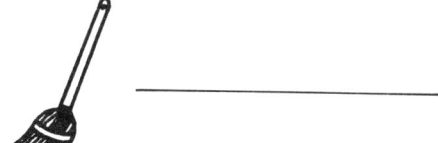 _____

 _____    _____

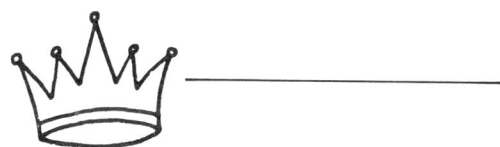 _____

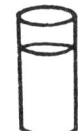 _____

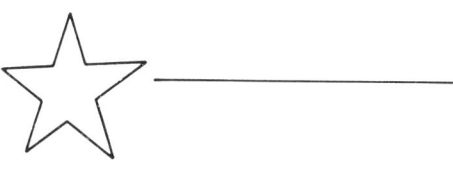 _____

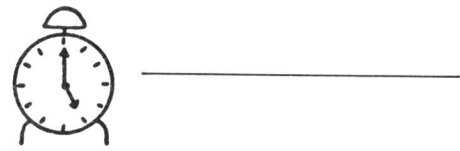 _____

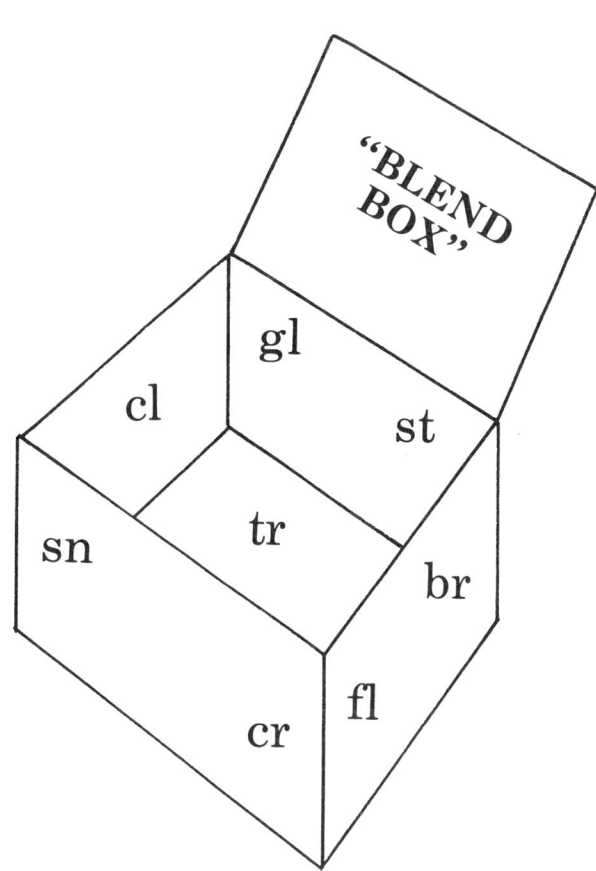

153

What Will We Ride Next?

Skill Reinforced: sight word knowledge

Grade Level: primary

Puzzle Description: The puzzle consists of 13 drawings and a list of words. The students match the drawings with their word names. If they are correct, the circled letters will spell the name of a ride in an amusement park.

Answer Key: The puzzle is self-correcting. As shown below, the words ROLLER COASTER will be spelled if the puzzle is completed correctly.

R	bi(r)d
O	h(o)use
L	(l)ightning
L	f(l)ower
E	f(e)ather
R	(r)ain
C	so(c)k
O	b(o)ok
A	st(a)r
S	gho(s)t
T	(t)en
E	tre(e)
R	th(r)ee

What Will We Ride Next?

Name _____

Date _____

Jim and Bob were at Fun Park. They rode on the merry-go-round and the train.

"Oh, look!" said Bob as they turned a corner.

"Oh, let's ride that!" said Jim.

What do you think the boys are going to ride next? You can find out! All you have to do is work the puzzle on this sheet.

Inside the merry-go-round you'll see a list of words that will help you to find the name of what the boys will ride next. Write the correct word next to each drawing. Circle the same letter in each word that is circled in the merry-go-round. If the words are in the correct order, the circled letters will spell the ride the boys will go on next.

so(c)k
f(e)ather
h(o)use   th(r)ee

f(l)ower   gho(s)t
bi(r)d   tre(e)
(r)ain   st(a)r   (t)en
(l)ightning
b(o)ok

Into the Harbor

Skill Reinforced: sight word knowledge

Grade Level: primary

Puzzle Description: The students are asked to help dock a ship by matching the word cards with the correct picture cards. They must cut out the word cards and paste them on top of the picture cards. One letter is circled on each word card. If the students are correct, the circled letters will spell the name of the person in charge of bringing the ship into the harbor.

Answer Key: The puzzle is self-correcting. As shown below, CAPTAIN JOE will be spelled if the puzzle is completed correctly.

C	so(c)k
A	b(a)ll
P	to(p)
T	ha(t)
A	c(a)t
I	f(i)sh
N	su(n)
J	(j)ar
O	mo(o)n
E	kit(e)

Into the Harbor

Name _____

Date _____

Help the ship make a perfect docking. Cut out the word cards and paste them over the correct picture cards. If you are correct, the circled letters will spell the name of the person who brings the ship into the harbor.

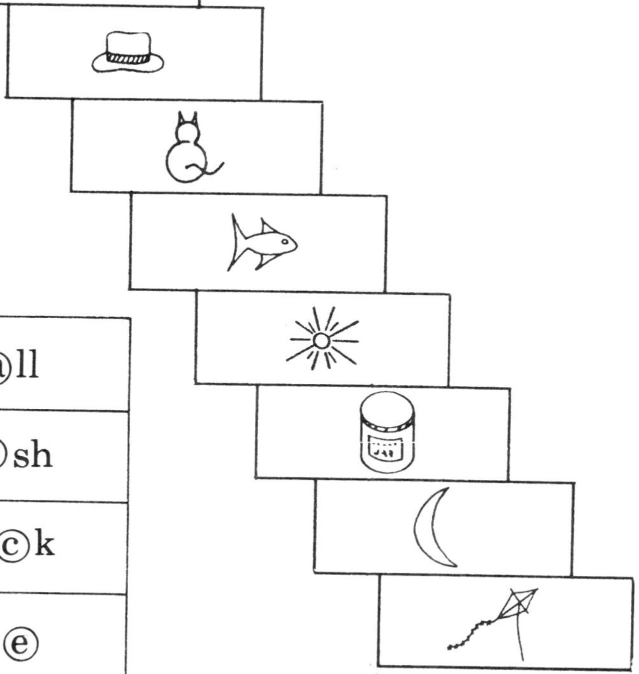

toⓟ	b@ll
mo⊙n	f①sh
c@t	so©k
su⓷	kit⊕
①ar	ha⊕

What Do You Want to Play?

Skill Reinforced: sight word knowledge

Grade Level: primary

Puzzle Description: The puzzle consists of two word lists. Students read the words in the first list and find the words in the "Word Box" which have the opposite meaning. They write these words in the appropriate spaces and circle the same letter in each word that is circled in the Word Box. If they complete the puzzle correctly, the circled letters will spell a game that children like to play.

Answer Key: The puzzle is self-correcting. As shown below, HIDE AND SEEK will be spelled if the puzzle is completed correctly.

H   ⓗard
I   bⓘg
D   enⓓ
E   latⓔ

A   wⓐlk
N   ⓝight
D   stanⓓ

S   yeⓢ
E   nⓔw
E   aftⓔr
K   taⓚe

What Do You Want to Play?

Name _____

Date _____

"What do you want to play?" asked Mike.
"Let's play jump rope," said Alice.
"Oh, I don't want to play that!" said Henry.
"I know, let's play baseball," said Sue.
"I'm not playing that!" said Joe.
"Well, then, what will we play?" asked Mike.

The children finally found a game that they all wanted to play. Can you guess what it is? If you work the puzzle below, you will find out!

Look at the first word in the list. Can you find a word in the Word Box that means the opposite? When you find one, write it in the space next to the first word. Be sure to circle the letter in the word that is circled in the Word Box. Continue doing this with all of the words. If you are correct, the circled letters will spell the game that the children played.

1. soft _____
2. little _____
3. begin _____
4. early _____
5. run _____
6. day _____
7. sit _____
8. no _____
9. old _____
10. before _____
11. give _____

WORD BOX
ⓝight
yeⓢ
latⓔ
bⓘg
stanⓓ
aftⓔr
ⓗard
nⓔw
wⓐlk
taⓚe
enⓓ

159

Are You Hungry?

Skill Reinforced: medial vowels

Grade Level: primary

Puzzle Description: The children read the riddles in each puzzle and look for the answers in the "Word Apples." When they find them, they write them in the spaces next to the riddles. If they are correct, the letters in the shaded spaces in each puzzle will spell the name of something that can be eaten.

Answer Key: The puzzle is self-correcting. As shown below, the words PEAR, PEACH, and BANANA will be spelled if the puzzle is completed correctly.

Puzzle 1

P	cu ⓟ
E	b ⓔ ll
A	f ⓐ n
R	ⓡ ed

Puzzle 2

P	ma ⓟ
E	b ⓔ d
A	m ⓐ n
C	ⓒ at
H	s ⓗ ut

Puzzle 3

B	ⓑ ag
A	tr ⓐ p
N	po ⓝ d
A	b ⓐ nk
N	ca ⓝ
A	h ⓐ m

Are You Hungry?

Name _____

Date _____

Below are three "Are You Hungry?" puzzles. Next to each puzzle is a Word Apple. If you can find the answer to each riddle in the apple, write it in the blanks. If you are correct, the letters in the shaded boxes will spell the names of things you can eat. Each puzzle will have its own answer.

Puzzle 1

1. You drink from it.
2. You can ring it.
3. It keeps you cool.
4. A color.

bell
fan
cup
red

Puzzle 2

1. It shows you where to go.
2. You sleep in it.
3. Your father.
4. It goes "meow."
5. You can do it to a door.

man
shut
map
cat
bed

Puzzle 3

1. You can put things in it.
2. You catch things with it.
3. Fish can live in it.
4. You put money in it.
5. Some food is sold in it.
6. You can eat it.

bank
trap
ham
bag
can
pond

161

Can You Find the Animals?

Skill Reinforced: word meaning

Grade Level: primary

Puzzle Description: The children read the riddles in each puzzle and look for the answers in the "Answer Box." When they find the answers, they write them in the spaces next to the riddles. If they are correct, the letters in the shaded spaces in each puzzle will spell the name of an animal.

Answer Key: The puzzle is self-correcting. As shown below, the words BIRD, MOOSE, and CAMEL will be spelled if the puzzle is completed correctly.

Puzzle 1
B   ⓑell
I   rⓘng
R   caⓡ
D   ⓓays

Puzzle 2
M   ⓜop
O   bⓞok
O   dⓞg
S   ⓢoap
E   pⓔncil

Puzzle 3
C   ⓒan
A   bⓐll
M   laⓜp
E   homⓔ
L   gⓛass

Name _____

Date _____

Can You Find the Animals?

Can you find the animals? They are somewhere on this sheet. You can find them by working the puzzles. Read the top line of the first puzzle. Now, look in the answer box for the answer. Can you find something you can ring? The word is BELL. This word has been written in the puzzle for you. See how each letter goes in a different box. Read the next lines and find the answers. Write them in the boxes just like the first one. If you are right, you will find an animal in the shaded boxes! You will find a different animal in each puzzle.

Puzzle 1

1. You can ring it.
2. You put it on your finger.
3. You can ride in it.
4. There are seven in one week.

ring
days
bell
car

Puzzle 2

1. You wash the floor with it.
2. You can read it.
3. It barks at strangers.
4. You wash with it.
5. You write with it.

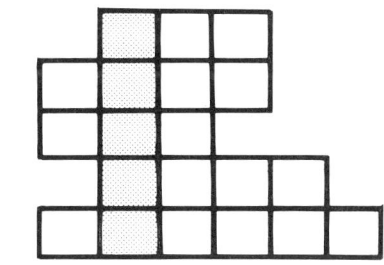

dog
book
soap
pencil
mop

Puzzle 3

1. Some food comes in it.
2. You hit it with a bat.
3. It gives you light.
4. You live in it.
5. You drink from it.

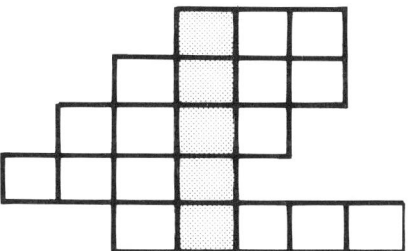

ball
home
glass
can
lamp

My Favorite Day

Skill Reinforced: vowel digraphs

Grade Level: primary

Puzzle Description: The puzzle consists of a list of 11 riddles. The children read each riddle and look through the "Word Box" for the correct answer. When they find the answers, they write them in the spaces provided. If they are correct, the circled letters will spell Dan's favorite day.

Answer Key: The puzzle is self-correcting. As shown below, the words HIS BIRTHDAY will be spelled if the puzzle is completed correctly.

H	teac(h)
I	ra(i)n
S	(s)oap
B	(b)oat
I	ta(i)l
R	(r)oad
T	(t)rain
H	w(h)eels
D	(d)ream
A	go(a)t
Y	da(y)

My Favorite Day

Name _____

Date _____

"I bet you can't guess what my favorite day is," said Dan.
"Is it Friday?" asked Jim.
"No."
"How about the Fourth of July?"
"No."

Well, can you guess what Dan's favorite day is? Below is a puzzle that will tell you.

Look at the first sentence in the puzzle. What does your teacher do? Look in the Word Box and see if you can find the answer. When you find the answer, print the letters in the spaces next to the first sentence. Now, do the rest of the sentences. If you are correct, the circled letters in the answers will spell Dan's favorite day.

1. What your teacher does. _ _ _ _ ○
2. It falls from clouds. _ _ ○ _
3. You wash with it. ○ _ _ _
4. You can sail in it. ○ _ _ _
5. A dog wags it. _ _ ○ _
6. Cars ride on it. ○ _ _ _
7. This runs on tracks. ○ _ _ _ _
8. A wagon has four of them. _ ○ _ _ _ _
9. You do this when you sleep. ○ _ _ _ _
10. It lives on a farm. _ _ ○ _
11. It has 24 hours. _ _ ○

WORD BOX
road
train
soap
rain
goat
tail
teach
dream
wheels
day
boat

Help Henry

Skill Reinforced: making inferences

Grade Level: primary

Puzzle Description: The children read six riddles, find their answers in Henry, and write them in the appropriate spaces. They circle the letter in each answer that is circled in Henry. If they are correct, the circled letters will spell the name of Henry's girlfriend.

Answer Key: The puzzle is self-correcting. As shown below, the circled letters will spell the word HOLLIS if the puzzle is completed correctly.

> H   Bert(h)a
> O   T(o)ny
> L   E(l)la
> L   Mo(l)ly
> I   Gerr(i)
> S   (S)ammy

Help Henry

Name _____
Date _____

Mo(l)ly the Monkey
T(o)ny the Tiger
(S)ammy the Seal
Berth(a) the Bunny
E(l)la the Elephant
Gerr(i) the Giraffe

Henry has many friends at his zoo. They have played a trick on him. Each has written down some things about himself or herself. Henry must guess who they are. You can help Henry!

Read each riddle and choose one of his friends. Their names are on Henry's side. Copy down the correct name under each riddle. Be sure to circle the letters that are circled on Henry. If you are correct, the circled letters will spell the name of Henry's girlfriend!

1. I can twitch my nose.
   I like to hop.
   I love to eat carrots.
   Who am I?

   _____

2. I live in a cage.
   I like to growl and scare people.
   Who am I?

   _____

3. I'm the biggest animal in the zoo.
   I can lift things with my trunk.
   Who am I?

   _____

4. I swing from trees.
   I love to eat bananas.
   Who am I?

   _____

5. I am very tall.
   I eat leaves off trees.
   Who am I?

   _____

6. I love to swim.
   I can balance things on my nose.
   Who am I?

   _____

Who Is Chickie Looking For?

Skill Reinforced: context clue usage

Grade Level: primary

Puzzle Description: The children follow Chickie's path. Each time they come to a sentence, they find the missing word in the barn and write it in the space provided. They circle the letter in each word that is circled in the barn. If they are correct, the circled letters will spell the name of the one Chickie is looking for.

Answer Key: The puzzle is self-correcting. As shown below, the circled letters will spell the words HIS MOTHER if the puzzle is completed correctly.

H	ⓗave
I	ⓘs
S	thoⓢe
M	ⓜy
O	wⓞuld
T	ⓣhey
H	tⓗan
E	therⓔ
R	hoⓡse

Who Is Chickie Looking For?

Name _____

Date _____

Follow Chickie's path. When you come to a sentence, read it and find the missing word in the barn. Be sure to circle the letter that is circled in the barn. If you are correct in filling in all of the missing words, the circled letters will spell the name of the one Chickie is looking for.

1. _____ you seen Farmer Jones?

2. I know where the fox _____ hiding.

3. Look out for _____ pigs.

4. Do you know where _____ hat is?

5. _____ you come to the barn with me?

6. Tell me when _____ come home.

7. My horse can run faster _____ yours.

8. Put it _____.

9. She is a pretty _____.

t(h)an
(i)s   (m)y
tho(s)e   ther(e)
ho(r)se
w(o)uld
(h)ave
(t)hey

Flying High

Skill Reinforced: story sequence

Grade Level: primary

Puzzle Description: The puzzle consists of an airplane's flight path and an airport containing sentences. These sentences will tell a story if they are put into the proper sequence. The children rearrange the sentences to form a story by following the airplane's path. Each time they come to a cloud, they write in the appropriate sentence. They circle the letter in each sentence that is circled in the building. If they are correct, the circled letters will spell out the name of the airplane.

Answer Key: The puzzle is self-correcting. As shown below, the circled letters will spell out the word LOOPY if the puzzle is completed correctly.

L Ⓛittle
O pilⓄt
O lⓄwer
P Ⓟilot
Y Ⓨelled

Flying High

Name _____

Date _____

Follow the airplane's path. Every time you come to a cloud, copy one of the sentences from the airport. You should try to put the sentences in the correct order so they form a story. Be sure to circle the letter in each sentence that is circled in the airport. If you do this correctly, the circled letters will spell the name of the airplane.

The ⓛittle airplane was flying high.

The ⓟilot aimed for the runway.

He began to fly the airplane lⓞwer and lower.

The people ⓨelled and cheered when he landed.

Then the pilⓞt saw the airport.

Who Did It?

Skill Reinforced: fact from fantasy

Grade Level: high primary

Puzzle Description: The puzzle consists of a list of 12 statements. Some of these statements are factual while others are pure fantasy. The children read each statement and decide whether it is fact or fantasy. They copy down the circled letter in each factual statement. If they are correct, the letters will spell a solution to a mystery.

Answer Key: The puzzle is self-correcting. As shown below, the words A MOUSE will be spelled if the puzzle is completed correctly.

A	t ⓐ ll
M	s ⓜ all
O	R ⓞ bert
U	ho ⓤ se
S	dres ⓢ ed
E	broth ⓔ r

Who Did It?

Josie lay in bed trying to go to sleep. Her parents had just tucked her in and had gone back downstairs. She was thinking about going to her friend's house tomorrow. She was going to spend the whole day with Sally. Then she heard a strange sound. It came from the attic. She stayed very quiet and she heard it again. She was getting scared and yelled for her parents.

Now, what do you think is making that strange sound? If you work the puzzle below, you will find out. Read each of the sentences. Decide if it could really happen or if it is just make-believe. If you think it could really happen, copy the circled letter in that sentence on a space at the bottom of this sheet. If you are correct, the circled letters will spell what is making the strange sound.

1. A bird flew over that t(a)ll tree.
2. The cow counted to te(n).
3. The s(m)all boy rode in his wagon.
4. That car smiled a(t) me.
5. I grew a pump(k)in so big it wouldn't fit in the barn.
6. R(o)bert and his sister went to the zoo.
7. Her father built her a tree ho(u)se.
8. The oak tree(d)anced and sang.
9. Julie turned(r)ocks into gold
10. I dres(s)ed like a ghost on Halloween.
11. A dragon wa(l)ked across our yard.
12. My broth(e)r is on the track team.

___ ___ ___

Going Swimming

Skill Reinforced: mood of a story

Grade Level: high primary

Puzzle Description: The puzzle consists of five brief statements made by children at a beach. Students determine how each child would be feeling when he or she made the statement. They do this by selecting one of the five faces on the sheet and writing the child's name under the statement. They are told to circle the letters in each name that are circled under the faces. If they are correct, the circled letters will spell the name of the beach where the children are.

Answer Key: The puzzle is self-correcting. As shown below, the word SANDY will be spelled if the puzzle is completed correctly.

S (S)am
A Ann(a)
N Bre(n)da
D (D)on
Y Dann(y)

Going Swimming

Name _____

Date _____

The following children are all at the beach. Look at their faces.

Dann(y)   Bre(n)da   (S)am   (D)on   Ann(a)

    You can tell how each one feels by looking at their faces, can't you? Below are things that were said by each of the children. Try to figure out how these children feel and write in their names on the spaces next to what they said. Be sure to circle the letter that is circled in each child's name above. If you are correct, the circled letters will spell the name of the beach where the children are.

1. "You'd better not splash me again! If you do, I'll tell your father!" _____

2. "I don't care if you do have a beach ball. I'm not going to play." _____

3. "My mother said I can't go swimming for two more hours." _____

4. "Look out! I think it's a shark!" _____

5. "Boy, this sure is fun. I'll race you down the beach!" _____

What Happened at the Zoo?

Skill Reinforced: main idea

Grade Level: high primary

Puzzle Description: The puzzle consists of two short stories each followed by three different story titles. The children read each story and decide which title is most appropriate for the story.

Answer Key: The puzzle is easily corrected. Simply check to see if the following titles were selected.

Story 1: A Good Day at the Zoo
Story 2: Monkey Mountain

Name _____

Date _____

What Happened at the Zoo?

Below are two things that happened at the zoo. Under each story are three titles. Choose the best title for each story and write it in the space above the story.

Story 1

_____

"What did you like best?" asked Cindy.
"Oh, the monkeys," said Dick.
"I liked the lions and tigers," said Helen.
"I guess I liked everything," said Cindy.
"It sure has been fun today," said Helen.
"I hope we can come back soon," said Dick.

TITLES
A Good Day at the Zoo
The Lions and Tigers
The Very Funny Monkeys

Story 2

_____

"Look over there," said Brenda.
"Oh, isn't that monkey cute," said Linda.
"Gosh, there must be a hundred monkeys on this mountain," said Brenda.
"They sure are fun to watch," said Linda.
"I like the ones on the swing," said Brenda.
"There is one hanging by his tail," said Linda.

TITLES
The Cute Monkey
Monkey Mountain
The Swing

Crazy Mixed-Up Words!

Skill Reinforced: context clue usage

Grade Level: high primary

Puzzle Description: The puzzle consists of eight sentences. The letters of one word in each sentence have been scrambled. The children read each sentence and then rewrite the scrambled word correctly on the spaces provided. If they are correct, the first letters of the rewritten words will spell what kind of work they did.

Answer Key: The puzzle is self-correcting. As shown below, the words VERY GOOD will be spelled if the puzzle is completed correctly.

V	very
E	eat
R	red
Y	yell
G	glad
O	old
O	off
D	deep

Crazy Mixed-Up Words!

Below are eight sentences. Each sentence has one "crazy mixed-up word." All of the letters are there but they are in the wrong order. Put them in the correct order on the space next to each sentence. If you are correct, the first letters of these words will tell you what kind of work you did.

1. I am going to try yrve hard. _____

2. Did you aet the candy? _____

3. My mother has a der rose bush. _____

4. I will leyl for him. _____

5. I'm lagd you are coming with me. _____

6. My grandmother is very lod. _____

7. Get that spider ffo the table. _____

8. How eped is that river? _____

Let's Take a Walk

Skill Reinforced: predicting outcomes

Grade Level: high primary

Puzzle Sheet Description: The puzzle consists of four story beginnings and four story endings. The children draw lines from each story beginning to its appropriate ending.

Answer Key: The puzzle is easily corrected. Simply check for the following beginning and ending combinations.

    1   C
    2   A
    3   B
    4   D

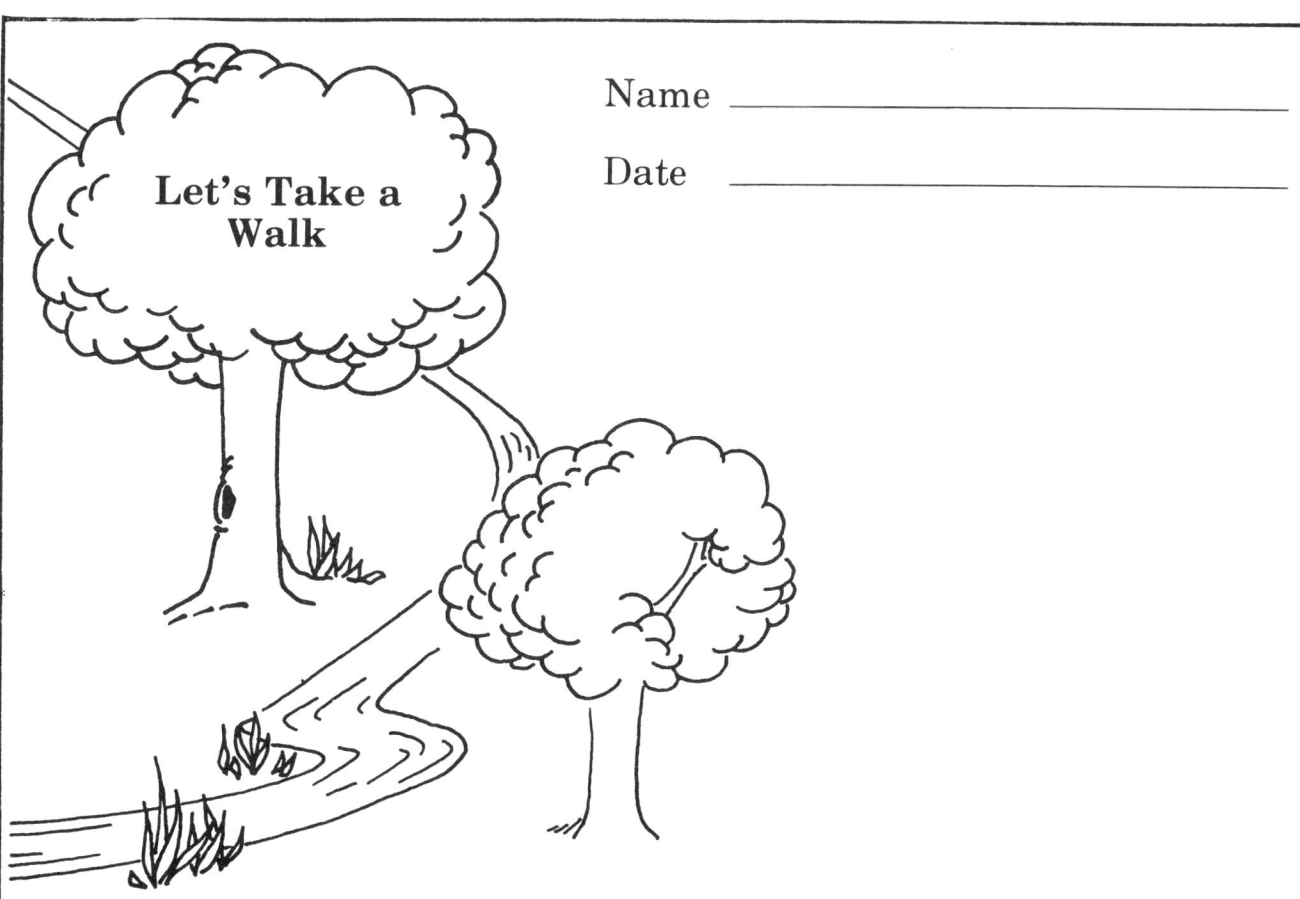

Name _____

Date _____

Draw a line from each story beginning to its correct ending.

Story Beginnings

1. The sun was out and the birds sang. It was nice as we walked through the field.
2. We were having fun on our walk. Then the wind began to blow. Dark clouds rolled across the sky.
3. We were walking through the forest. All at once we heard a strange sound.
4. We were walking along the river. The rocks were very wet and slippery.

Story Endings

A. We ran for home, but we still got very wet.

B. My little brother jumped out from behind a tree. "Boo!" he yelled.

C. We picked flowers and took them home to our mothers.

D. My mother was mad. I was all wet and covered with mud.

Compound Pictures

Skill Reinforced: compound words

Grade Level: high primary

Puzzle Description: The puzzle consists of a list of words and a list of pictures. The students draw lines from the words to the pictures so that compound words are formed.

Answer Key: The puzzle is easily corrected. Simply check for the following compound words.

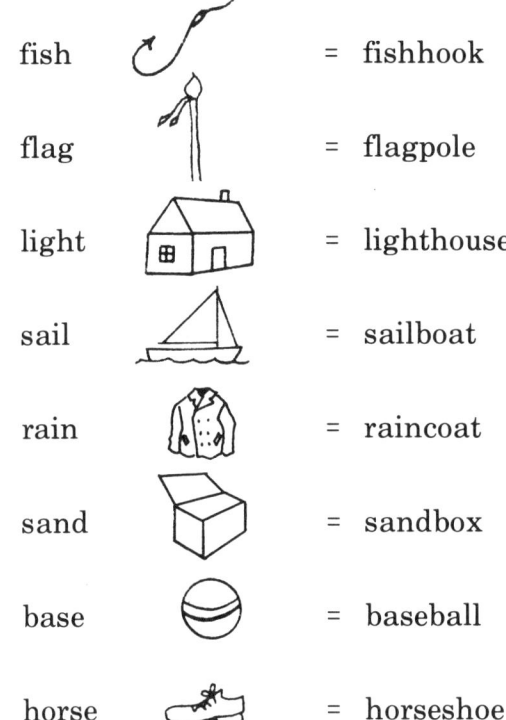

fish		= fishhook
flag		= flagpole
light		= lighthouse
sail		= sailboat
rain		= raincoat
sand		= sandbox
base		= baseball
horse		= horseshoe

Compound Pictures

Name _____

Date _____

Do you know what a compound picture is? Well, here is one:

mail +

Do you know what word this compound picture is? Mailbox! Now draw a line from each of the following words to a picture so that they make a compound word.

fish •   •

flag •   •

light •   •

sail •   •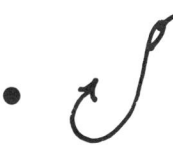

rain •   •

sand •   •

base •   •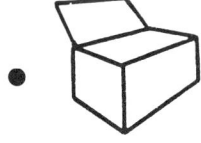

horse •   •

Our Picnic Mess

Skill Reinforced: story sequence

Grade Level: high primary

Puzzle Description: The puzzle consists of a story followed by a list of events taken from the story. The students rearrange the list of events so that they are in the same order as in the story. They circle the letter that is circled in each event. If they are correct, the circled letters will spell what the children ate on their picnic.

Answer Key: The puzzle is self-correcting. As shown below, the circled letters will spell HOT DOGS if the puzzle is completed correctly.

H	t(h)e
O	d(o)wn
T	le(t)
D	hoppe(d)
O	st(o)pped
G	(G)rover's
S	kid(s)

Our Picnic Mess   Name _____

Date _____

Read the following short story:

"Oh, look," said Jim. "There's the lake!"

We were going to have a picnic at Grover's Lake. We had been walking a long way and were glad to get there.

"This is a good place to eat our picnic lunch," said Sue. She sat down under a big tree next to the lake.

Just as Jim got everything out of the sack, Benny let out a yell. I turned around and saw him jumping up and down on one foot. "A bee! A bee!" he yelled, and went on jumping around. In fact, he went on jumping right into the potato salad and cake. Jim thought this was funny. But I didn't, since I was really hungry and the cake had looked good.

When Benny stopped yelling, I went around the lake to Grover's Store. I got something for our picnic and took it back.

"Hooray!" yelled Jim and Sue when I got back. "We sure are hungry!"

Now, let's see how well you remember what happened in this story. Below is a list of the things that happened on the picnic. But the things are not in the right order. Put them in the same order as they happened in the story. Write them in the spaces from top to bottom. Be sure to circle the letter in each one that is circled in the list. If you are correct, the circled letters will spell what the children ate. Try to do it without looking back at the story!

Benny le(t) out a yell.   _____

Benny st(o)pped yelling.   _____

The kid(s) yelled when I got back.   _____

Jim saw t h e lake.   _____

I went to (G)rover's Store.   _____

Benny hoppe(d) into the cake.   _____

Sue sat d(o)wn under a tree.   _____

185

IV
Bulletin Boards

The bulletin boards in this section are designed to encourage children to read. Each example includes a list of materials needed to construct the bulletin board. The sizes of these items will depend on your bulletin board space. You will also find simple directions for constructing each bulletin board.

Bulletin Board	*Grade Level*
Balloon Fun!	low primary
Shivers Up Your Spine	primary
You've Seen Them on TV	primary
Children's Book Week	primary
Gerald Knows ... Do You?	primary
A Hoppin' Good Book	primary
How High Can We Build the Tower?	primary
Reach for the Stars	primary
Vote for Your Favorite Dr. Seuss Book!	primary
It's Grrreat to Write to an Author!	high primary

Balloon Fun!

Materials Needed:

white background paper
felt-tipped pens in various colors
construction paper in various colors
ditto box
ditto master
ditto paper
scissors
tape
stapler

Construction Directions:

1. Use an opaque projector to trace the lettering, clown, and circus tent on page 190 on the background paper. Use appropriate colors.
2. Cut the ditto box in half (widthwise), cover with yellow construction paper, print "Eager Reader Sheets" on the front, and attach it to the board.
3. Duplicate copies of the "Eager Reader Sheet" on page 191, and place a supply in the bulletin board box.
4. Cut and mark the construction paper using the balloon pattern on page 189. Attach a few of these to the board as shown in the bulletin board illustration. Keep the remainder in your desk, ready to give to "eager readers."

Bulletin Board Use: This bulletin board may be used by low primary children. The children take a sheet and draw a picture of something from a book that they have just read. When they are finished, return the sheet so that you may give them an "Eager Reader Balloon."

SUGGESTION: *Young children will love to have the balloons pinned to their clothing to wear around school.*

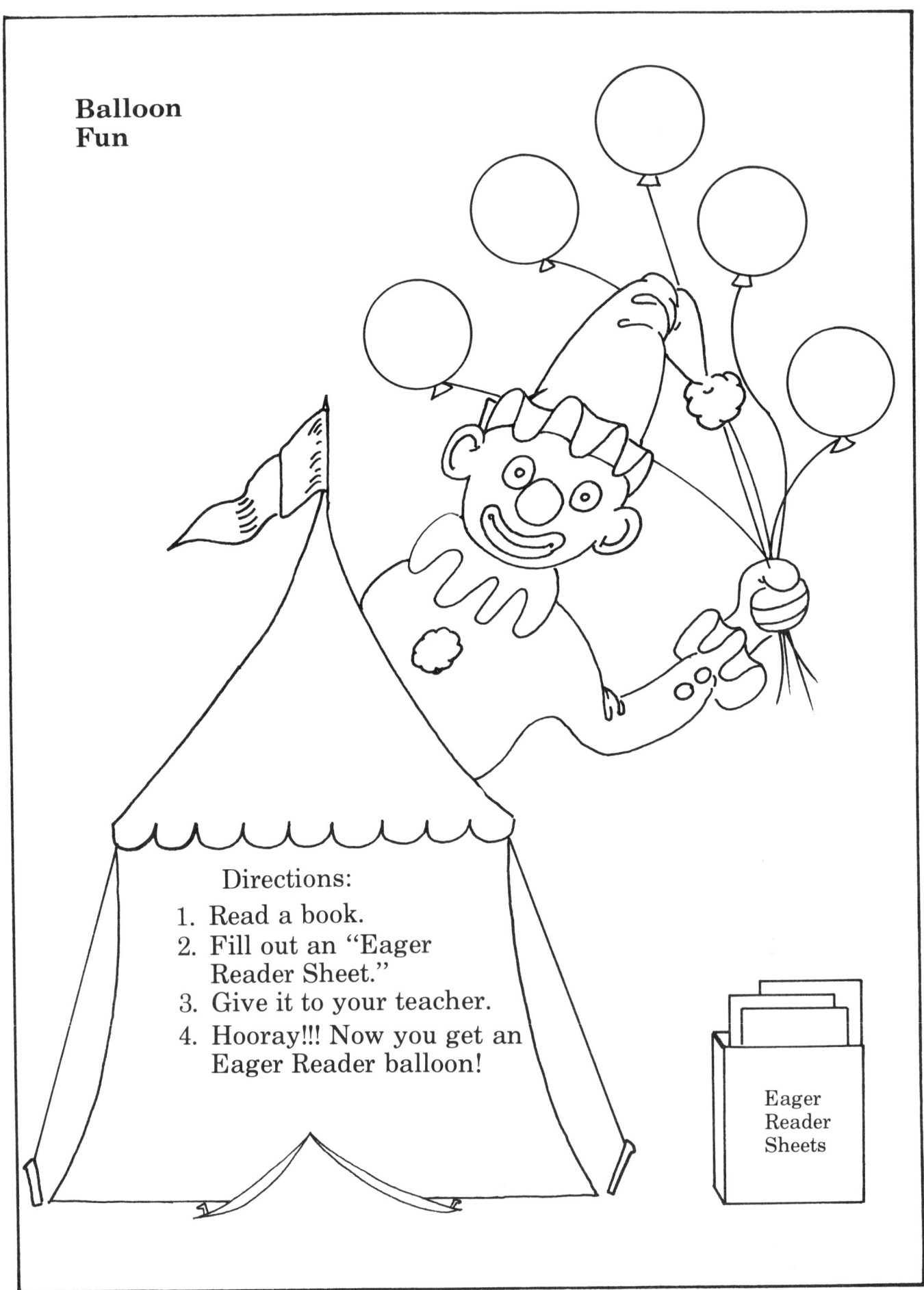

Name _____

Date _____

Eager Reader Sheet

Book _____

Author _____

I'll draw my favorite part of the book inside this circus tent.

Shivers Up Your Spine

Materials Needed:

> white background paper
> black construction paper
> gray construction paper
> straight pins
> felt-tipped pens in various colors
> scissors
> ditto box
> ditto master
> ditto paper
> stapler
> tape

Construction Directions:

1. Using an opaque projector, copy the house and lettering on the background paper. Use appropriate colors.
2. Cut out the letters from the black construction paper and attach them to the bulletin board. You may use the letter patterns provided on page 195 or use other appropriate patterns. Attach these to the bulletin board using the straight pins. Pull the letters away from the bulletin board to the heads of the pins. This will give a three-dimensional effect.
3. Cut the ditto box in half (widthwise), cover with the gray construction paper, print "Shiver Sheets" on the front, and attach it to the board.
4. Duplicate copies of the "Shiver Sheet" on page 194 and place a supply in the bulletin board box.

Bulletin Board Use: This bulletin board may be used by primary children. The children must read a mystery book or a scary story and fill in one of the sheets. Each child who does this may add something to the bulletin board. Just watch the scene expand as the month progresses!

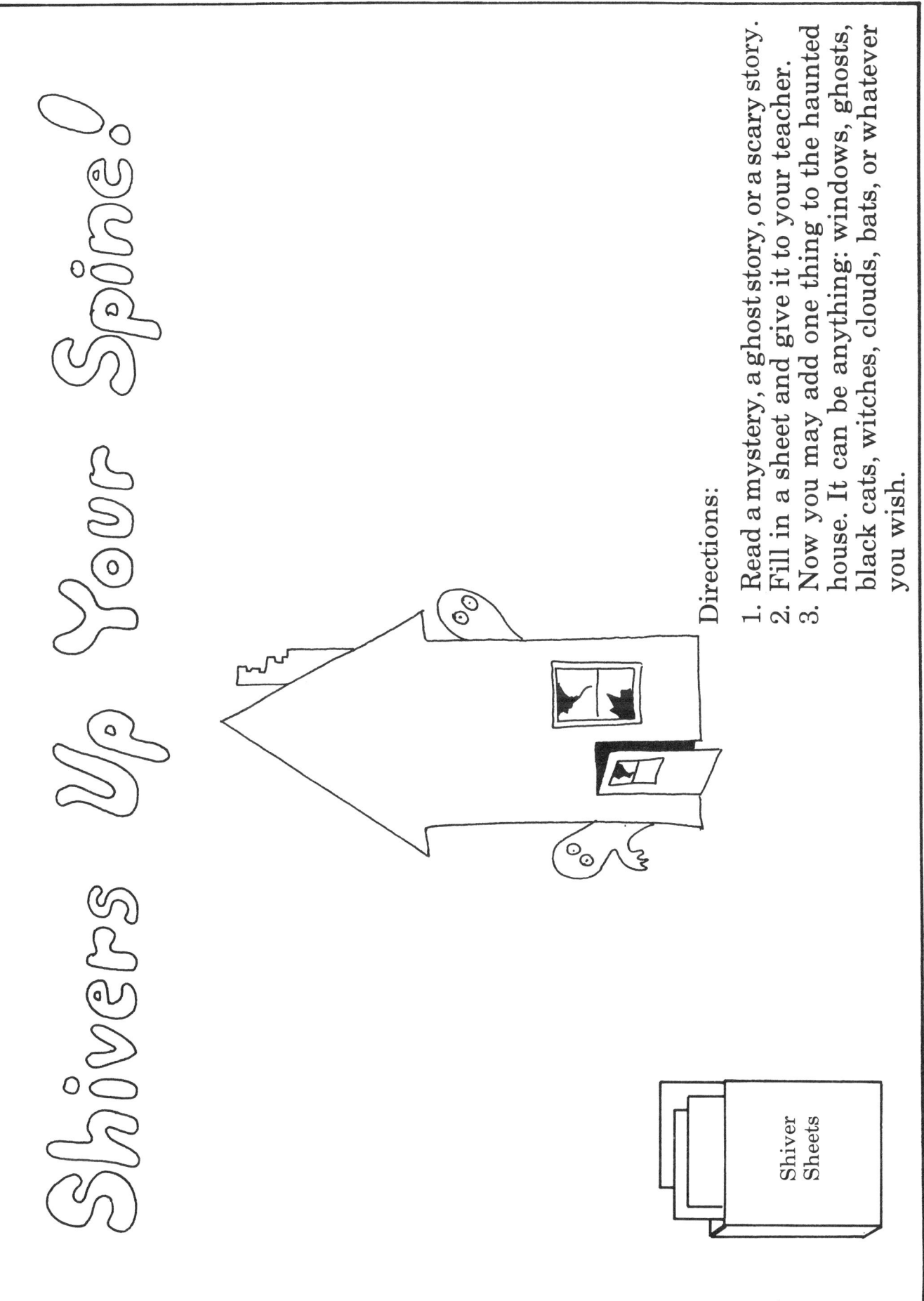

Name _____

Date _____

Shiver Sheet

The book I read is:
_____

It was written by:
_____

It was about:
_____
_____
_____

The scariest thing in the story was:
_____
_____
_____

Here is a drawing of one of my favorite characters in the story.

You've Seen Them on TV

Materials Needed:
  yellow background paper
  brown construction paper
  white construction paper
  four cereal boxes
  black felt-tipped pen
  scissors
  stapler
  tape
  glue

Construction Directions:

1. Cover the cereal boxes with brown construction paper. Cut the white construction paper and glue it to the boxes. Mark the knobs as shown here.

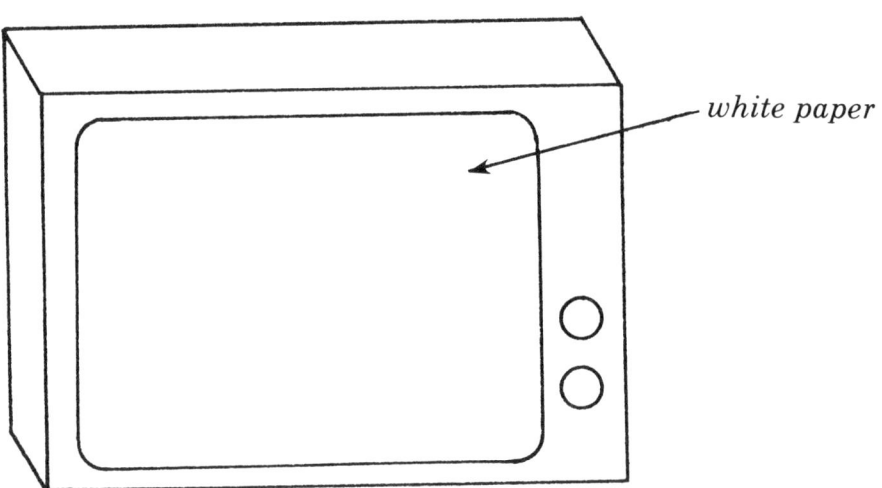

2. Copy the information onto these television sets as shown in the bulletin board illustration.
3. Attach the television sets to the board.
4. Use an opaque projector and copy the lettering and the TV onto the background paper.

Bulletin Board Use: This bulletin board may be used to stimulate interest in reading with primary children.

The Cat in the Hat
by Dr. Seuss

Little House in the Big Woods
by Laura Wilder

Winnie-the-Pooh
by A.A. Milne

READ THEM

You've Seen Them
On TV... Now

The Lorax
by Dr. Seuss

Children's Book Week

Materials Needed:
- white background paper
- felt-tipped pens in various colors

Construction Directions: Use an opaque projector to trace the bulletin board onto the background paper. Use appropriate colors for the figures.

Bulletin Board Use: This bulletin board may be used to stimulate interest in reading with primary children.

Gerald Knows ... Do You?

Materials Needed:
- white background paper
- felt-tipped pens in various colors
- ditto box
- scissors
- stapler
- tape
- ditto master
- ditto paper
- yellow construction paper

Construction Directions:

1. Use an opaque projector to trace the lettering and giraffe onto the background paper. Use appropriate colors for the giraffe.
2. Cut the ditto box in half (widthwise), cover with yellow construction paper, print "Gerald Knows Sheets" on the front, and attach it to the board.
3. Duplicate copies of the "Gerald Knows Sheet" on page 202 and place a supply in the bulletin board box.
4. Fill out two of the sheets, as shown in the illustration, and attach them to the board.

Bulletin Board Use: This bulletin board may be used by primary children. The children take a sheet and make up a riddle about one of their favorite story characters. They also draw a picture of this character. When they are finished, they return the sheet so that you may attach it to the bulletin board.

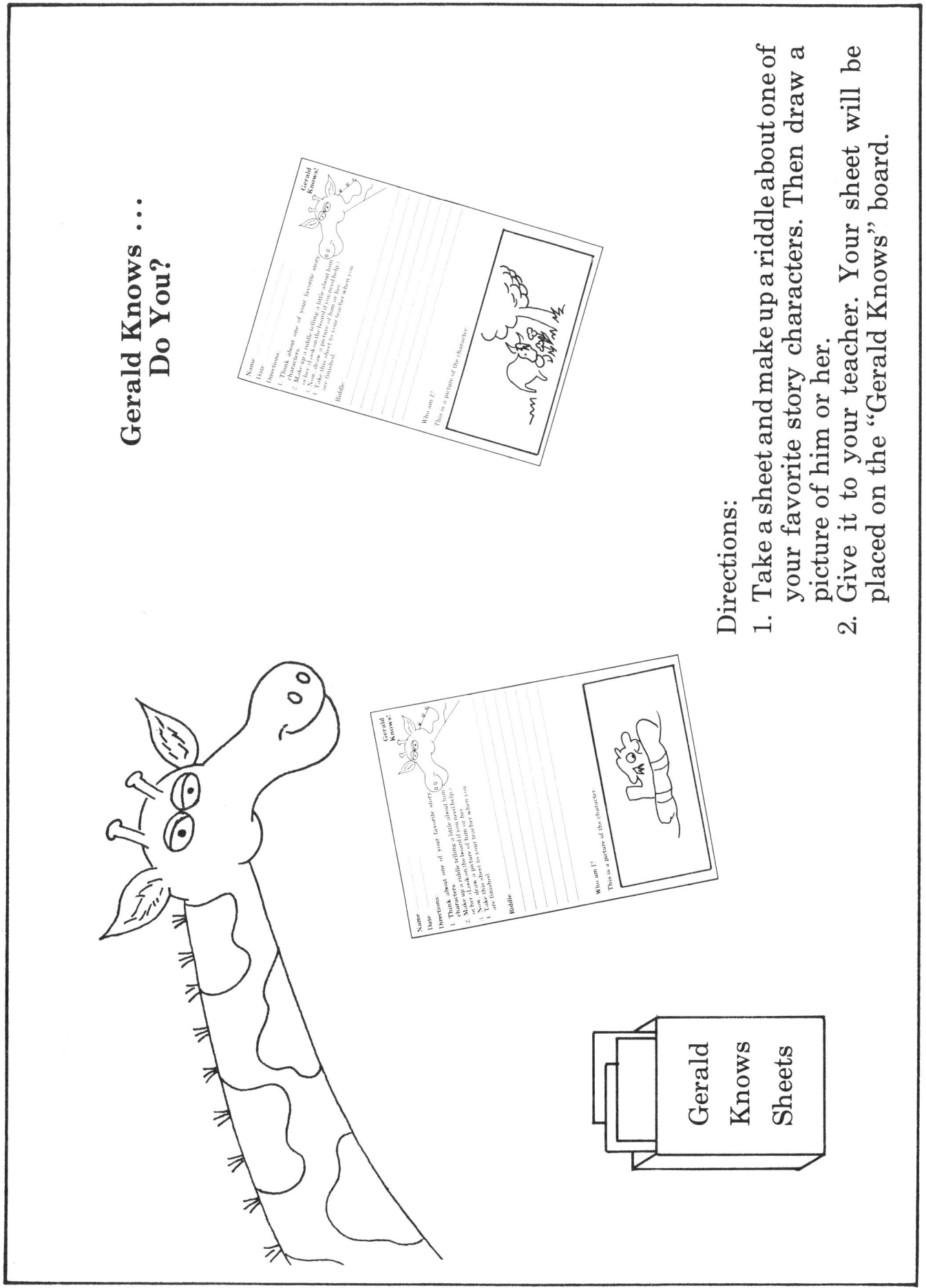

Name _____

Date _____

Gerald Knows!

Directions:

1. Think about one of your favorite story characters.
2. Make up a riddle telling a little about him or her. (Look on the board if you need help.)
3. Now, draw a picture of him or her.
4. Take this sheet to your teacher when you are finished.

Riddle: _____

_____

_____

_____

_____

_____

_____

Who am I?

This is a picture of the character:

A Hoppin' Good Book

Materials Needed:
white background paper
felt-tipped pens in various colors
green construction paper
stapler
scissors
tape
ditto box
ditto master
ditto paper
straight pins

Construction Directions:
1. Use an opaque projector and copy the lettering and figures onto the background paper. Use appropriate colors. Do not copy the frog on the lily pad.
2. Cut and mark the green construction paper using the frog pattern shown on the bulletin board illustration. Attach the frog to the board by using the straight pins and pulling the paper away from the board to the heads of the pins. This will give a three-dimensional effect.
3. Cut the ditto box in half (widthwise), cover with green construction paper, print "Hoppin' Good Books" on the front, and attach it to the board.
4. Duplicate copies of the "Hoppin' Good Books" sheet on page 205 and place a supply in the bulletin board box.

Bulletin Board Use: This bulletin board may be used by primary children. The children fill in "Hoppin' Good Book" sheets and return them to you. These sheets should be displayed on the bulletin board.

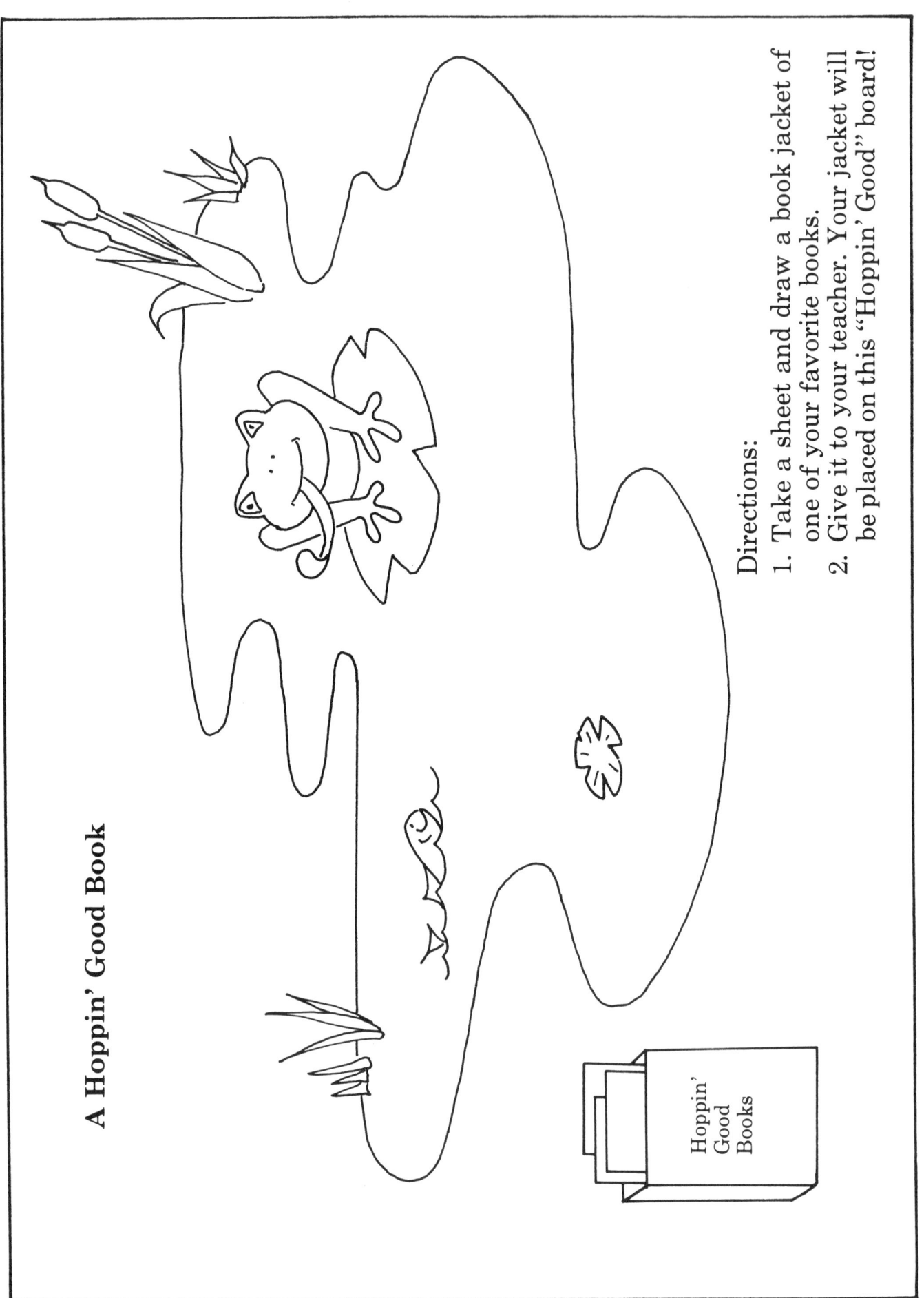

Name _____

Date _____

**Hoppin'
Good
Books**

Draw a book jacket for one of your favorite books. When you are finished, give it to your teacher. It will be placed on the "Hoppin' Good" board.

How High Can We Build the Tower?

Materials Needed:
- white background paper
- yellow construction paper
- felt-tipped pen
- ditto box
- ditto master
- red ditto paper
- scissors
- tape
- stapler

Construction Directions:

1. Use an opaque projector to trace the lettering and tower outline onto the background paper.
2. Cut the ditto box in half (widthwise), cover with yellow construction paper, print "Building Bricks" on the front, and attach it to the board.
3. Duplicate copies of the "Building Bricks" sheet on page 208 and place a supply in the bulletin board box.

Bulletin Board Use: This bulletin board may be used by primary children. The children take a sheet, cut out the brick, and fill it out. When they are finished, they return the brick so that you may attach it to the board. Begin at the bottom of the tower and build layer upon layer. See how high the tower can be built.

NOTE: *Don't let the size of your bulletin board stop the growth of the tower. Continue taping bricks right up the wall!*

How High Can We Build the Tower?

Directions:
1. Read a book.
2. Fill out one of the bricks and give it to your teacher.
3. It will help to build the tower.

Building Bricks

Name _____

Date _____

Title: _____

Author: _____

The book is about: _____

Reach for the Stars

Materials Needed:
- black background paper
- white construction paper
- scissors
- felt-tipped pen
- ditto master
- ditto paper

Construction Directions:

1. Using an opaque projector, cut and mark the white construction paper to form the stars, moon, and cloud, as shown in the bulletin board illustration.
2. Attach these to the board.
3. Duplicate copies of the star on page 211 and keep for future use.

Bulletin Board Use: This bulletin board may be used by primary children. They keep a list of all the books they read during a designated time span. At the end of this time, these lists are turned in to you. You fill in a star for each child. Return the sheets and have the children cut out the stars and attach them to the board.

SUGGESTION: *You might keep track of the total books your class reads during one week and then try to improve this figure during the second week.*

Reach for the Stars

Directions:
1. Make a list of all the books you read this week. See how many you can read.
2. Give the list to your teacher next Monday. Then wait to see what happens right here on this board!

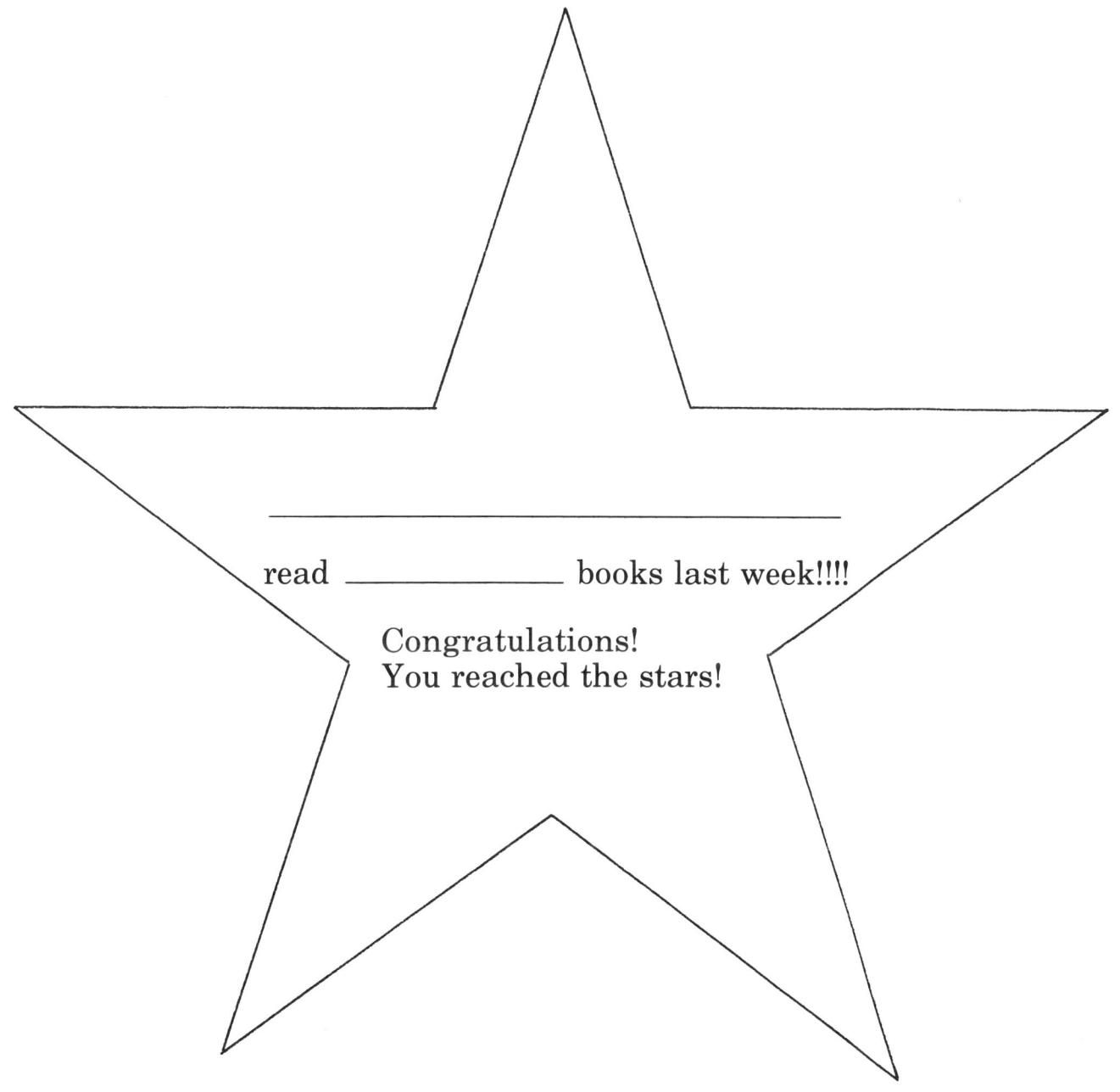

Vote for Your Favorite Dr. Seuss Book!

Materials Needed:

    white background paper

    felt-tipped pens in various colors

    ditto box

    scissors

    red construction paper

    ditto master

    ditto paper

    stapler

    tape

    shoe box

Construction Directions:

1. Use an opaque projector to trace the figures and lettering onto the background paper.
2. Cut the ditto box in half (widthwise), cover with red construction paper, print "Dr. Seuss Ballots" on the front, and attach it to the board.
3. Duplicate copies of the "Official Dr. Seuss Ballot" sheet on page 214 and place a supply in the bulletin board box.
4. Cover the shoe box with red construction paper and cut a large slit through the top. Print "Ballot Box" on it and place it near the bulletin boards.

Bulletin Board Use: This bulletin board may be used by primary children. The children take a ballot and vote for their favorite book.

SUGGESTION: *The bulletin board display should go up several weeks before the voting. Allow only a few days for the voting and post the winner after the ballots are counted.*

Name _____

Date _____

Vote for Your Favorite Dr. Seuss Book!

On Beyond Zebra
Horton Hatches the Egg
The Lorax
The Cat in the Hat
Thidwick, the Big-Hearted Moose
Horton Hears a Who
McElligot's Pool
How the Grinch Stole Christmas
And to Think That I Saw It on Mulberry Street
Green Eggs and Ham
The 500 Hats of Bartholomew Cubbins

Directions:
1. Take a ballot and vote for a Dr. Seuss book.
2. Fold the ballot and place it in the ballot box.

Official Dr. Seuss Ballot

- ☐ On Beyond Zebra
- ☐ Horton Hatches the Egg
- ☐ The Lorax
- ☐ The Cat in the Hat
- ☐ Thidwick, the Big-Hearted Moose
- ☐ Horton Hears a Who
- ☐ McElligot's Pool
- ☐ How the Grinch Stole Christmas
- ☐ And to Think That I Saw It on Mulberry Street
- ☐ Green Eggs and Ham
- ☐ The 500 Hats of Bartholomew Cubbins

It's Grrreat to Write to an Author!

Materials Needed:
- white background paper
- one large paper plate
- felt-tipped pens in various colors
- writing paper
- stapler

Construction Directions:

1. Attach the paper plate, bottom side away from the board, and mark it as shown here. Use appropriate colors.

2. Using an opaque projector, finish drawing the tiger and adding the lettering to the board.
3. Print a letter like the one on page 216 on a sheet of the writing paper and attach it to the board.

Bulletin Board Use: This bulletin board may be used with high primary children. When they turn in copies of their letters, they should be attached to the board.

Directions:

1. Write to your favorite author.
2. Be sure to make a copy of your letter and give it to your teacher. It will be placed on this board.

V
Learning Boards

While bulletin boards can help to stimulate an interest in reading, this does not have to be their sole function. You can construct bulletin boards that will help to reinforce the reading skills you are currently teaching your students.

Fifteen examples of learning boards that reinforce reading skills are described in this section. Each example includes a list of materials needed to construct the learning board. The sizes of these items will depend on your bulletin board space. You will also find simple directions for constructing each learning board and instructions for using the board to reinforce a specific reading skill.

The following reading skills are reinforced by the designated learning boards.

Learning Board	*Reading Skill*	*Grade Level*
Find Humpty-Dumpty's Cousins!	visual discrimination	low primary
Marvin Mouse and His Friends	alphabet knowledge	low primary
Bells Are Ringing	auditory discrimination	low primary
Fido's Treat	initial consonants	primary
Spin a Vowel	medial vowels	primary
Jack and the Beanstalk	final consonants	primary
Down the Chute!	consonant blends	primary
Panda's Problem	main idea	primary
Help Henrietta Find Her Baby!	sight word knowledge	primary
Fish Bubbles	contractions	primary
Hang Glider	story sequence	primary
Fill 'er Up!	context clue usage	high primary
Hello ... Operator	compound words	high primary
Apples, Apples, and More Apples	word meaning	high primary
The Old Train	fact from fantasy	high primary

Find Humpty-Dumpty's Cousins!

Reading Skill Reinforced: visual discrimination

Grade Level: low primary

Materials Needed:
- yellow background paper
- white posterboard
- small Jell-O or cereal boxes
- felt-tipped pens in various colors
- stapler
- scissors
- legal-size envelope
- 10 straight pins
- paper hole punch

Construction Directions:

1. Use an opaque projector to trace the brick wall and lettering onto the background paper. Use appropriate colors.
2. Use the opaque projector to trace the Humpty-Dumpty figure on the white posterboard. Attach the small Jell-O boxes to the board and glue the Humpty-Dumpty to these. This will give a three-dimensional effect.
3. Attach the straight pins over the brick wall as shown in the illustration.
4. Cut, punch, and mark the white posterboard using the Humpty-Dumpty pattern on page 219.
5. Print each of the following words on a different Humpty-Dumpty as shown.

dog	big
dig	log
fog	pig
bat	mat
sat	fat

6. Mark "Humpty-Dumpty" on the envelope, attach it to the board, and place all of the Humpty-Dumpties in it.

Learning Board Use: Children take the Humpty-Dumpties out of the envelope and match the words on these pieces with the words on the bricks. To do this they hang the Humpty-Dumpties on the hooks above the appropriate bricks.

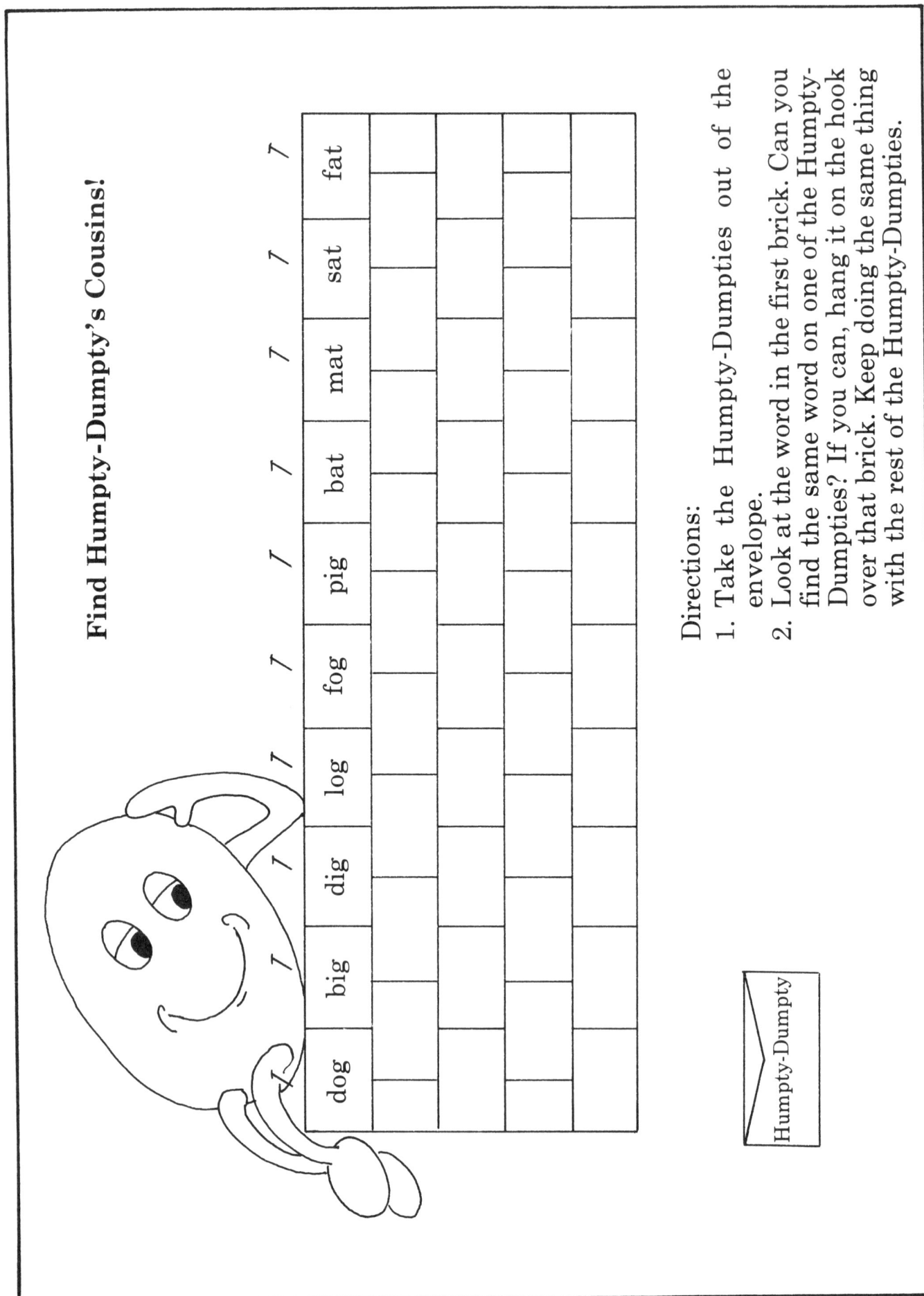

Marvin Mouse and His Friends

Reading Skill Reinforced: alphabet knowledge
Grade Level: low primary
Materials Needed:
    white background paper
    felt-tipped pens in various colors
    yellow construction paper
    scissors
    paper hole punch
    straight pins
    legal-size envelope
    stapler

Construction Directions:

1. Use an opaque projector to trace the figures and lettering onto the background paper. Use appropriate colors.
2. Cut, punch, and mark the yellow construction paper using the cheese pattern shown here. Make eight pieces of cheese and copy the first eight letters of the alphabet, in their lower-case forms, each on a different piece.

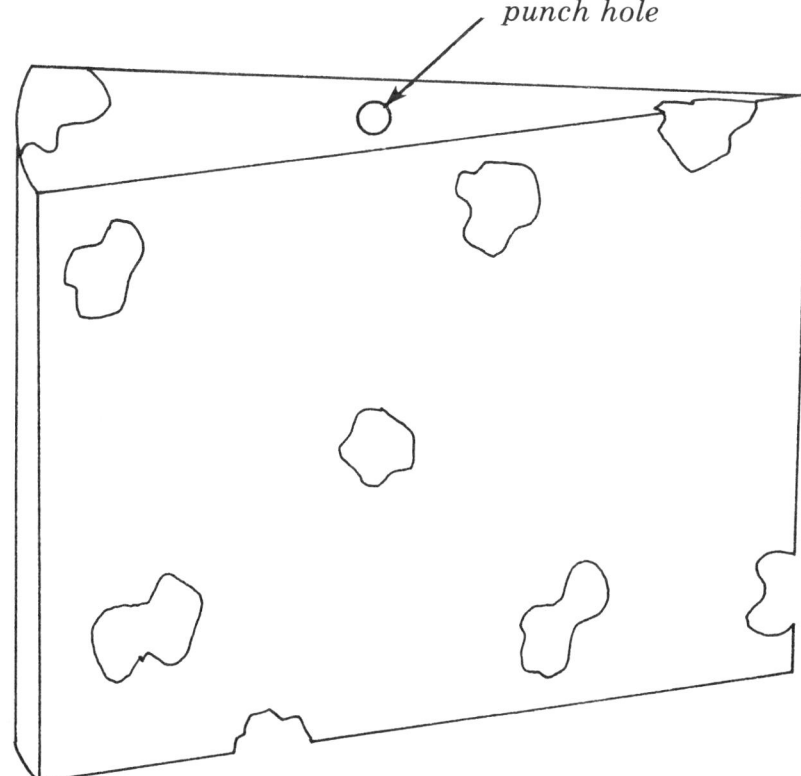

3. Mark the word "Cheese" on the large envelope, attach it to the board, and place the pieces of cheese in it.
4. Fold the yellow construction paper to form an Answer Key and mark the front as shown in the illustration. Copy the following on the inside of the Answer Key.

A	a
B	b
C	c
D	d
E	e
F	f
G	g
H	h

Learning Board Use: Children take the cheese out of the envelope and match the lower-case letters on the cheese with the upper-case letters on the mice. They do this by hanging the cheese on hooks next to the mice. When they finish, they may use the Answer Key to correct themselves.

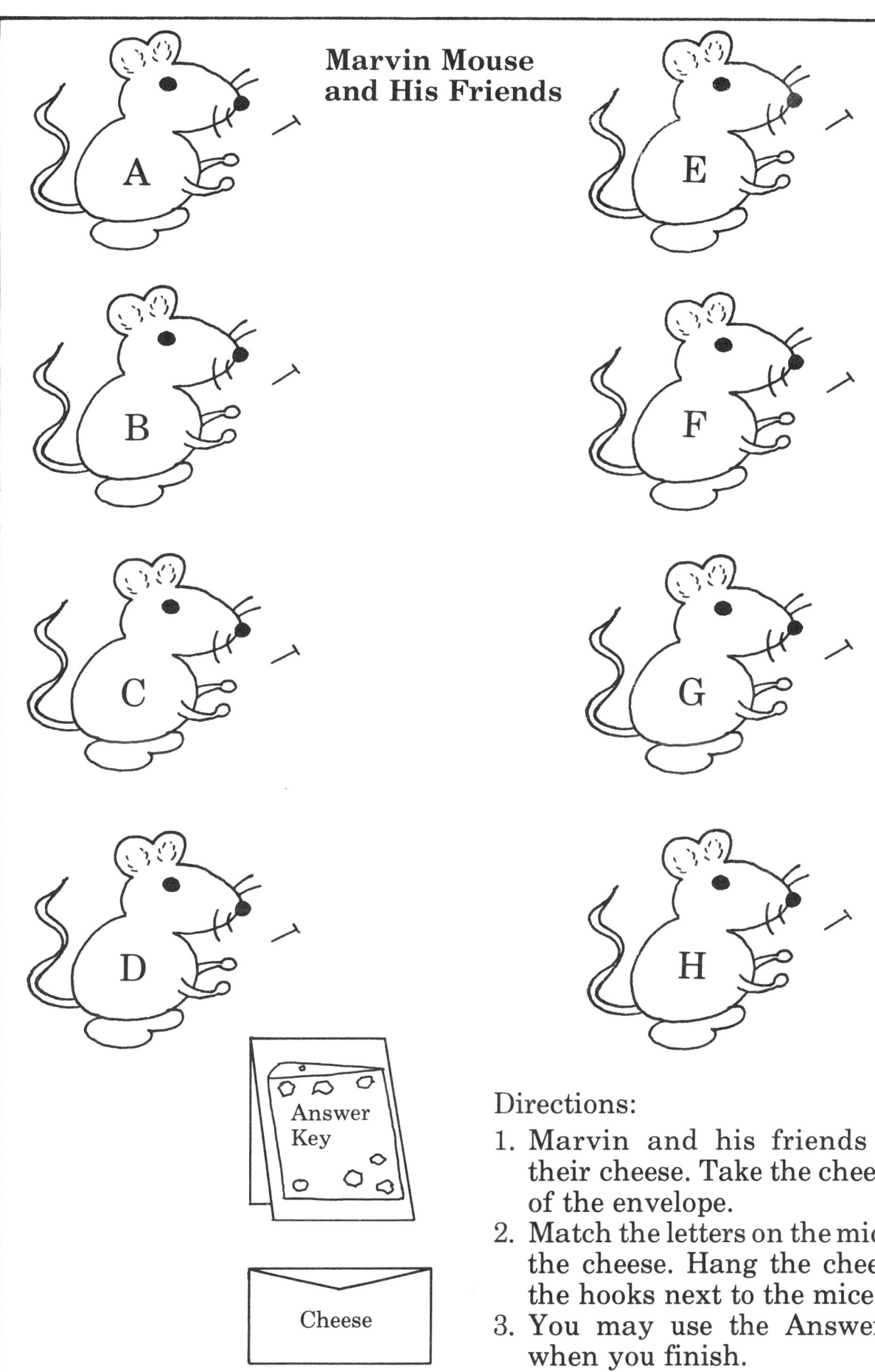

Marvin Mouse and His Friends

Directions:

1. Marvin and his friends want their cheese. Take the cheese out of the envelope.
2. Match the letters on the mice and the cheese. Hang the cheese on the hooks next to the mice.
3. You may use the Answer Key when you finish.

Bells Are Ringing

Reading Skill Reinforced: auditory discrimination
Grade Level: low primary
Materials Needed:
   white background paper
   red posterboard
   red construction paper
   felt-tipped pens in various colors
   long thumbtacks
   small Jell-O boxes
   scissors
   stapler

Construction Directions:

1. Use an opaque projector to trace and cut the three large bells from the red posterboard. Attach the small Jell-O boxes to the board and glue the bells to these. This will give a three-dimensional effect.
2. Cut and mark the red posterboard using the bell pattern below.

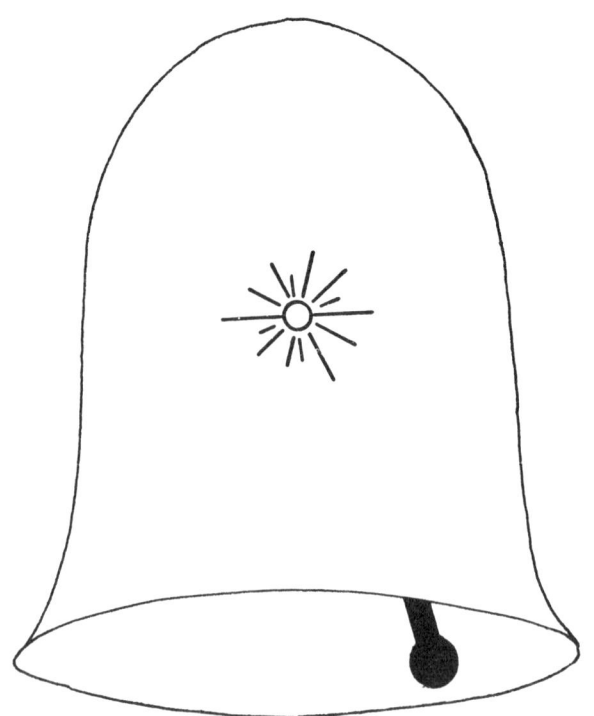

3. Copy each of the following drawings on a different bell as shown in the illustration.

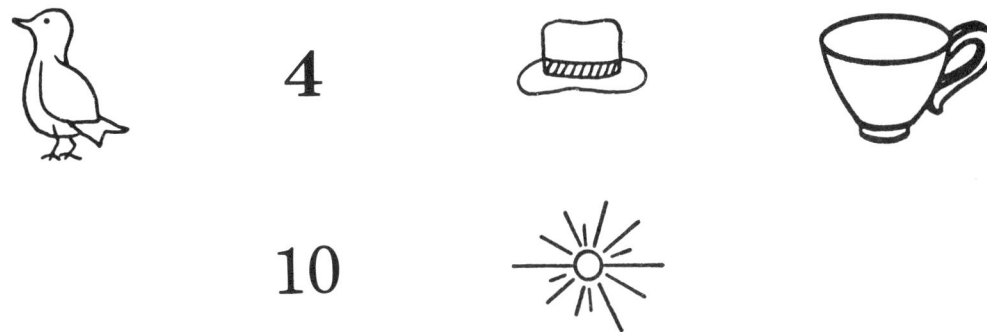

4. Attach these to the board by using the thumbtacks as shown on page 226.
5. Use an opaque projector to finish tracing the figures and lettering as shown in the illustration.
6. Fold the red construction paper to form an Answer Key and mark the front cover as shown. Mark the following on the inside and attach to the board.

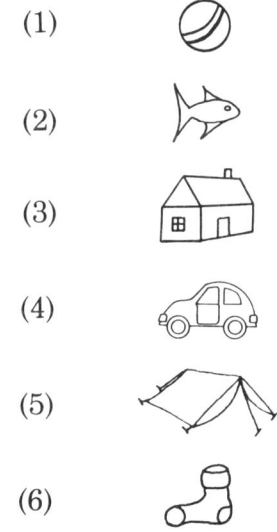

Learning Board Use: Children look at the drawings on the bells and match the beginning sounds with the beginning sounds of the objects in the drawings on either side. They do this by swinging the bells toward the appropriate drawings. They may use the Answer Key when they are finished.

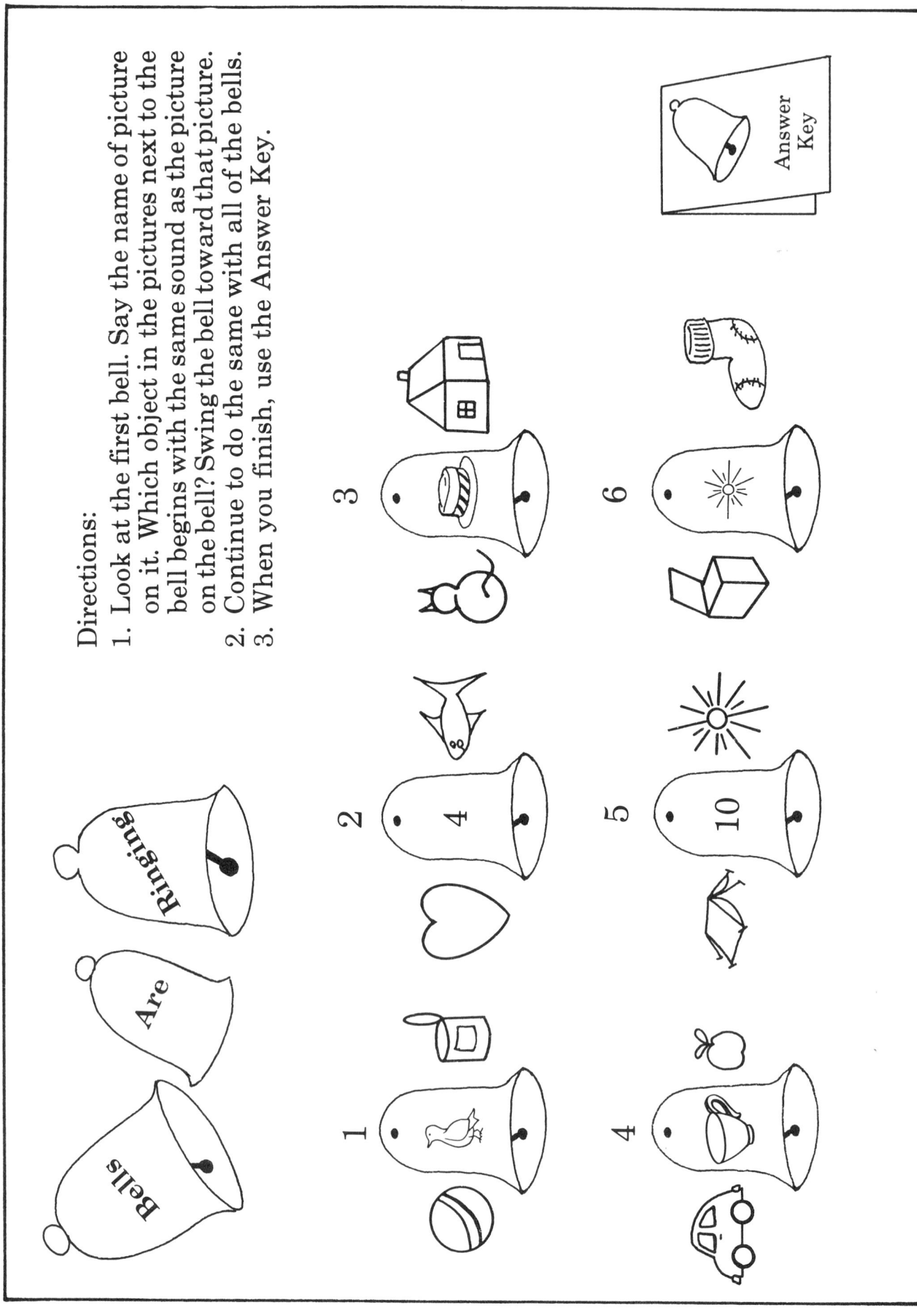

Fido's Treat

Reading Skill Reinforced: initial consonants
Grade Level: primary
Materials Needed:
  white background paper
  felt-tipped pens in various colors
  red construction paper
  white construction paper
  scissors
  paper hole punch
  legal-size envelope
  straight pins
  stapler

Construction Directions:

1. Use an opaque projector to trace the figures and lettering onto the background paper. Use appropriate colors. Attach the straight pins as shown.
2. Cut and punch the white construction paper using the bone pattern shown here. You will need ten bones.

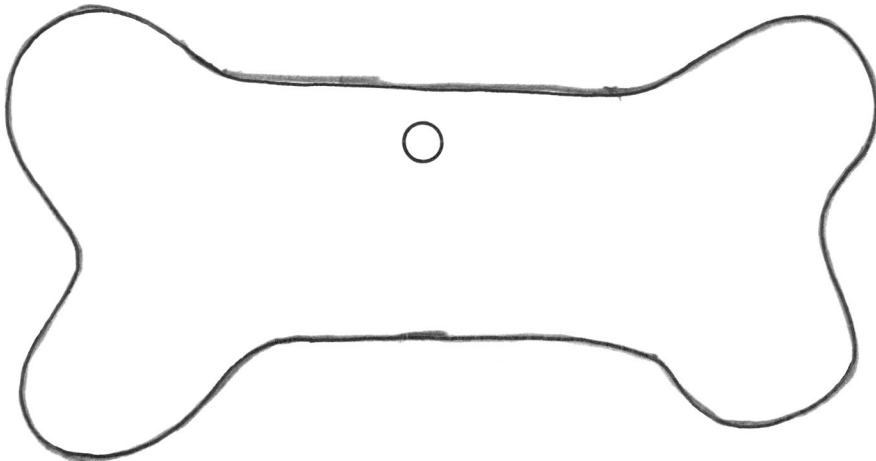

3. Mark each of the following drawings on a different bone.

4. Mark the word "Bones" on the large envelope, attach it to the board, and place the bones in it.
5. Fold the red construction paper to form an Answer Key and mark the front as shown in the board illustration. Copy the following on the inside of the answer key.

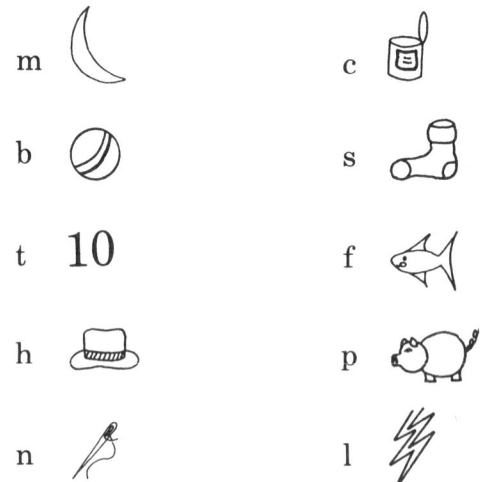

Learning Board Use: Children take the bones out of the envelope and match the beginning sounds on the bones with the letters on the dogs. They do this by hanging the bones on hooks under the dogs. When they finish, they may use the Answer Key to correct themselves.

Fido's Treat!

Answer Key

Bones

Directions:
1. Take the bones out of the envelope.
2. Look at the drawing on one of them. Find a dog with the beginning letter of that drawing. Hang the bone under that dog. Do the rest the same way.
3. When you finish, check the Answer Key.

Spin a Vowel

Reading Skill Reinforced: medial vowels
Grade Level: primary
Materials Needed:
- yellow background paper
- large sheet of black posterboard
- long tack
- felt-tipped pens in various colors
- tan construction paper
- stapler

Construction Directions:
1. Use an opaque projector to trace the vowel wheel, figures, and lettering onto the background paper.
2. Cut out a spinner arrow from the posterboard and attach it to the learning board with a long thumbtack.
3. Fold a sheet of tan construction paper. Mark "Answer Key" on the front and the following picture-vowel list on the inside. Attach this to the board as shown in the illustration.

(lock) = o   (clock) = o

(box) = o   (hat) = a

(can) = a   (sun) = u

(jug) = u   (tent) = e

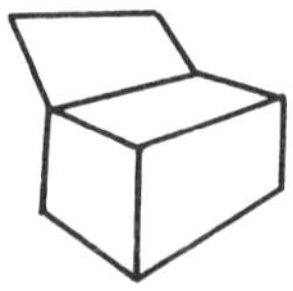

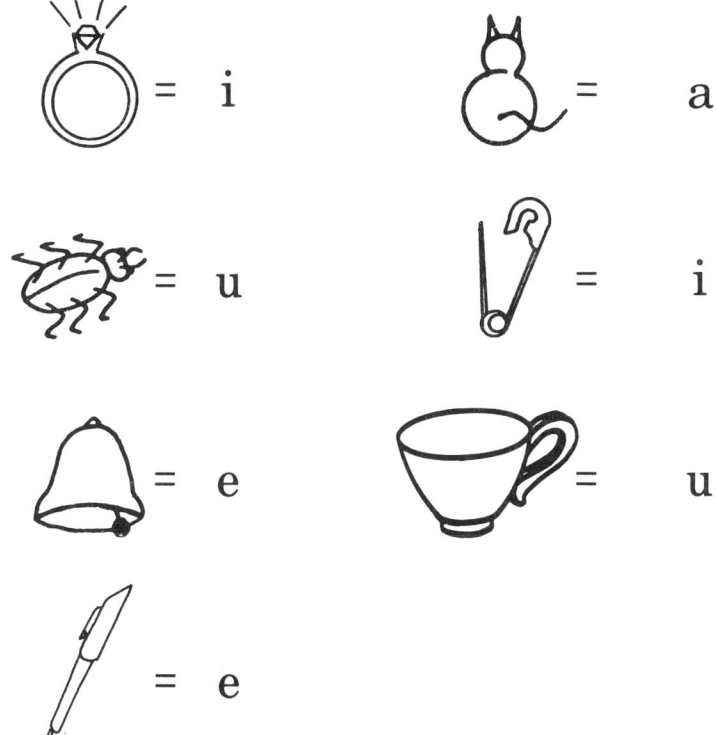

Learning Board Use: Children spin the arrow. When it stops on a vowel, they must find a picture of something whose name contains that particular vowel sound. When they finish, they may use the Answer Key to correct themselves.

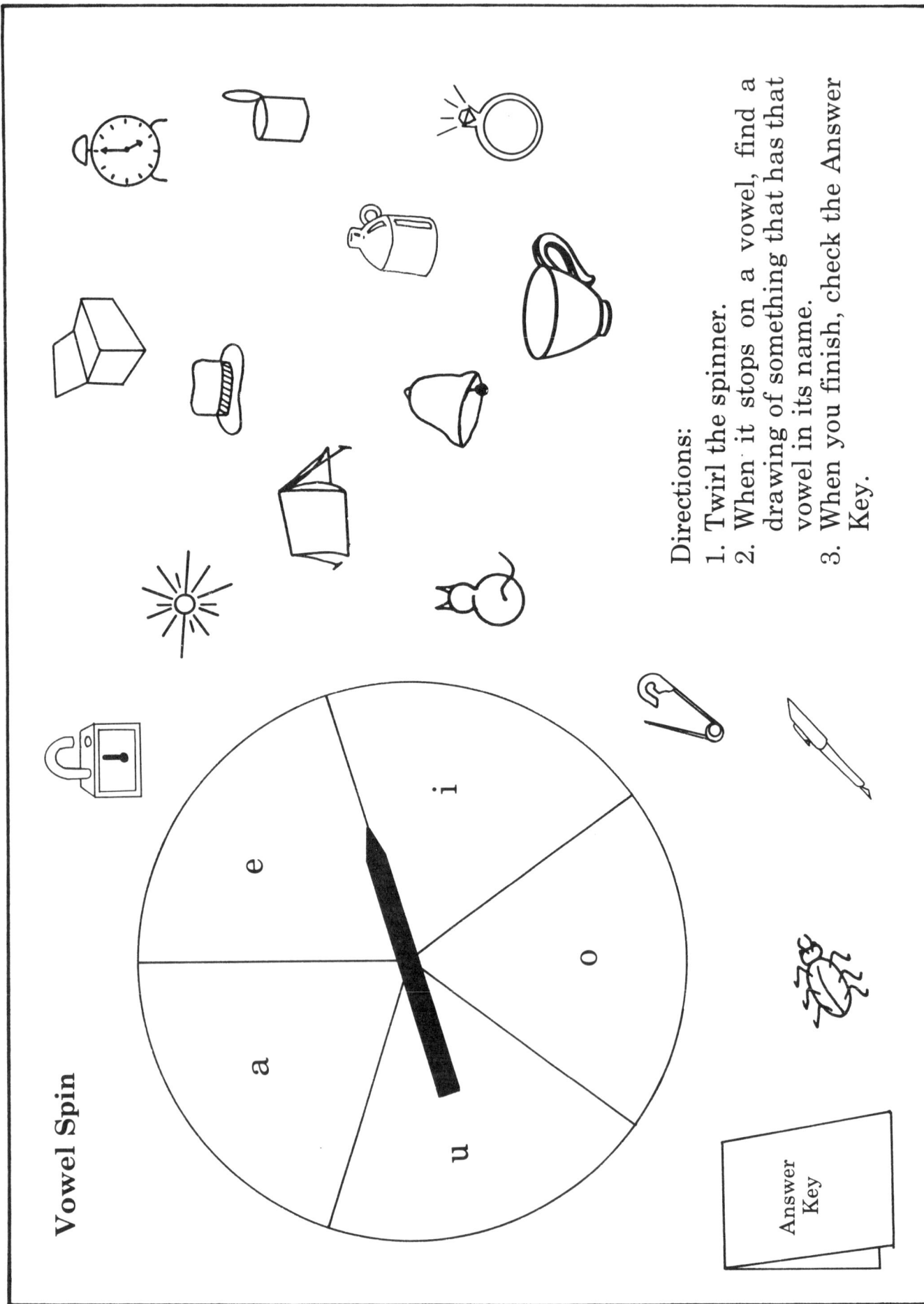

Jack and the Beanstalk

Reading Skill Reinforced: final consonants
Grade Level: primary
Materials Needed:
>   green background paper
>   felt-tipped pens in various colors
>   green construction paper
>   7 library book card pockets
>   legal-size envelope
>   scissors
>   stapler

Construction Directions:

1. Use an opaque projector to trace the figures and lettering onto the background paper.
2. Mark the book card pockets and attach them to the board as shown in the illustration.
3. Cut the green posterboard using the following leaf pattern. You will need seven leaves.

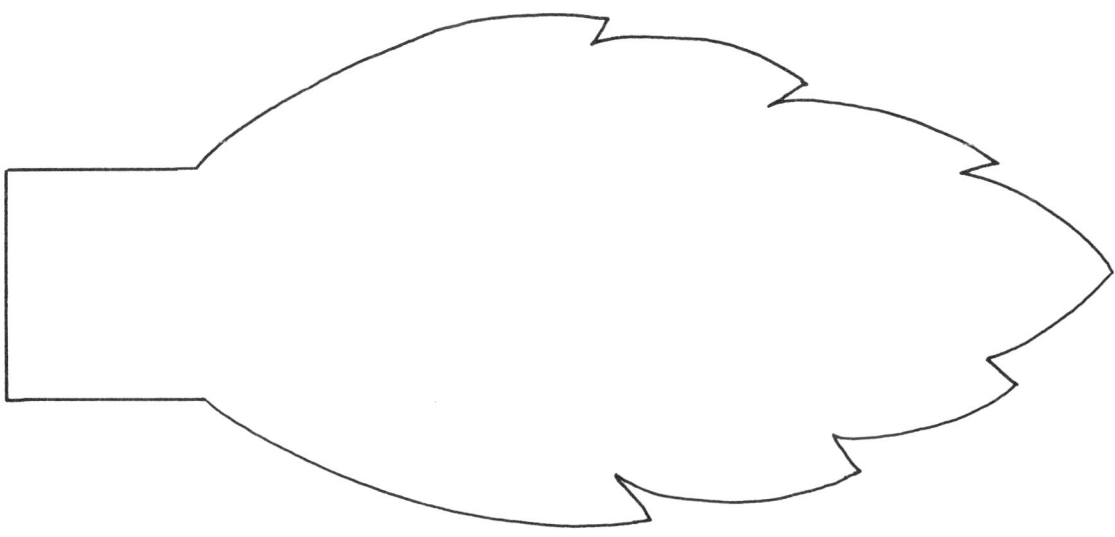

4. Copy each of the following drawings on a different leaf.

5. Mark "Leaves" on the envelope, attach it to the board, and place the leaves in it.
6. Fold the green construction paper to form an Answer Key and mark the front cover as shown in the illustration. Copy the following on the inside of the Answer Key and attach it to the board.

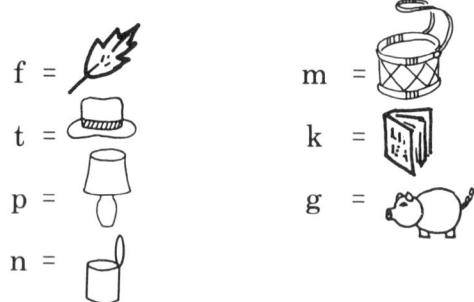

Learning Board Use: Children take the leaves out of the envelope and climb the beanstalk by matching the ending sound of the drawings on the leaves to the consonants on the pockets. They place one leaf in each pocket as they climb. When they finish, they may use the Answer Key to correct themselves.

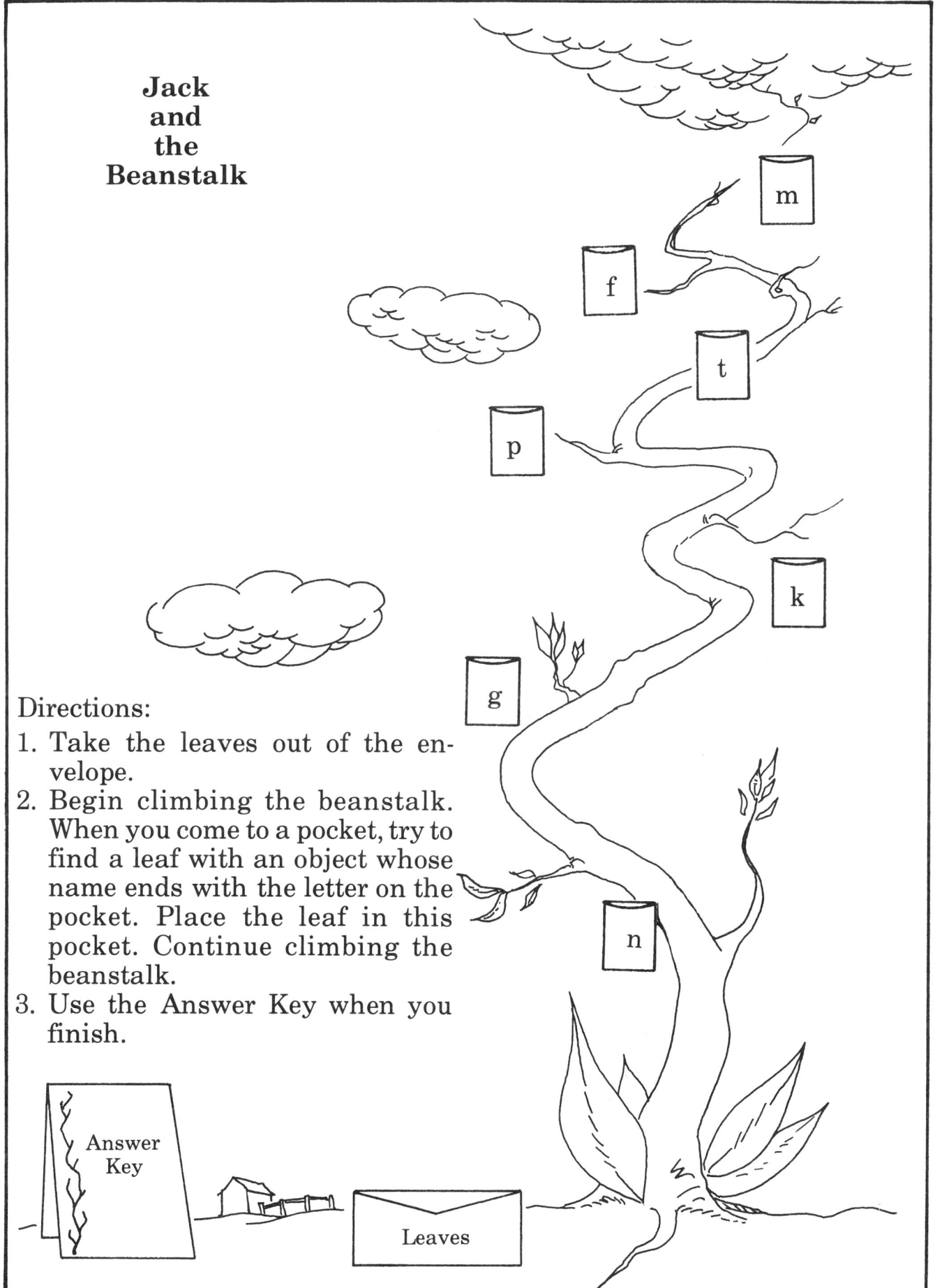

Down the Chute!

Reading Skill Reinforced: consonant blends
Grade Level: primary
Materials Needed:
    yellow background paper
    felt-tipped pens in various colors
    9 round potato chip cans
    green posterboard
    green construction paper
    legal-size envelope
    long thumbtacks
    stapler
    scissors
    green Con-Tact paper

Construction Directions:
1. Use an opaque projector to trace the lettering onto the background paper.
2. Cover the potato chip cans with the green Con-Tact paper and cut out part of the side as shown here.

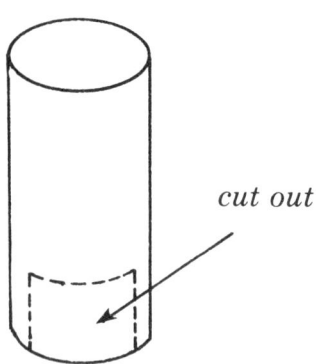

cut out

3. Mark each of the following blends on a different can and attach them to the board as shown in the illustration. Use the thumbtacks to attach them.

        tr   sp   br   sn   st   cl   fl   cr   gl

4. Cut nine circles with 2″ diameters from the green posterboard. Copy each of the following drawings onto a different circle.

5. Mark "Picture Circles" on the large envelope, attach it to the board, and place the circles in it.
6. Fold the green construction paper and mark "Answer Key" on the cover. Copy the following onto the inside of the Answer Key and attach it to the board.

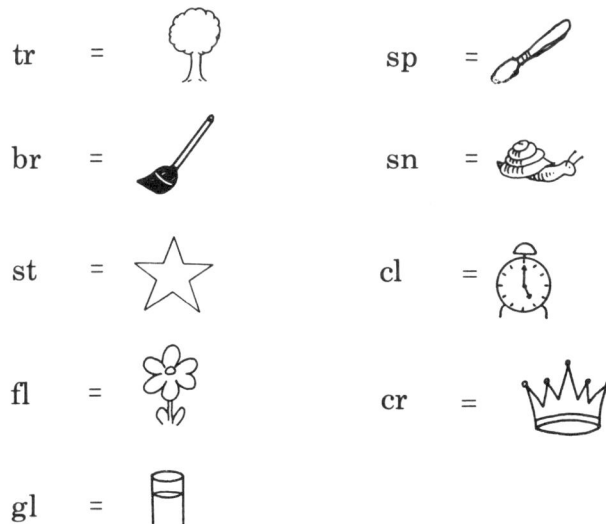

Learning Board Use: Children take the picture circles out of the envelope and match the beginning sounds on these circles with the blends on the chutes. They do this by dropping the circles down the chutes. When they finish, they may use the Answer Key.

Down the Chute

Directions:
1. Take the circles out of the envelope.
2. Look at the first one. Can you find a blend on one of the chutes that sounds like the beginning of the name for that picture? If you can, drop it down that chute. Continue doing this with all of the circles.
3. You may use the Answer Key when you finish.

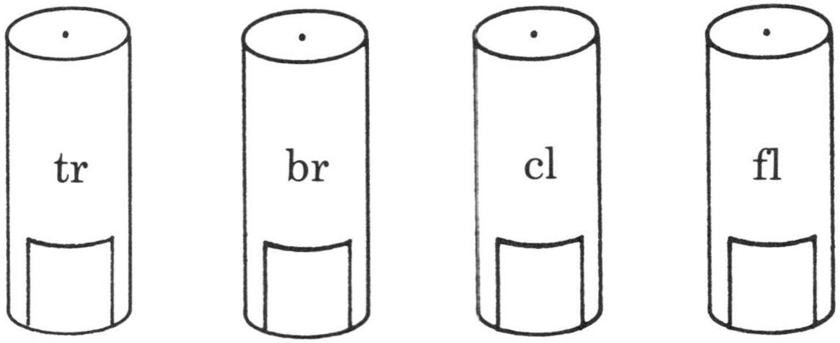

tr br cl fl

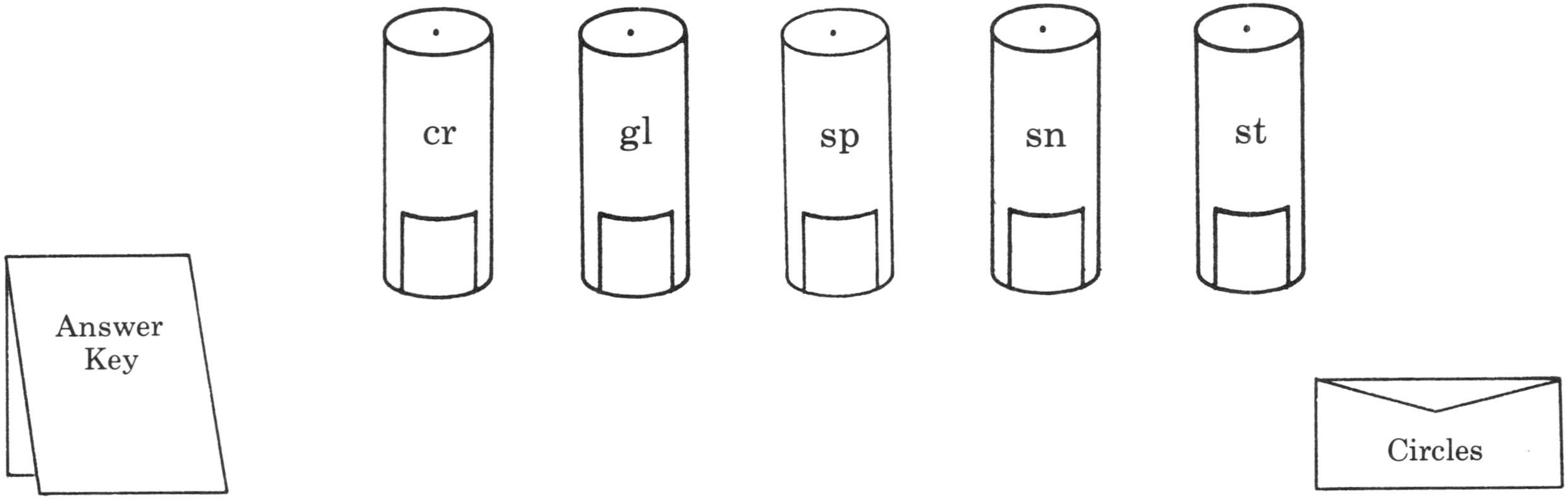

       gl sp sn st

cr

Circles

Answer Key

Panda's Problem

Reading Skill Reinforced: main idea
Grade Level: primary
Materials Needed:
> white background paper
> 6 pictures
> 6 library book card pockets
> legal-size envelope
> stapler
> felt-tipped pen
> 6 strips of 2″ × 8″ posterboard
> blue construction paper

Construction Directions:

1. Use an opaque projector to trace the lettering and panda onto the background paper. Use appropriate colors.
2. Cut out pictures from old basal readers or magazines and mount them as shown.
3. Mount a card pocket under each picture and print a numeral on it as shown in the illustration.
4. Print a sentence describing one of the pictures on each strip of posterboard.
5. Mark the word "Sentences" on the large envelope, attach it to the board, and place the sentence strips in it.
6. Fold the blue construction paper and mark "Answer Key" on the cover. Copy the sentences next to the correct numeral on the inside of the Answer Key and attach it to the board.

Learning Board Use: Children take the sentence strips out of the envelope and attempt to match each sentence with the picture it describes. When they think they know the answer, they place the sentence strips in the pockets under the appropriate picture. When they are finished, they may use the Answer Key.

Help Henrietta Find Her Baby!

Reading Skill Reinforced: sight word knowledge
Grade Level: primary
Materials Needed:
- white background paper
- felt-tipped pens in various colors
- 8 library book card pockets
- legal-size envelope
- red construction paper
- 8 strips of 2" × 6" posterboard
- stapler

Construction Directions:

1. Use the opaque projector to trace the lettering and figures onto the background paper. Use the felt-tipped pens and color appropriately.
2. Attach the library book card pockets to the learning board as shown in the illustration. Print one of the following words on each card pocket.

high	come
cold	tall
win	night
winter	fast

3. Print one of the following words on each of the posterboard strips.

low	go
hot	short
lose	day
summer	slow

4. Fold the red construction paper and mark "Answer Key" on the front. Copy the following on the inside and attach to the board.

    high—low
    cold—hot
    win—lose
    winter—summer
    come—go
    tall—short
    night—day
    fast—slow

5. Attach the large envelope to the board and place the word cards in it.

Learning Board Use: Children take the word cards out of the envelope. Following Henrietta's path, they try to find an antonym for each word card pocket. The children place the word cards in the correct pockets. When they finish, they may use the Answer Key.

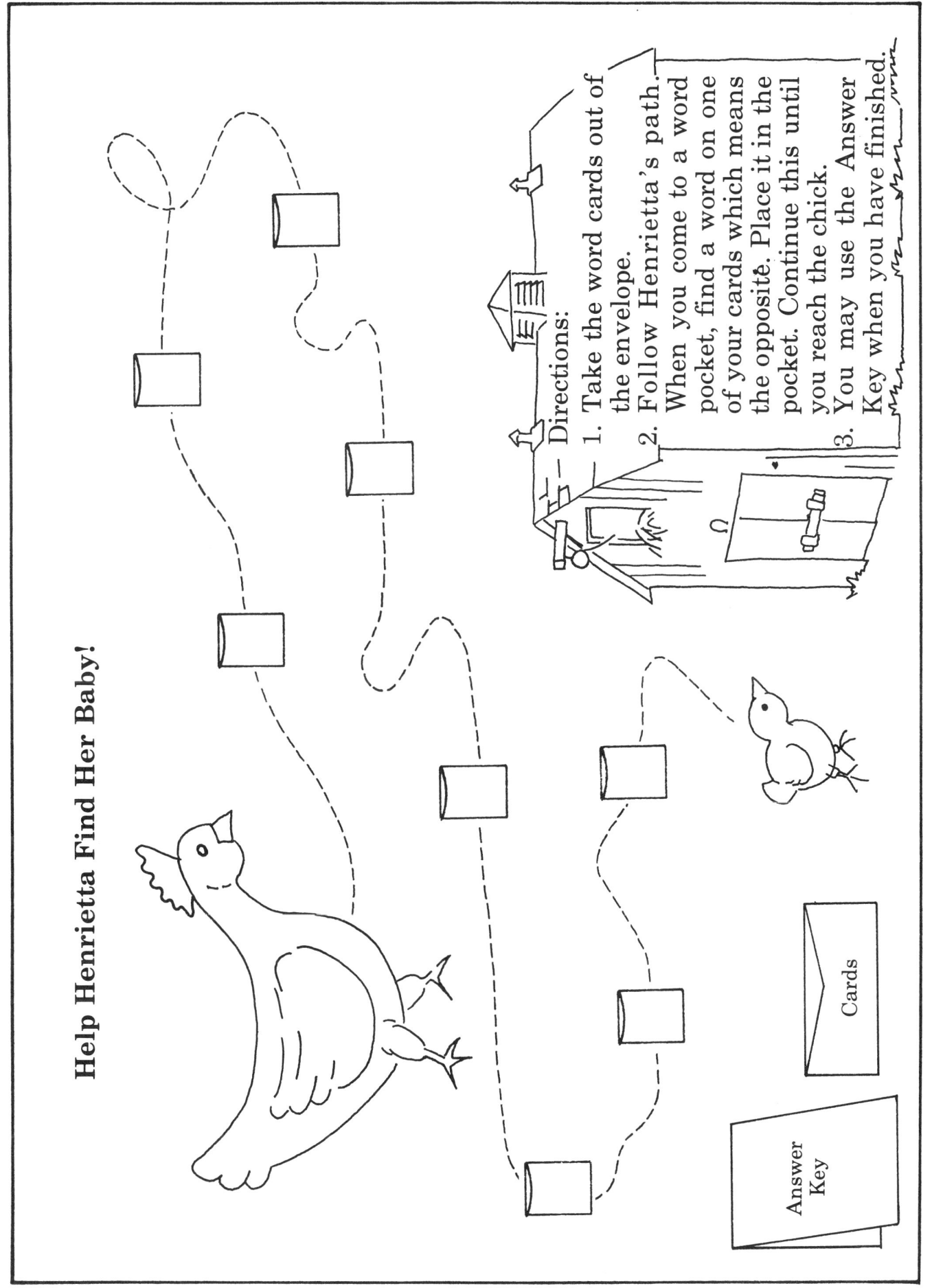

Fish Bubbles

Reading Skill Reinforced: contractions
Grade Level: primary
Materials Needed:
- blue background paper
- felt-tipped pens in various colors
- 10 straight pins
- blue construction paper
- blue posterboard
- paper hole punch
- scissors
- stapler
- legal-size envelope

Construction Directions:

1. Use an opaque projector to trace the figures and lettering onto the background paper. Use appropriate colors.
2. Attach the straight pins as shown in the illustration.
3. Cut and punch the blue posterboard using the following bubble shape.

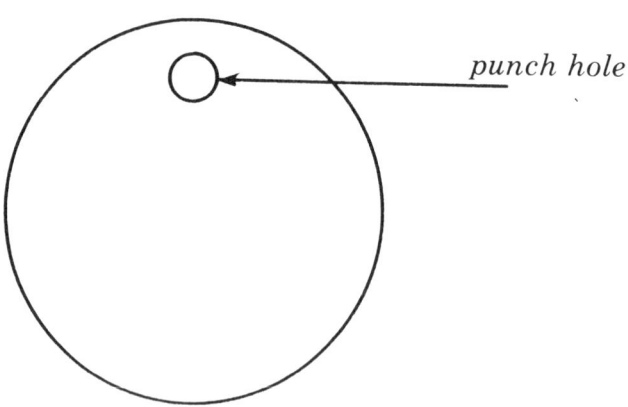

4. Copy each of the following contractions onto a different bubble.

wouldn't	they've
I'd	didn't
isn't	I'll
I'm	you're
it's	can't

5. Print "Bubble" on the envelope, attach it to the board, and place the bubbles inside.
6. Fold the blue construction paper to form an Answer Key and mark the cover as shown in the illustration. Mark the following on the inside and attach to the board.

> would not = wouldn't
> they have = they've
> I would = I'd
> did not = didn't
> is not = isn't
> I will = I'll
> I am = I'm
> you are = you're
> it is = it's
> can not = can't

Learning Board Use: Children take the bubbles out of the envelope and match the contractions with the words on the fish. They do this by hanging the bubbles on hooks over the fish. When they finish, they may use the Answer Key to correct themselves.

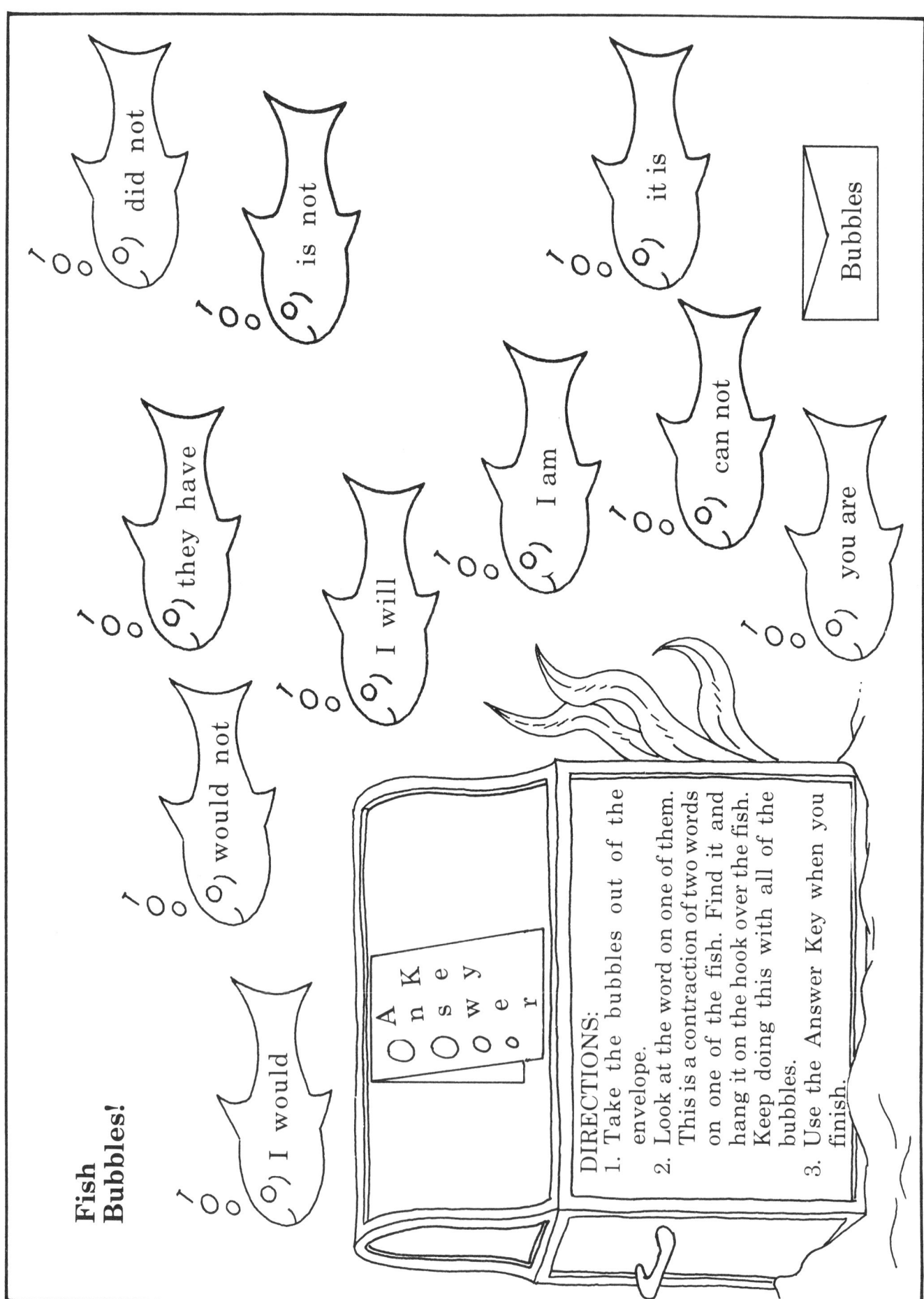

Hang Glider

Reading Skill Reinforced: story sequence
Grade Level: primary
Materials Needed:

>   white background paper
>   6 library book card pockets
>   blue construction paper
>   legal-size envelope
>   scissors
>   stapler
>   felt-tipped pens in various colors

Construction Directions:

1. Use an opaque projector to trace the figures and lettering onto the background paper.
2. Attach and number the library book card pockets as shown in the illustration.
3. Cut six 2½″ × 8″ strips from the blue construction paper. Copy each of the following sentences onto a strip.
   (1) "Help me get this hang glider to the edge of the cliff, Bob," said William.
   (2) Bob and William pushed and pulled until William's hang glider was close to the edge.
   (3) "Oh, gosh," said Bob, "you couldn't pay me to push off this cliff."
   (4) "Oh, it's fun," laughed William. "Now give me a push."
   (5) Bob pushed as the hang glider and William left the cliff.
   (6) Out over the ocean the hang glider soared under William's control.
4. Mark "Sentences" on the envelope, attach it to the board, and place the sentence strips in it.
5. Fold the blue construction paper and mark "Answer Key" on the front cover. Copy the sentences and their corresponding numbers (in step 3) on the inside and attach to the board.

Learning Board Use: Children take the sentence strips out of the envelope and arrange them in a sequence so that they form a story. They do this by following the hang glider's path and putting the strips in the pockets. When they finish, they may use the Answer Key.

Hang Glider

Directions:
1. Take the story strips out of the envelope.
2. Read through them and place them in the correct order so that they form a story. Place them in the pockets in the path of the hang glider.
3. Now, use the Answer Key to see if you're correct.

Answer Key

Sentences

Fill 'er Up

Reading Skill Reinforced: context clue usage
Grade Level: high primary
Materials Needed:

    white background paper
    felt-tipped pens in various colors
    straight pins
    posterboard in various colors
    scissors
    paper hole punch
    red construction paper
    legal-size envelope
    stapler

Construction Directions:

1. Use an opaque projector to trace the figures and lettering onto the background paper. Attach the straight pins as shown in the illustration.
2. Cut and punch the posterboard using the car pattern below. You will need 12 cars.
3. Print each of the following words on a car as shown in the illustration.

where	going
are	that
saw	off
horses	no
is	don't
near	could

4. Mark "Cars" on the envelope, attach it to the board, and place the cars in it.
5. Fold the red construction paper and mark "Answer Key" on the front cover. Print the following on the inside and attach to the board.

W	where
A	are
S	saw
H	horses
I	is
N	near
G	going
T	that
O	off
N	no
D	don't
C	could

Learning Board Use: Children take the cars out of the envelope. They are then told to follow the car's path. When they come to a gas pump they read the sentence and look for the missing word on one of their cars. They hang it on the hook in that gas pump. If they fill in all of the missing words correctly, the first letters of these words will spell where the car is going.

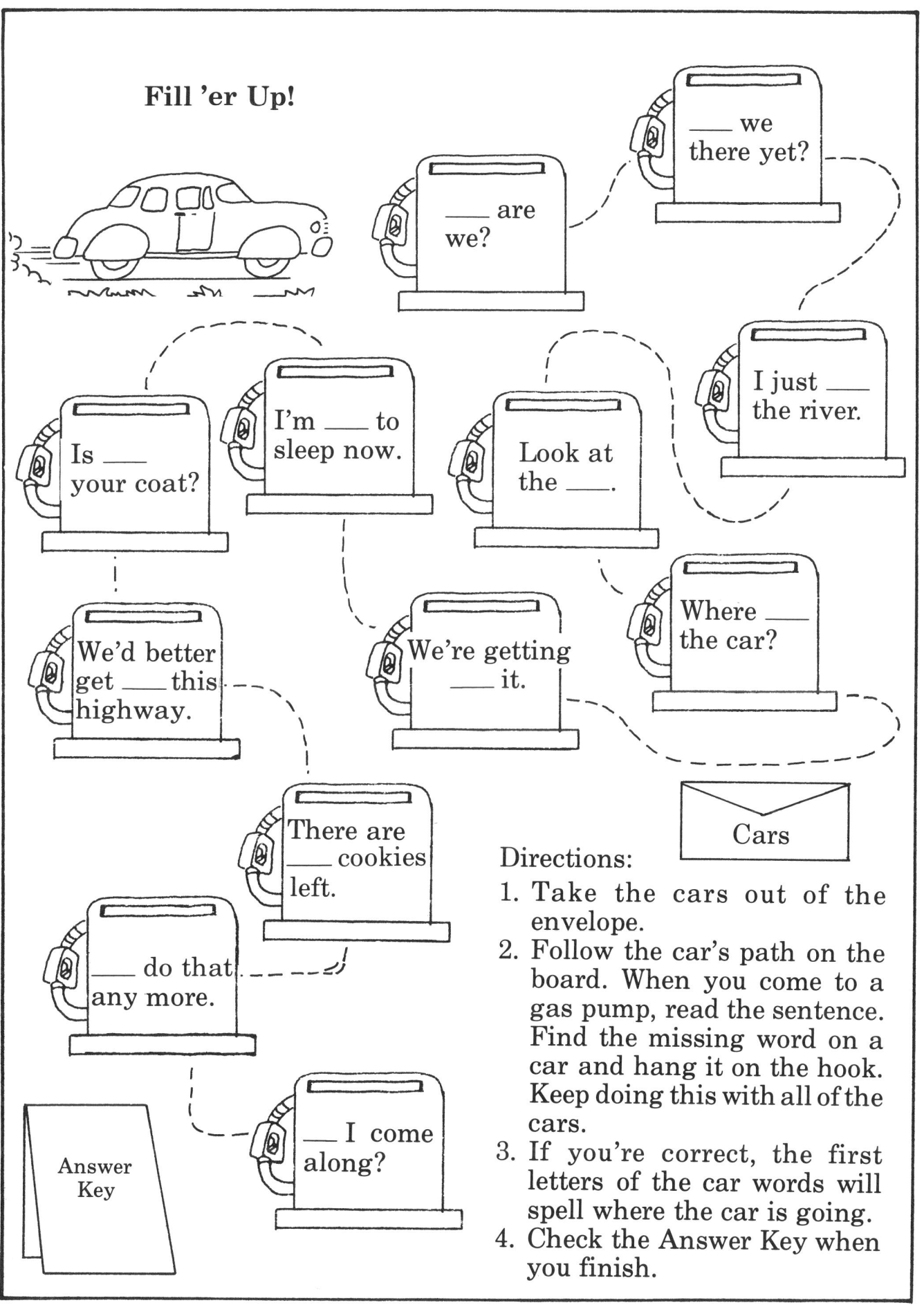

Hello ... Operator

Reading Skill Reinforced: compound words
Grade Level: high primary
Materials Needed:

    red background paper
    felt-tipped pens in various colors
    large detergent box
    brown construction paper
    tape
    thumbtacks
    stapler
    scissors
    long shoelaces

Construction Directions:

1. Use an opaque projector to trace the telephones and lettering onto the background paper.
2. Cover the large box with brown construction paper. Cut eight small holes and mark the front as shown in the board illustration. Attach the box to the board.
3. Attach each of the shoelaces to a telephone by using the thumbtacks as shown in the illustration.
4. Fold the brown construction paper to form an Answer Key and mark the front cover as shown in the illustration. Mark the following on the inside and attach to the board.

        anyway
        something
        airport
        himself
        birthday
        without
        afternoon
        railroad

Learning Board Use: Children make compound words by matching the word on a telephone with one on the switchboard. They then "plug in" to the appropriate word. When they are finished, they may use the Answer Key.

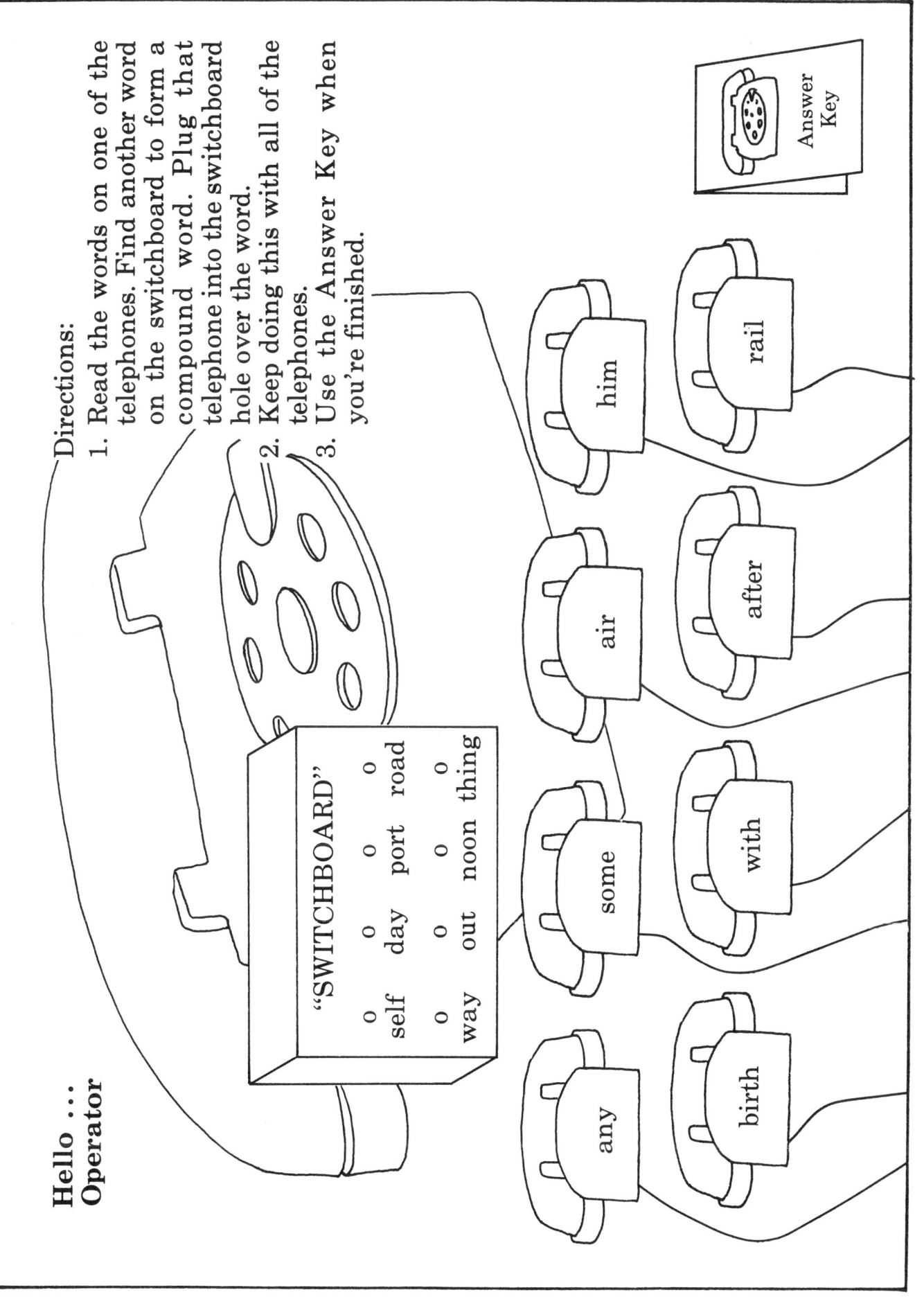

Apples, Apples, and More Apples

Reading Skill Reinforced: word meaning
Grade Level: high primary
Materials Needed:

    white background paper
    felt-tipped pens in various colors
    red construction paper
    red straight pins
    legal-size envelope
    scissors
    stapler
    paper hole punch

Construction Directions:

1. Use an opaque projector to trace the figures and lettering onto the background paper. Use appropriate colors.
2. Attach the straight pins above the words in the tree as shown in the illustration.
3. Cut, punch, and mark the red construction paper using the apple pattern below. You will need ten apples.

4. Print each of the following words on an apple.

    eight   tail
    new   sea
    right   weak
    won   deer
    our   through

5. Mark the word "Apples" on the large envelope, attach it to the board, and place the apples in it.

6. Fold the red construction paper and mark the front as shown in the board illustration. Copy the following on the inside and attach it to the board.

    eight—ate
    tail—tale
    new—knew
    sea—see
    right—write
    weak—week
    won—one
    deer—dear
    our—hour
    through—threw

Learning Board Use: The children take the apples out of the envelope and attempt to match the words on the apples with the homonyms on the tree. They do this by hanging the apples on the hooks under the words. When they finish, they may use the Answer Key.

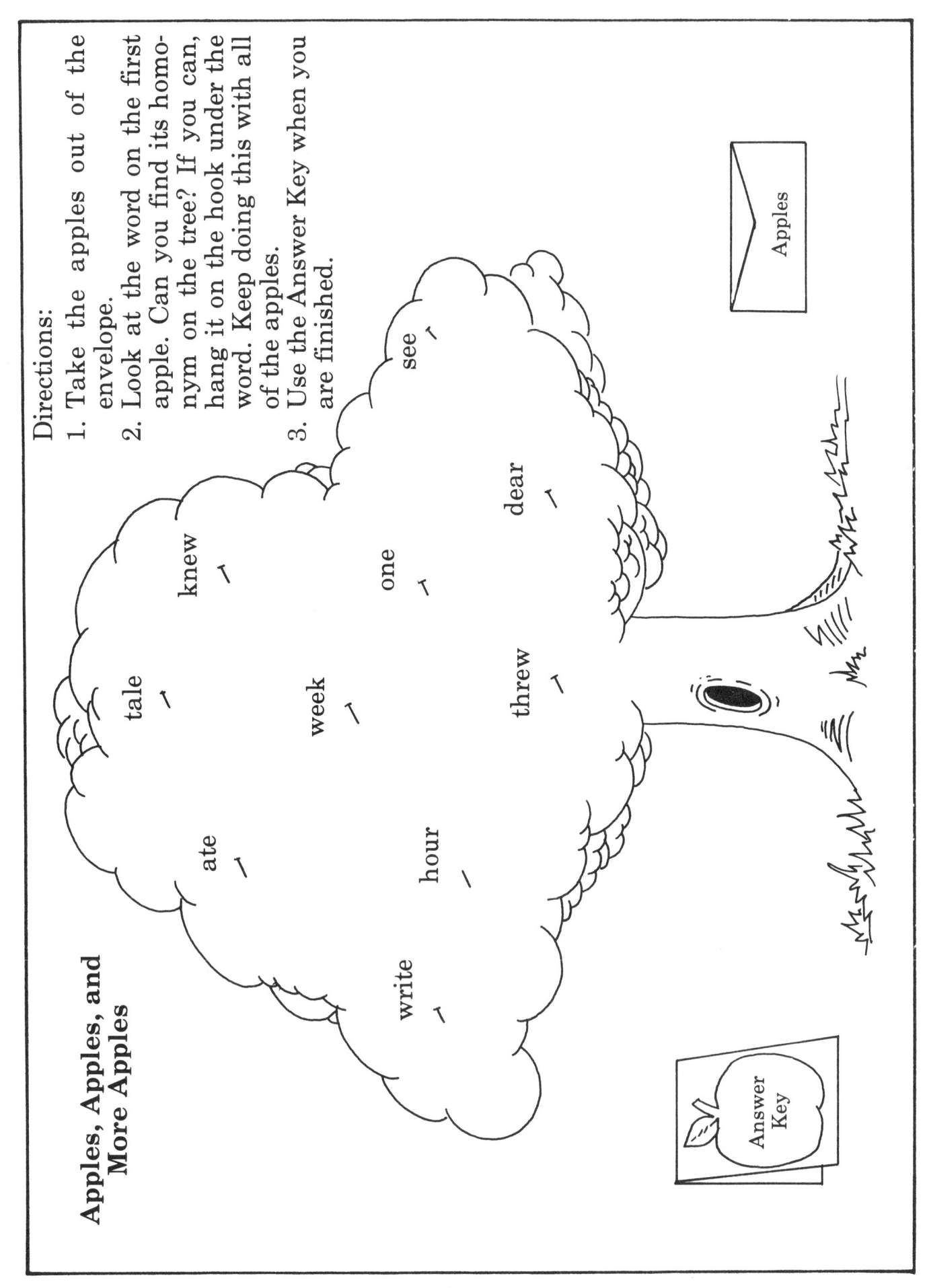

The Old Train

Reading Skill Reinforced: fact from fantasy
Grade Level: high primary
Materials Needed:
   white background paper
   felt-tipped pens in various colors
   gray construction paper
   scissors
   stapler

Construction Directions:
1. Use an opaque projector to trace the figures and lettering onto the background paper. Color the train and station appropriately.
2. Cut, number, and attach the flaps as shown here, using the gray construction paper.

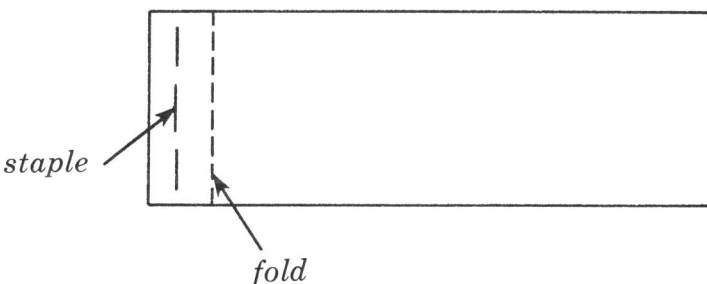

3. Copy one of the following sentences under each flap.

   (1) The old train rode down the tracks.

   (2) The old train winked at me as it passed.

   (3) The old train was mad and wouldn't pull the cars.

   (4) The old train pulled the cars up the steep hill.

   (5) The old train's whistle is very loud.

4. Fold the gray construction paper to make the Answer Key and mark the front as shown in the illustration. Copy the following on the inside and attach it to the board.

   (1) fact
   (2) fantasy
   (3) fantasy
   (4) fact
   (5) fact

Learning Board Use: Children lift up the flaps on the train and read the sentences. They decide whether the statements are factual or fantastic. When they finish, they may use the Answer Key to correct themselves.

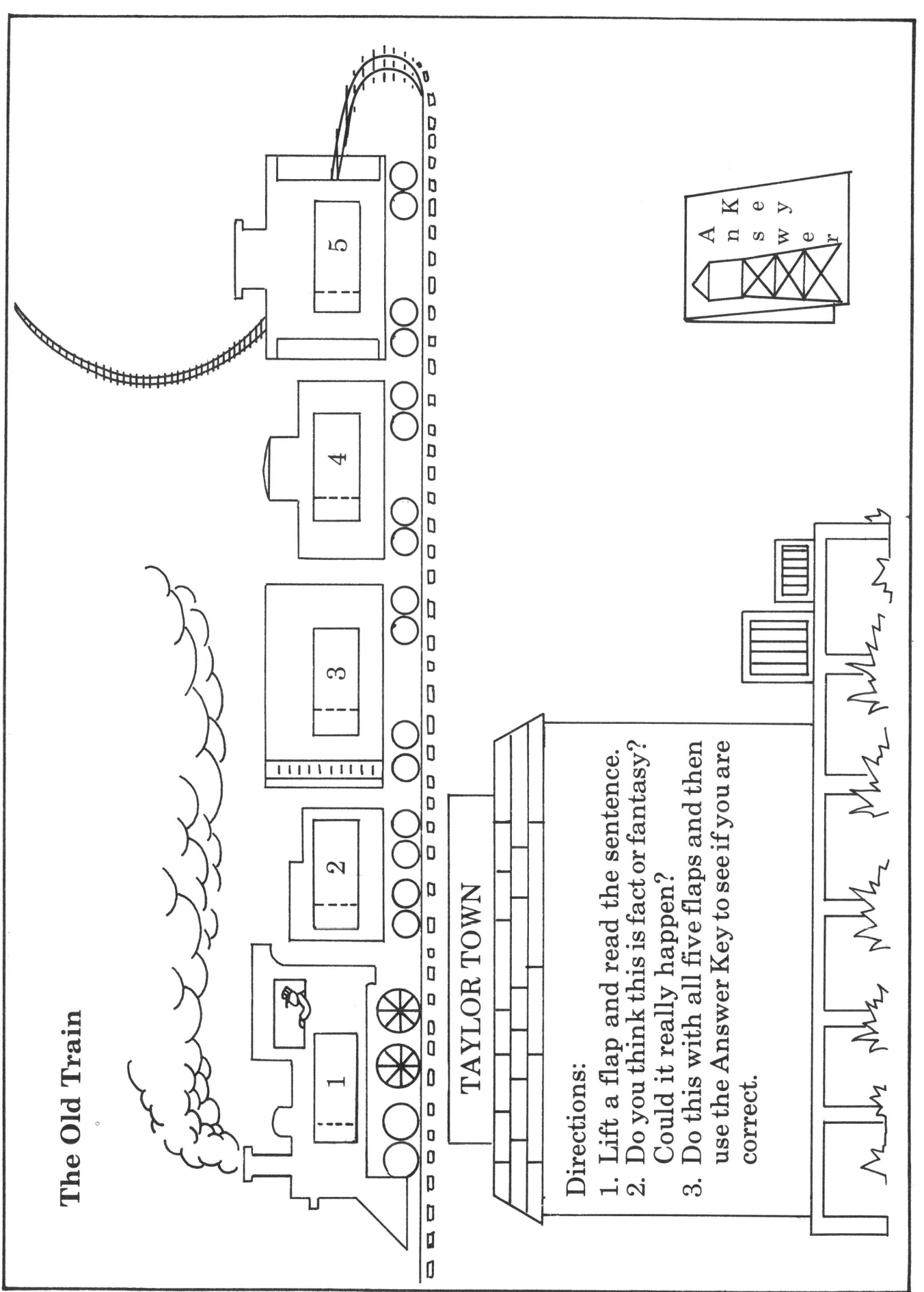

VI
Special Motivators

The activities in this section are designed to motivate children to *want* to read. The potpourri of ideas ranges from individual activities to activities which will include your entire class. Complete directions are included for each activity, along with the recommended grade level. Sample a few of these ideas and just watch your children's interest in reading grow.

The following reading motivators are provided in this section.

Motivator	*Grade Level*
Shhh .. I Can't Hear What the Book's Saying!	low primary
I Think I Can	low primary
Book Displays	primary
A "Bunch" of Mysteries	primary
Magic Well	primary
Bertrum Bug's Book Club	primary
Bookmark Factory	primary
Fabulous Foxy Award	primary
Month of the Super Sillies	primary
The Tiger's Tale	primary
And the Books Roll On	high primary
Read All About It!	high primary
Want Ads	high primary
Hidden Books!	high primary

SHHHH...I Can't Hear What the Book's Saying!

(Low Primary)

Arrange a listening post in a corner of your classroom. A couple of pillows, a playback tape deck, and appropriate books and tapes are all you need. You might want to attach a sign, similar to the one shown here, close to the listening post.

I Think I Can

(Low Primary)

You can make an irresistible reading nook with the help of a large cardboard box, a razor blade knife, felt-tipped pens, and tape. Simply turn the box on its side and then cut and assemble as shown on the next page. Throw in a few pillows and watch the children take turns reading in the engine.

IMPORTANT: *Be sure to tape one side of the engine to the wall for stability.*

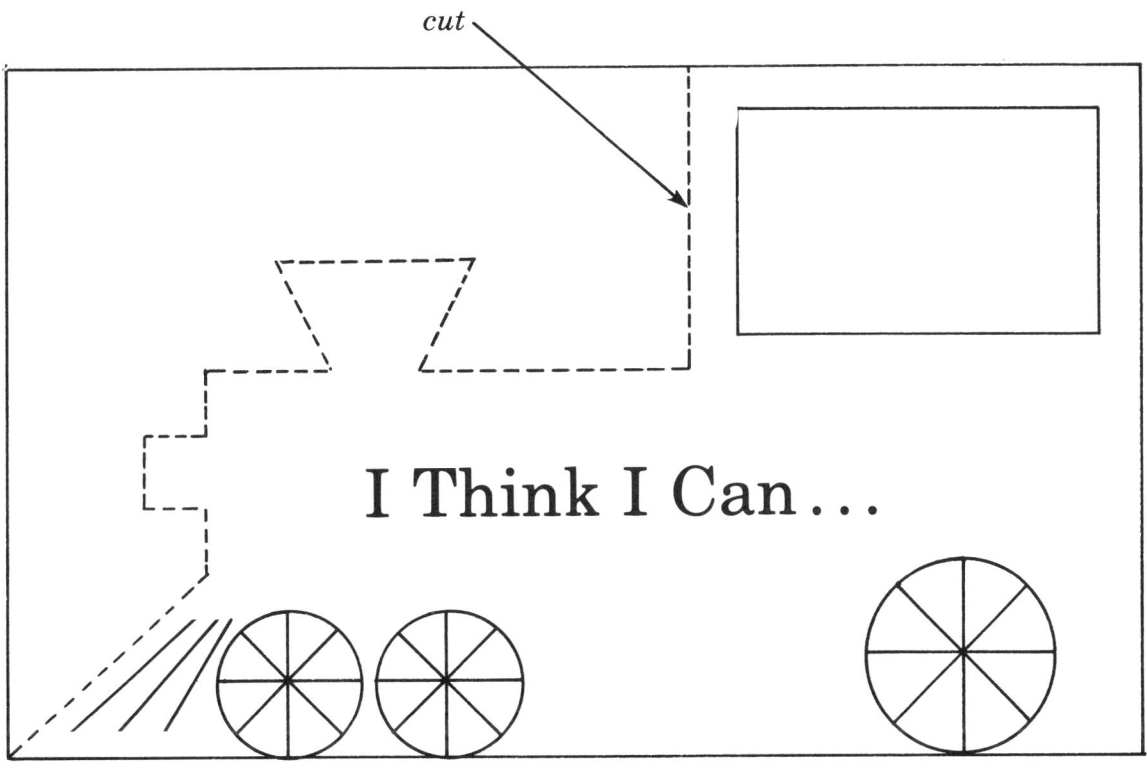
side view

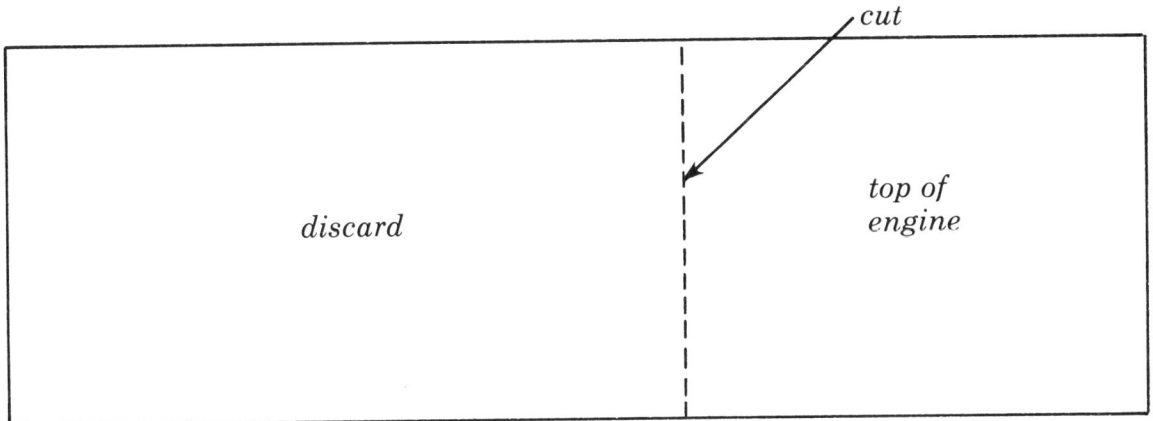
top view

Book Displays

(Primary)

Attractive book displays are a simple way to interest children in reading. Try one of the examples shown on the next few pages and just see if it doesn't spark an interest in reading.

CAUTION: *Book displays must be changed often to maintain the children's interest.*

Children can make dragons out of rolled newpapers, egg cartons, and pâpier-maché. Felt-tipped pens give the final touch.

Books you might want to include in this display are:

Mr. Drackle and His Dragons, by Elizabeth Froman
The Dragon of an Ordinary Family, by Margaret Mahy
The 14th Dragon, by James Seidelman and Grace Mintoyne
The Popcorn Dragon, by Jane Thayer
The Reluctant Dragon, by Kenneth Grahame

Encourage children to bring in things they've read about in some of these books.

Books you might want to include in this display are:

Katy and the Big Snow, by Virginia Lee Burton
The Little House, by Virginia Lee Burton
Mike Mulligan and His Steam Shovel, by Virginia Lee Burton
The Little Engine That Could, by Watty Piper
Little Toot, by Hardie Gramatky
Loopy, by Hardie Gramatky
Sparky, by Hardie Gramatky
The Velveteen Rabbit, by Margery Williams
Charles, by Liesel Skorpen
Corduroy, by Don Freeman

Children may add items found on a nature walk or "treasures" from past vacations.

Books you might want to include in this display are:

The Dead Tree, by Alvin Tresselt
The Beaver Pond, by Alvin Tresselt
The Old Bullfrog, by Berniece Freschet
The Turtle Pond, by Berniece Freschet
All Upon a Stone, by Jean George
The Last Free Bird, by A. Harris Stone
The Mountain, by Peter Parnall
The Lorax, by Dr. Seuss
The Web in the Grass, by Berniece Freschet

But don't stop with these book displays. Create your own. You might ask your children for suggestions and even take straw votes to determine the next few book displays.

NOTE: *The older primary children can form committees, each responsible for a different book display. As usual, the teacher must be an integral part of these committees with children of this age group.*

A "Bunch" of Mysteries

(Primary)

This motivator is best done on a wall but a bulletin board will work if necessary. Using green construction paper, tape a grapevine up one of your classroom walls...from the floor to the ceiling. Attach large green leaves using the leaf pattern on the next page.

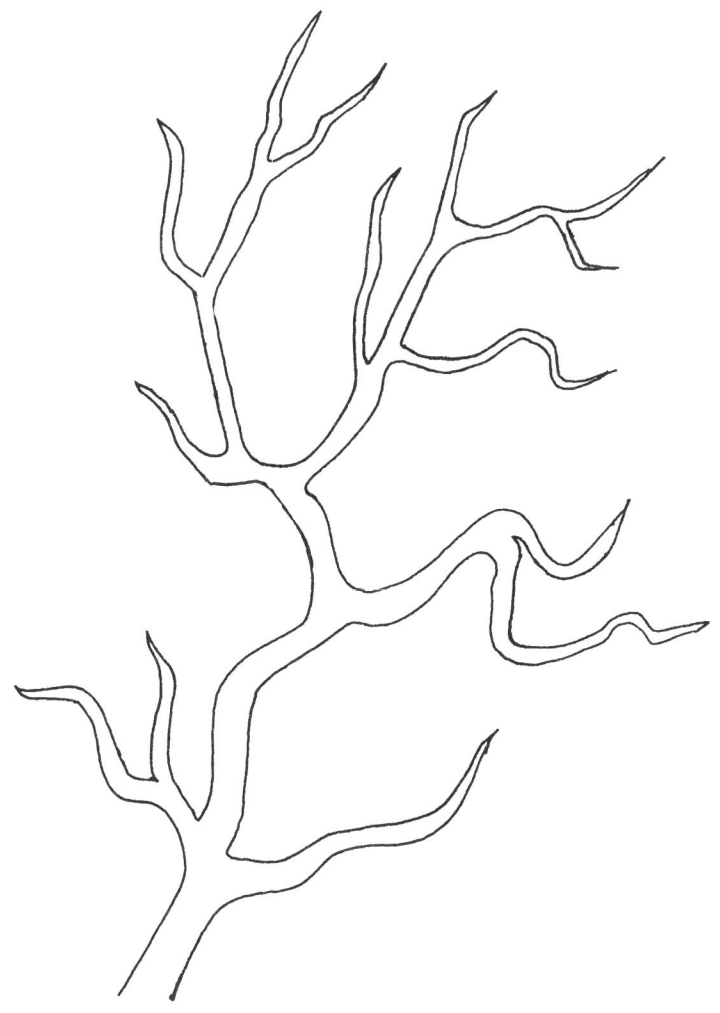

Cut bunches of grapes out of purple construction paper using the following pattern.

Print a title and author of a mystery book on each of these bunches of grapes and tape them on the grapevine. Here are a few good mystery books you might want to use for primary children:

The Tree House Mystery, by Carol Beach
The Case of the Cat's Meow, by Crosby Bonsall
The Case of the Dumb Bells, by Crosby Bonsall
The Case of the Hungry Stranger, by Crosby Bonsall
The Case of the Scaredy Cats, by Crosby Bonsall
The Case of the Long-Lost Twin, by Dan Cohen
Something Queer at the Ball Park, by Elizabeth Levy
Something Queer at the Library, by Elizabeth Levy
Something Queer Is Going On, by Elizabeth Levy
Something Queer on Vacation, by Elizabeth Levy
The Homework Caper, by Joan Lexau
The Rooftop Mystery, by Joan Lexau
The Secret Three, by Mildred Myrick
The Case of the Stolen Code Book, by Barbara Rinkoff
Inspector Rose, by Ben Shector
Lucy, by Catherine Storr
The Case of the Missing Kittens, by Mark Taylor

Make a large sign to place near this display that says, "Here's a BUNCH of Good Mysteries!"

Magic Well

(Primary)

A small tub is perfect for this project. Simply cover it with "brick" Con-Tact paper. Yardsticks, tape, string, and a large paper cup are the other materials you'll need in order to finish your well.

Make the following poster and place it near the well.

Fill up the well with good fantasy for your children. Here are some very popular fantasy books for children to help you get started:

The Emperor's New Clothes, by Hans Christian Andersen
The Runaway Bunny, by Margaret Wise Brown
Andy and the Lion, by James Daugherty
The Mouse and His Child, by Russell Hoban
Fish Is Fish, by Leo Lionni
Frederick, by Leo Lionni
Frog and Toad Are Friends, by Arnold Lobel
The Plain Princess, by Phyllis McGinley
Little Bear, by Else Minarik
Amelia Bedelia, by Peggy Parish
The Tale of Peter Rabbit, by Beatrix Potter
Curious George, by Hans Rey
Where the Wild Things Are, by Maurice Sendak
The 500 Hats of Bartholomew Cubbins, by Dr. Seuss
The Amiable Giant, by Louis Slobodkin
Anatole, by Eve Titus
You Look Ridiculous Said the Rhinoceros to the Hippopotamus,
    by Bernard Waber
The Velveteen Rabbit, by Margery Williams
Mr. Rabbit and the Lovely Present, by Charlotte Zolotow

Bertrum Bug's Book Club

(Primary)

Encourage your students to join Bertrum Bug's Book Club, whereby they pledge to read a certain number of books each month. Upon joining the book club, they receive a bookmark, as shown below, and a "Tell Bertrum Bug" sheet, as shown on page 272.

SUGGESTION: *Copy the bookmark on a ditto master and run off copies using construction paper. The children can cut them out and color them.*

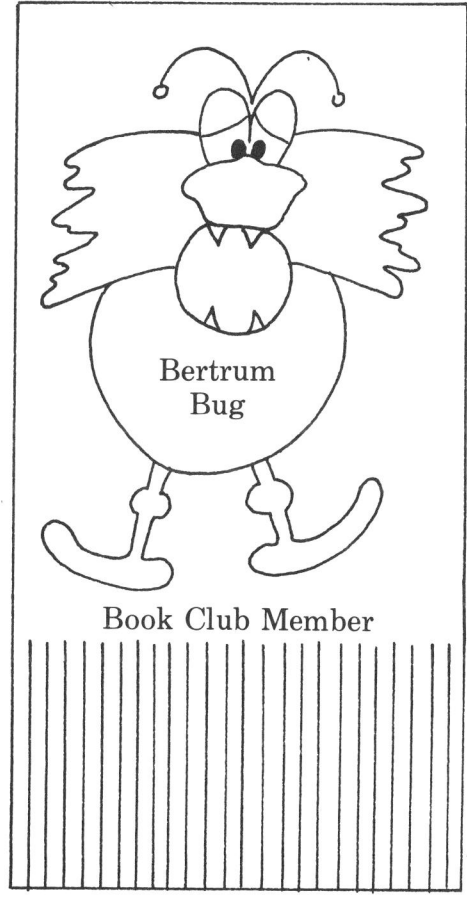

After a child finishes a book, he or she should fill in the "Tell Bertrum Bug" sheet and return it to you. At this time the child receives another sheet for a future book. By using a class list and check marks, you can record how many books each child has read. When children reach a certain number of books read, reward them with a "Bertrum Bug Book Award." This is a certificate of merit found on page 273.

Tell Bertrum Bug!

Tell me all about the book you just read and then draw me a picture of your favorite part.

Book _____

Author _____

_____
_____
_____
_____

Bertrum Bug Reading Award

_____ has earned this award for reading _____ books.

_____
Teacher

_____
Date

Bookmark Factory

(Primary)

Provide your students with a bookmark factory. Simply attach a sign to an extra desk and chair in a corner of your room.

Have a supply of construction paper, scissors, and felt-tipped pens available at the factory. Hang the following poster on a wall next to your factory and watch the "Busy Bookmark Factory" come alive!

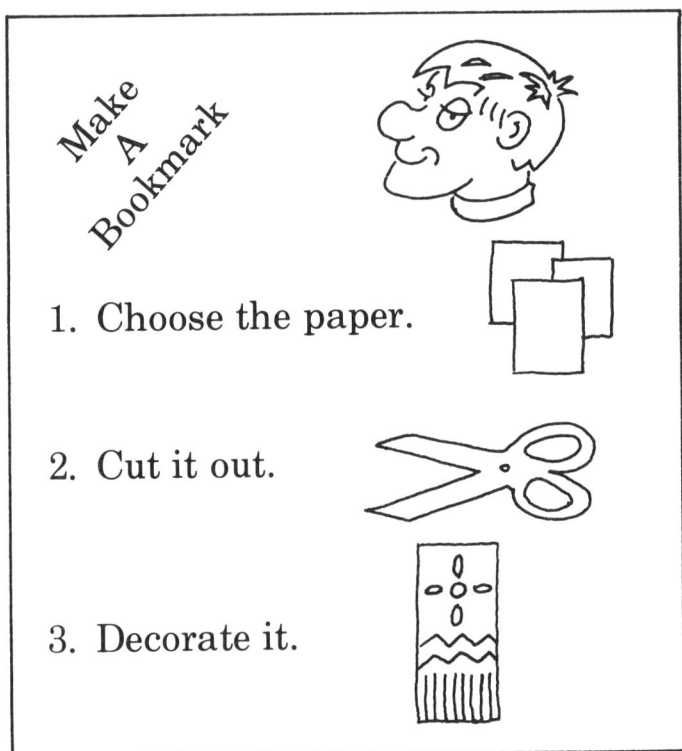

VARIATION: *For high primary children, you might suggest that they choose a book they've read and design a bookmark for it. The bookmark could contain a quotation from the book, an illustration of a character, or a picture of an interesting event.*

Fabulous Foxy Award

(Primary)

Ask each child to nominate several favorite books by using the "Fabulous Foxy Nomination Form" on the following page. List the ten most frequently named books on the "Official Fabulous Foxy Ballot" on page 276. Pass out the ballots and have the children vote for their favorite book.

NOTE: *You may want to have children bring in copies of these books and tell about them before they vote. Be sure to allow several days for this sharing activity.*

The winner, along with the first four runners-up, could be displayed in your school library or a hall showcase, along with appropriate posters made by your children. A typical display might look something like the illustration on page 277.

**Fabulous Foxy
Nomination Form**

I, _____ , nominate the

following three books for the "Fabulous Foxy Award."

    1. _____

       by _____

    2. _____

       by _____

    3. _____

       by _____

**Official
Fabulous
Foxy
Ballot**

NOTE: *You can make the award ribbons using the pattern shown here.*

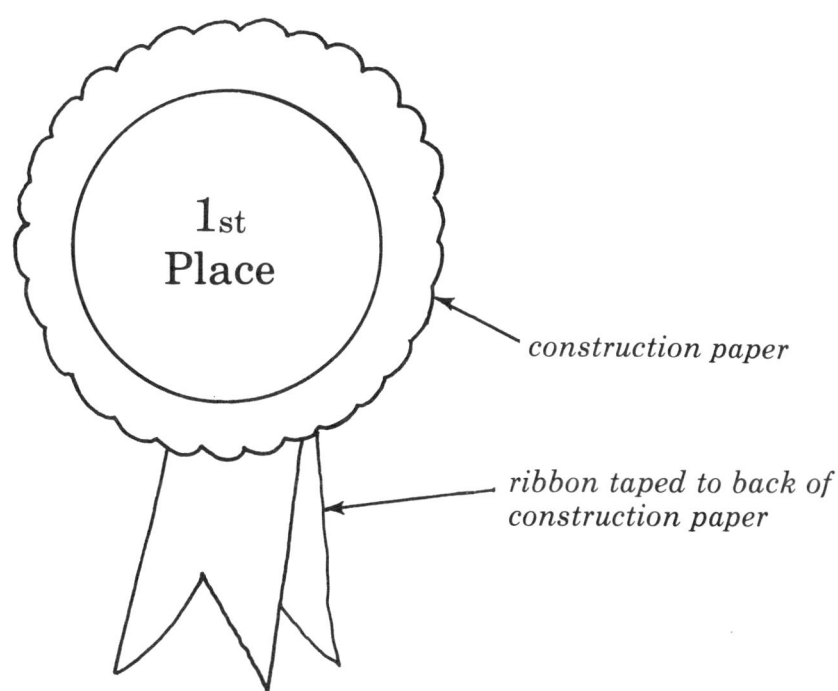

Month of the Super Sillies

(Primary)

Have a month of Super Sillies! Here are several ideas to help you have a fun month with humorous and often downright silly stories.

BOOK LIST: *Start the month off by duplicating the book list of Super Sillies on the next page for your students. Use colorful paper for added appeal.*

NOTE: *The books on this list are commonly found in most libraries for children. You might want to check with your school librarian before handing out the book list so that he or she may be prepared to help locate the Sillies.*

Duplicate the "Super Sillies" activity sheets, shown on page 280, and have them available for children to complete after reading a silly book. Attach the completed sheets to the bulletin board display as shown on page 281.

We dare you to read just one of these silly books and not giggle, grin, or laugh your head off!

Allard, Harry, *The Stupids Step Out*, Houghton Mifflin (1974)
Balian, Lorna, *The Aminal,* Abington Press (1972)
Christian, Mary, *Nothing Much Happened Today,* Addison-Wesley (1973)
Flory, Jane, *We'll Have a Friend for Lunch,* Houghton Mifflin (1974)
Hoban, Russell, *A Baby Sister for Frances,* Harper & Row (1964)
Hoban, Russell, *Dinner at Alberta's*, Crowell (1975)
Hutchins, Pat, *Don't Forget the Bacon*, Greenwillow (1976)
Kent, Jack, *The Egg Book*, Macmillan (1975)
Krahn, Fernando, *Who's Seen the Scissors?*, Dutton (1975)
Marshall, James, *George and Martha*, Houghton Mifflin (1972)
Mayer, Mercer, *Hiccup*, Dial (1976)
Mayer, Mercer, *One Frog Too Many*, Dial (1975)
Mayer, Mercer, *There's a Nightmare in My Closet*, Dial (1968)
Raskin, Ellen, *Nothing Ever Happens on My Block*, Atheneum (1971)
Sharmat, Marjorie, *Goodnight Andrew, Goodnight Craig,* Harper & Row (1969)
Supraner, Robyn, *It's Not Fair*, Warne (1976)
Tobias, Tobi, *A Day Off*, Putnam (1973)
Viorst, Judith, *Alexander and the Terrible, Horrible, No Good, Very Bad Day,* Atheneum (1972)
Zolotow, Charlotte, *Someday*, Harper & Row (1965)

Super Sillies

Name _____

Date _____

I just finished reading a very silly book called: _____

_____

It was written by: _____

_____

I (did/did not) like it because: _____

_____

_____

_____

_____

Here is a picture of the part I liked best:

© 1981, by The Center for Applied Research in Education, Inc.

Super Silly Mobile

NOTE: *Make this mobile out of posterboard and string. List a different book on each side of the figures.*

Super Silly Button

I just read a

SUPER SILLY Book

NOTE: *Make this button out of construction paper and pin one on each "special" reader of silly books!*

Make a Super Silly Reading Center

As shown in the illustration, a large cardboard box can be easily transformed into the front and sides of a "Big Top." Simply use a razor blade knife to cut out the door. Then, add a "silly circus" effect by illustrating the box with latex paint. Fold back the sides of the box and use masking tape to attach the sides to the wall.

"Spin a Silly"

Skill Reinforced: sight word knowledge

Grade Level: primary

Materials Needed:

    10 sheets of 5" × 8" yellow posterboard

    10 white posterboard circles with 4" diameters

    10 paper fasteners

    felt-tipped pen

    scissors

    ruler

Construction Directions:

1. Cut and mark the yellow posterboard pieces as shown on the next page.
2. Print each of the following word groups on a game piece. The three words in each list go on the circle as shown here. Do not print the words on the circle until you have attached it to the large game piece so that they will be visible through the cutout. Print the correct answer on the back of the circle as a self-check.

in	out	over	under
	top		house
	the		that
day	night	big	little
	there		bottom
	play		over
long	short	cool	warm
	front		big
	winter		work
wet	dry	good	bad
	bad		girl
	none		poor
high	low	begin	end
	lost		sit
	slow		hard

Game Play

1. Take one of the game boards and read the word on the "Super Silly's" head. Turn the white wheel until you find a word that means the opposite.
2. When you think you've found it, turn over the game board. The correct answer is on the back of the wheel.

The Tiger's Tale

(Primary)

A newsletter is just the thing to stimulate your children to read *and* write. This is usually a one- or two-sheet publication that could be printed on the school's duplicator every six or nine weeks.

IMPORTANT: *Be sure to include children's work, both drawings and written material. Several children could be asked to write about new books they have just read.*

It is probable that you will want to run a few of the columns on a regular basis. For example, "From the Teacher" and "New to Read" could possibly be found in all issues.

For added appeal, you might want to print your newsletter on colored paper and place it in a central location for easy access. A bulletin board like the one below could be used for this.

NOTE: *An example of a typical newsletter may be found on the next page.*

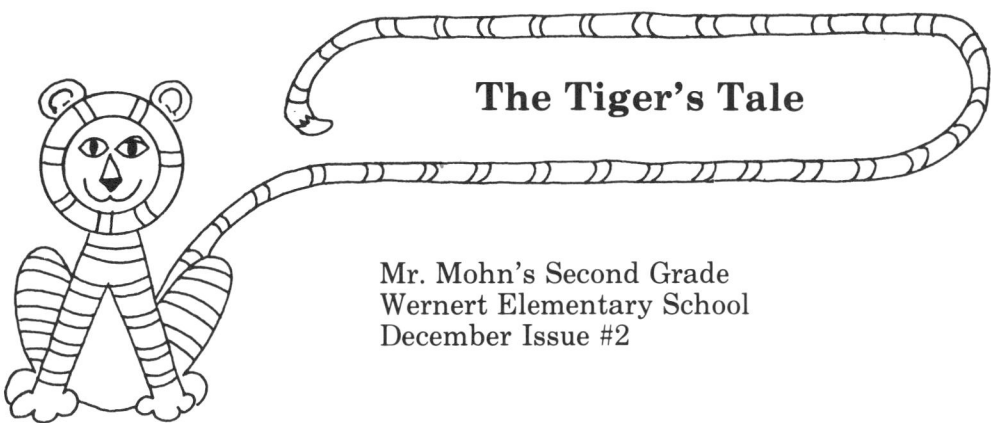

The Tiger's Tale

Mr. Mohn's Second Grade
Wernert Elementary School
December Issue #2

I Just Read
by
Cindy Smith

I just read *Nothing Ever Happens on My Block,* by Ellen Raskin. It was a very funny book. This boy, named Chester, sits on a curb and complains that there is nothing to do on his block. All the while funny and exciting things are happening all around him. He doesn't see any of it! I really like the haunted house. I hope Santa brings me this book for Christmas!

From the Teacher

I just read some books by Mercer Mayer and now I'm hooked. I like them all!!! Some of them don't have any words and are called wordless picture books. I have them on display if you are interested and want to read some of them. I wish some of you would write stories to go along with the wordless picture books. If you do, we'll make a bulletin board display so that everyone can enjoy them.

A Christmas Poem
by
Bobby Brown

I can hardly wait,
For Christmas to come,
Last year I got,
Toys, candy and gum.

Our tree is up,
All decorated and
  bright,
When Santa comes,
He'll see a real sight.

Christmas Puzzle

Fill in the correct words and the shaded boxes will spell someone who comes at Christmas!

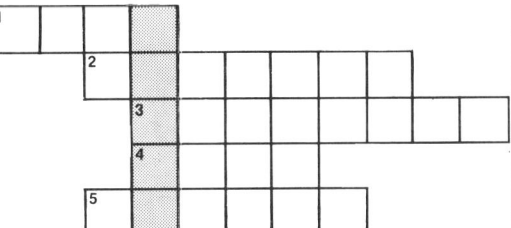

1. Sometimes you get these for Christmas.
2. This is the month after December.
3. This is the month before December.
4. They are decorated for Christmas.
5. We sing them at Christmas.

Basketball Mania!

Would you like to know more about basketball? Well, here are two books that will give you a lot of facts! Look in our class library or ask Mrs. Shelden, our school librarian. She can suggest others!

All About Basketball, by
  Henry Haskil
Basketball Is Fun, by
  Sue Tomkin

New to Read

Here are some new books you might like to read!

The Stupids Have a Ball,
  by Harry Allard
Anno's Journey, by Anno

© 1981, by The Center for Applied Research in Education, Inc.

287

And the Books Roll On

(High Primary)

A fun way of sharing recently read books is to make a movie roll. Children who want to do this simply illustrate the most important parts or main ideas of the story. They arrange them in proper sequence and then tape the sheets together. Next, they must tape each end to a different paper towel roll and then roll it onto the roll at the story's end. With a helper or two, the children tell the story as it is rolled from left to right.

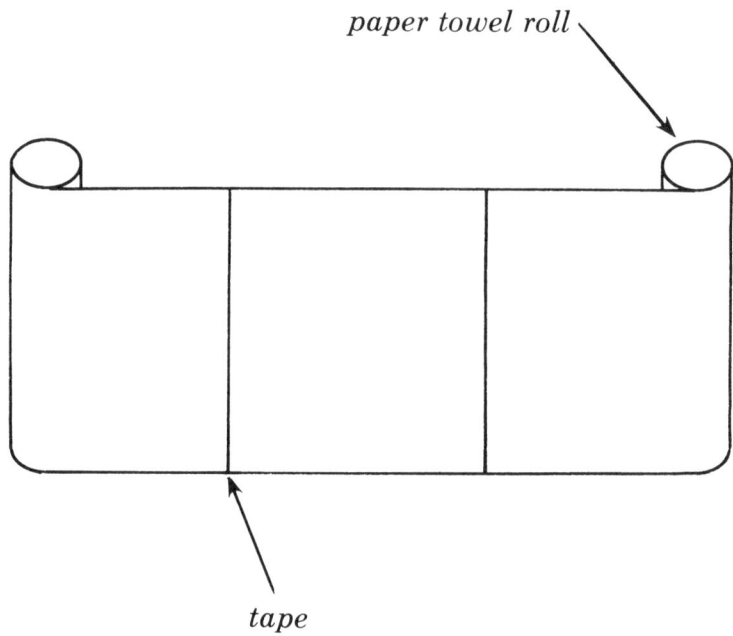

paper towel roll

tape

Read All About It!

(High Primary)

Tell the children to pretend that the events in a story or book really happened. Ask them to write a newspaper article about these events. They should tell the story as if it were a serious news item. They should also write a brief, newsy headline, such as "Little Old Man Brings Home Millions of Cats" (*Millions of Cats*, by Wanda Gag).

You might want to develop interest in the project by using the bulletin board on the following page.

IMPORTANT: *Be sure to attach the children's articles as they turn them in.*

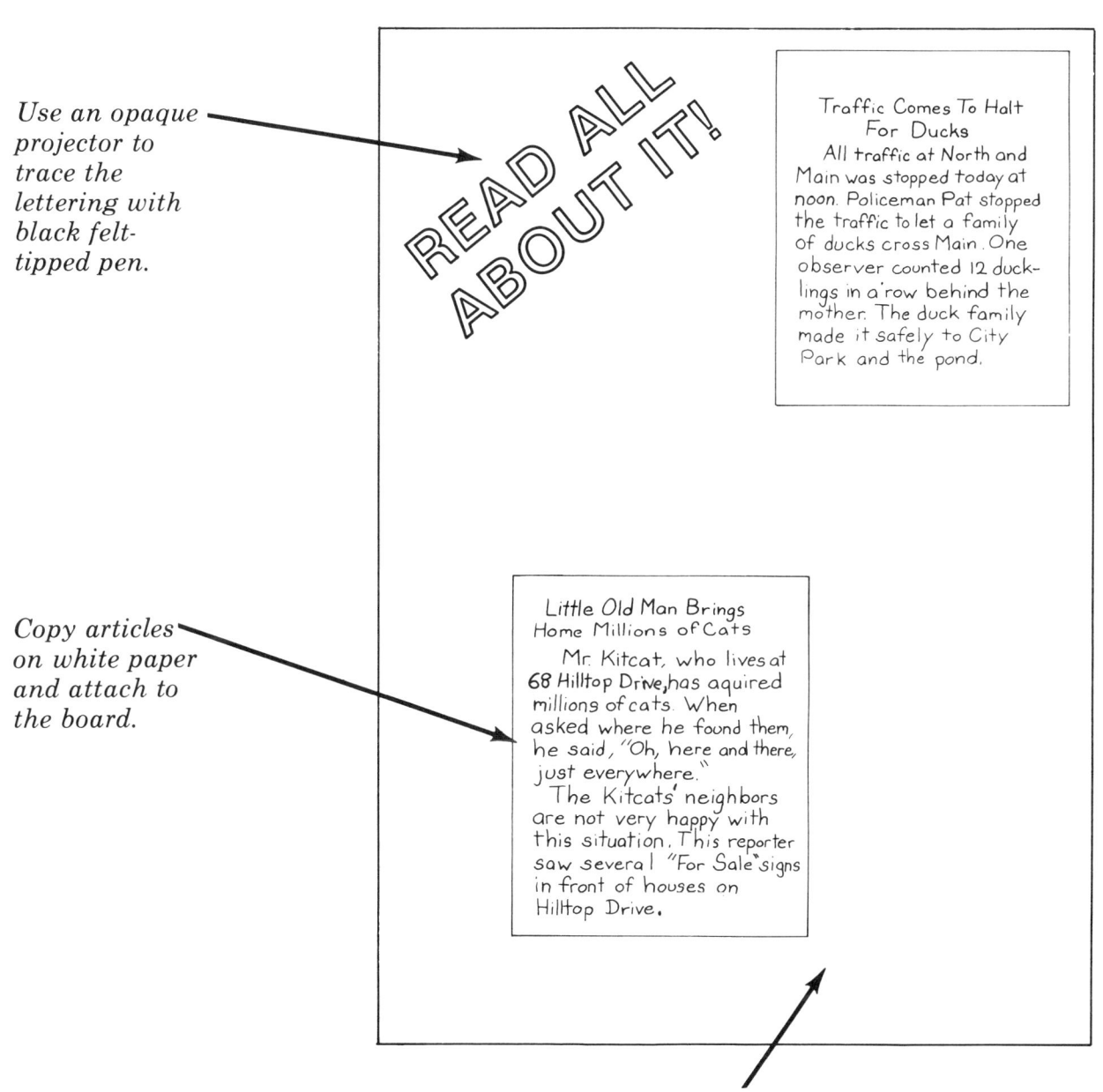

Use an opaque projector to trace the lettering with black felt-tipped pen.

Copy articles on white paper and attach to the board.

Use newspapers for the background paper.

Want Ads

(High Primary)

Have your students write a want ad for the main character from a book. Ask them to describe what they want, the reasons why they want it, and how it will be used. Here are a couple of examples to help get your students in gear!

> **Wanted** ...
> I am looking for two new brothers, ones who will read books to me and play games with me ... and not cheat!
> If interested, call 123-4567 before 8 P.M. (my bedtime!). Ask for Alexander.

> **Wanted** ...
> A new cork tree. I have one but I want a bigger one ... It must be taller than a house! I want to sit under it so I can smell the flowers. Please keep the bees!
> Call 999-2345. Do not call in the afternoon ... I take a nap. Ask for Ferdinand the Bull.

Hidden Books!

(High Primary)

The word puzzle on page 291 uses book titles that are very popular with children. The children look through the group of letters and find as many of these book titles as possible. You might have a class contest to see who can find the most book titles in a limited amount of time.

The following book titles may be found in the puzzle.

Madeline's Rescue	*The Biggest Bear*
The Little House	*Thy Friend Obadiah*
Petunia	*The Beaver Pond*
The Happy Lion	*Crowboy*
Little Toot	*Curious George*
Frederick	*The Happy Owls*
Horton Hatches the Egg	*The Snowy Day*
Anatole	*Pet of the Met*
I'll Fix Anthony	*Once a Mouse*

Name _____

Date _____

Hidden Books!

Here is a group of letters that look like they are all mixed up. But don't let that fool you! If you look closely enough, you will find many of your favorite book titles hidden among these letters. See how many you can find!

```
M A D E L I N E S R E S C U E B T L O M
A M T O T H E L I T T L E H O U S E C V
H B K S D D I C U A E I P E T U N I A T
C N T H E H A P P Y L I O N D F H J L P
B Q S R T L I T T L E T O O T A C F V W
V W Z T I U M P R B A F R E D E R I C K
H O R T O N H A T C H E S T H E E G G T
C H I K N R W Y D A N A T O L E I F E G
T Y I L L F I X A N T H O N Y C S W I P
A W P X T T H E B I G G E S T B E A R I
T H Y F R I E N D O B A D I A H L K J H
Q W E T H E B E A V E R P O N D E R T Y
P O I U Y T R E W Q C R O W B O Y H G J
A S D F G C U R I O U S G E O R G E B N
M N B V T H E H A P P Y O W L S S D F G
J H T H E S N O W Y D A Y P O I U Y T R
Y H B G T R F V P E T O F T H E M E T Y
I K M J O N C E A M O U S E E D C W S X
```

Reading Skills Index

Alphabet Knowledge

Beautiful Butterflies 22
Choo Choo! 134
Eggs in the Basket 85
The Island 138
The Lost Caboose 28
Marvin Mouse and His Friends 221
Sailing, Sailing 26
Sew an Alphabet 87

Auditory Discrimination

Bells Are Ringing 224
Bunch of Balloons 89
Diving for Pearls 15
Mitten Match 20
Peek in the Windows 18
Wild Windows 140

Categorization

Bigger Than I Am 30
Elmo's Peanut Game 97
Something in Common 33

Compound Words

Compound Pictures 182
Hello ... Operator 252
Watch the Forest Grow 116

Consonant Blends

Blend Box 152
Down the Chute! 236
Roll a Blend 102
Take Daffy Swimming 65

Context Clue Usage

Crazy Mixed-Up Words!	178
Crossing the Ocean	122
Fill 'er Up	249
Help the Bluebird	77
Ride the Streetcar	75
Who Is Chickie Looking For?	168

Contractions

Fish Bubbles	244
Toby's Problem	114

Fact from Fantasy

Going Fishing	129
The Old Train	257
Who Did It?	172

Final Consonants

Flying High	106
Jack and the Beanstalk	233
Mail the Letters	56
Meet the Frog Family	59
Rocket Puzzle	148

Fine Motor Skills

Follow Suzy	142

Initial Consonants

All Aboard!	146
Can You See It?	144
Do a Daisy	53
Fido's Treat	227
Let Toby Help	50
The Magic Hat	99

Main Idea

Panda's Problem	239
Picture Plus	125
What Happened at the Zoo?	176

Making Inferences

Help Henry	166
Old Oak Tree	126

Medial Vowels

Are You Hungry?	160
Polly Wants a Cracker	62

Road Signs 104
  Spin a Vowel 230
  Twirl a Vowel 150

Mood of Story

  Going Swimming 174

Predicting Outcomes

  Let's Take a Walk 180

Sentence Structure

  Silly Seal 80

Sequence

  Flying High 170
  Form a Picture 71
  Hang Glider 247
  The Long Train 119
  Marching Toy Soldiers 73
  Our Picnic Mess 184

Sight Word Knowledge

  Busy As a Bee 46
  Egg Carton Picture Game 112
  Help Henrietta Find Her Baby! 241
  Inside—Outside 42
  Into the Harbor 156
  Stop and Go 37
  Swimmy Flips His Fins 40
  Turn On the Light 48
  What Do You Want to Play? 158
  What Will We Ride Next? 154
  Word Fit 36

Visual Discrimination

  Birds in the Tree 92
  Build a Ship 95
  Button Up 7
  Colorful Garden 136
  Find Humpty-Dumpty's Cousins! 218
  Ladybug Match 12
  Marble Match 5
  The Pumpkin Parade 3
  Snowman Shapes 9

Vowel Digraphs

  My Favorite Day 164

Reading Skills Index   **295**

Word Meaning

Apples, Apples, and More Apples 254
Can You Find the Animals? 162
A Flock of Birds 109
Magic Pictures 107
Time for Baseball 68